Introducing AutoCAD® Civil 3D® 2009

JAMES WEDDING, P.E.

DANA PROBERT, E.I.T.

WILEY

Wiley Publishing, Inc.

Senior Acquisitions Editor: Willem Knibbe
Development Editor: Kathryn Duggan
Technical Editor: Rick Graham
Production Editor: Rachel McConlogue
Copy Editor: Kathy Carlyle-Grider
Production Manager: Tim Tate
Vice President and Executive Group Publisher: Richard Swadley
Vice President and Executive Publisher: Joseph B. Wikert
Vice President and Publisher: Neil Edde
Book Designer: Caryl Gorska
Compositor: Chris Gillespie, Happenstance Type-O-Rama
Proofreader: Jen Larsen, Word One
Indexer: Jack Lewis
Project Coordinator, Cover: Lynsey Stanford
Cover Designer: Ryan Sneed
Cover Image: (top) Jupiter Images, (bottom row) iStockPhoto

Copyright © 2008 by Wiley Publishing, Inc., Indianapolis, Indiana

Published simultaneously in Canada

ISBN: 978-0-470-37316-3

For general information on our other products and services or to obtain technical support, please contact our Customer Care Department within the U.S. at (800) 762-2974, outside the U.S. at (317) 572-3993 or fax (317) 572-4002.

Wiley also publishes its books in a variety of electronic formats. Some content that appears in print may not be available in electronic books.

Library of Congress Cataloging-in-Publication Data

Wedding, James, 1974-

Introducing AutoCAD Civil 3D 2009 / James Wedding, Dana Probert. — 1st ed.

p. cm.

ISBN-13: 978-0-470-37316-3 (paper/website)

ISBN-10: 0-470-37316-4 (paper/website)

1. Civil engineering—Computer programs. 2. Surveying—Computer programs. 3. Three-dimensional display systems. 4. AutoCAD Civil 3D (Electronic resource) I. Probert, Dana, 1976- II. Title.

TA345.W44 2009

624.0285'536—dc22

2008032266

10 9 8 7 6 5 4 3 2 1

Dear Reader,

Thank you for choosing *Introducing AutoCAD Civil 3D 2009*. This book is part of a family of premium-quality Sybex books, all of which are written by outstanding authors who combine practical experience with a gift for teaching.

Sybex was founded in 1976. More than thirty years later, we're still committed to producing consistently exceptional books. With each of our titles we're working hard to set a new standard for the industry. From the paper we print on, to the authors we work with, our goal is to bring you the best books available.

I hope you see all that reflected in these pages. I'd be very interested to hear your comments and get your feedback on how we're doing. Feel free to let me know what you think about this or any other Sybex book by sending me an email at nedde@wiley.com, or if you think you've found a technical error in this book, please visit http://sybex.custhelp.com. Customer feedback is critical to our efforts at Sybex.

Best regards,

Neil Edde
Vice President and Publisher
Sybex, an Imprint of Wiley

For our fellow users.

Acknowledgments

As with Mastering AutoCAD Civil 3D 2009, Dana and I had a lot of help in putting this text together. Thanks to Willem Knibbe for being our friend in the publishing business, and defender at the deadline meeting. Thank you to Rick Graham and Kathryn Duggan, our front line of editorial review—their dedication and efforts helped to make this book possible. Thank you to Jason Schmidt, Bobby Procter, and the other folks at Jacobs Carter Burgess for allowing us to use their project for our instructional data set. We absolutely owe thanks to our team at Engineered Efficiency, Inc.: Mark Scacco, Marc Meyers, Jason Hickey, Eric Chappell, and Joshua Modglin. Their efforts and work are what make it possible for Dana and me to tackle a project like this. Finally, thank you to all of the readers and members at Civil3d.com. Your encouragement and enthusiasm for AutoCAD Civil 3D are what make all the effort worthwhile.

About the Authors

This book was written as a team effort from day one, but here's a bit more about the two names on the cover.

James Wedding, P.E., spent nearly a decade in the Dallas/Fort Worth land development industry before partnering with Engineered Efficiency (EE) in February 2006. A graduate of Texas Tech with a BSCE in 1997, he worked as a design engineer focused on private development. His design experience includes small commercial to multiphase single-family and master planned communities. James has served as president of the Preston Trail Chapter of the Texas Society of Professional Engineers and was selected their Young Engineer of the Year in 2003.

One of the earliest gunslingers for the Civil 3D product, James has worked extensively with the Autodesk product team to shape and guide the software's development. James is a highly rated repeat presenter at Autodesk University and a presenter on the Friday Civil 3D webcasts.

Dana Probert, E.I.T., received her BSCE from Georgia Tech in 1998. Since then she has worked for consulting engineers in the United States and Canada, doing a variety of civil projects such as large planned residential communities, small subdivisions, commercial site design, stormwater management, road design, sanitary sewer networks, stream restoration projects, and municipal GIS. For most of this work, she has used AutoCAD-based products, including Land Desktop, Civil Design, Raster Design, Autodesk Map, and Civil 3D. Dana began instructing Civil 3D users in October 2004, and since then has used Civil 3D herself for subdivision-layout design, road design, grading, stormwater management, and utility projects.

In addition to her own design work, Dana has been working closely as a team member with several firms on their Civil 3D pilot projects and implementation plans, and taught many Civil 3D training classes. Oh, and she also built the best 52-baseline corridor known to man.

CONTENTS AT A GLANCE

Contents

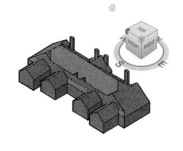

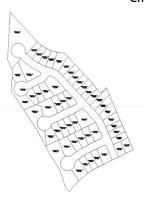

Introduction

If you haven't hidden your head in the sand the last few years, you know the world of land development is all about going 3D. It's the next jump from the board to CAD to the model. The magic question of course is, "How do I get there?" If you're part of the Autodesk world—as so many engineers, land planners, and surveyors are—then the answer to that question is *AutoCAD Civil 3D.*

With the growing maturity of the Civil 3D product, more and more users are making the jump from AutoCAD Land Desktop or other civil engineering software suites, and that means the user base is growing. Part of that growth is the new or occasional user who just wants to understand what all the hubbub is about, and how to make some use of all this modeling information. Civil 3D is a complicated product, and after five years, most users will still say they learn something every day, in spite of being the experts in their office. This book isn't for them. This book is for the project manager who needs to understand what his engineers and designers are doing. This is for the engineer who has moved more into a team-management role, but still contributes to the design process. This is for the new student who wants to get a feel for all the pieces that make up a Civil 3D model, and why all these tools are used instead of just lines, arc, and polylines. If you're looking to get a basic understanding of what Civil 3D is all about, and to get a quick peek at the full toolset from points to project data management, then this is the book for you.

How to Use This Book

This book covers the basics of creating, editing, and using the elements that make up the Civil 3D universe. You won't find every setting covered in detail or presented with the most complex uses. You'll find straightforward examples and language that give you a clear path to understanding and a level of confidence to begin taking on bigger tasks within your Civil 3D designs.

The book is essentially a catalog of tools, arranged according to features and object sets. Each chapter describes an object and a bit about why it's different from your stock AutoCAD objects. You'll get some discussion, and then go right into step-by-step exercises that walk you through the creation of most objects types in a couple of different ways. You'll look at some of the most common creation options, with further exercises that let you explore these as well. After you have created some Civil 3D objects, you'll move to editing and styling objects to suit your needs. Each chapter wraps with a quick summary to help you remember all that was covered and the purpose a given feature serves.

This book assumes a basic understanding of the core AutoCAD package and Microsoft Windows. Although you won't get into complex AutoCAD commands or sequences, this book assumes that you can draw lines and arcs, copy objects, and use osnaps within the program.

Running Civil 3D is not a job for your old computer. Although the models and exercises presented here are very basic, hardware deficiencies are some of the most common sources of frustration with Civil 3D. It's simply a very demanding application even in basic design models. In case you're curious, here's a list of the recommended specifications according to Autodesk:

- Microsoft Window Vista Ultimate/Business/Enterprise or XP (SP2)
- Intel Pentium 4 (3GHz or higher) or AMD Athlon
- 3GB RAM
- 5GB free disk space for installation
- 1,280 × 1,024 display with true color, 1,600 × 1,200 or greater recommended (OpenGL® accelerator with full OGL ICD support not required)
- Microsoft® Internet Explorer® 6.0 (SP1 or later)
- DVD drive

You can (and should) visit the Autodesk website (www.autodesk.com) and review system requirements for any changes since this publication.

What's Inside

Before you even flip through the rest of this introduction, point your web browser to www.sybex.com/go/introducingcivil3d2009 and begin downloading the data and drawings that go along with the exercises. This way, once you're done with this introduction, you'll be ready to roll right into the text.

This book moves through the Civil 3D program in a way that seems to match the way most people use and learn it. It starts with the general setup, and then moves on to points, surfaces, and corridors, and ends with team data management. Each chapter covers a general feature, and although some chapters build on skills or concepts covered in previous chapters, most stand alone as well. If you're set on hitting a specific topic right off the bat, we'd still suggest that you start with Chapter 1 just to get familiar with the Civil 3D environment—you're not in AutoCAD anymore, Toto.

The first two chapters cover the changes to the Civil 3D environment:

Chapter 1: Welcome to the Civil 3D Environment discusses the Prospector and Panorama, along with the other interfaces you'll use to understand and build your Civil 3D model. You'll also explore Civil 3D styles, and how they make the display of your models easier than ever to manage.

Chapter 2: General Tools covers tools you'll use throughout your Civil 3D experience, including the Civil 3D–specific Inquiry and Tool Palettes. You'll also explore some standard AutoCAD tools that are part of the Civil 3D package, but you might not have used them before.

Unlike the core AutoCAD product, AutoCAD Civil 3D has not adopted the ribbon interface.

The next few chapters look at getting the initial data into the model:

Chapter 3: Lines and Curves teaches you how to use existing legal descriptions or linework to begin creating your Civil 3D drawing data and how some Civil 3D tools can be applied to regular AutoCAD linework.

Chapter 4: Survey takes the model from the outside world into your computer. Working with field books and figures, you'll see how to translate basic on-the-ground survey data into the basis for a Civil 3D model.

Chapter 5: Points, gives you hands-on practice importing points from outside data, creating points for your own modeling use, and labeling them as needed.

With a basic idea of the site in place, you'll want to look at setting out your site and reviewing it. The next two chapters tell you how:

Chapter 6: Parcels covers the creation of parcels and getting your basic labeling together to create plans you can submit for review.

Chapter 7: Surfaces begins to get to the heart of the 3D environment. You'll explore how to build a basic surface from Google Earth information and from points. You'll also explore how contouring and labeling can help you understand this surface better.

The next two chapters work hand-in-hand to help you begin your design work:

Chapter 8: Alignments gives you hands-on practice creating alignments from existing linework and from scratch, as well as labeling and stylizing them to meet your requirements.

Chapter 9: Profiles and Profile Views shows you how to cut profiles, and then lay in a design profile to describe your proposed model. You'll also learn how to manipulate the profile views, setting different scales and attaching labels to make the data more understandable.

With the basic elements of Civil 3D in place, you'll begin looking at all the parts that make up the finished model.

Chapter 10: Assemblies and Corridors is all about Road Design in Civil 3D. You'll build a typical cross-section called an assembly, and use the alignment and profile data to create a 3D model of that road. You'll also look at creating a surface from the corridor, the first step in preparing a final ground model.

Chapter 11: Sections walks you through the process of cutting sections, displaying them in your drawing, and making arrays of sections to make plotting easier.

Chapter 12: Grading covers feature lines and grading groups, the two primary tools for building the part of your model that isn't defined in a corridor. You'll create feature lines from objects and alignments and use a single feature line to set the grades for others. You'll also make a grading group based on a feature line, building a drainage channel as a function of a single feature line and some parameters. Finally, you'll put both the feature lines and grading group into a composite finished ground model and run a quick earthworks analysis.

Chapter 13: Pipes walks you through picking the parts for your pipe network, the layout of your network, and getting it displayed just right. You'll also push those pipes and manholes into a profile view and explore the relationship between plan and profile as you edit.

Chapter 14: Projects looks a bit outside the technical engineering aspect of Civil 3D and at how to pull the team together using the data shortcuts feature. You'll see how to make a typical project folder structure, how to make a new project within Civil 3D, and how to share your design data with other members of your team.

How to Contact the Authors

The idea for this book came from the growing number of users who have said, "I wish I had some way to explain the basics of Civil 3D to my boss and the new guys." We've attempted to incorporate the things that make us excited about Civil 3D, and what we would show to someone who asked us to explain why we're so excited to be involved with this product. With that in mind, there are always things that could be covered in more detail, or perhaps features that we should include here. If you have ideas on how to improve this text, please contact us both at introducing@eng-eff.com. Although we can't reply to every message, we do read every one and we value your feedback.

Sybex strives to keep you supplied with the latest tools and information you need for your work. Please check their website at www.sybex.com, where we'll post additional content and updates that supplement this book if the need arises. Enter **Civil 3D** in the Search box (or type the book's ISBN—**9780470373163**) and click Go to get to the book's update page. You can also find updates and more information at www.civil3d.com/errata.

Thank you for picking up *Introducing AutoCAD Civil 3D 2009*. We appreciate it.

—James Wedding, P.E. and Dana Probert, E.I.T.

CHAPTER 1

Welcome to the Civil 3D Environment

To paraphrase, Civil 3D isn't your father's AutoCAD. If you're just getting into the Civil 3D environment, want to learn how to get around in models, and would like to understand the object styles and labels, then this is the place to start. Even if you've had a class or two, this chapter will provide a good review of some definitions, terms, and techniques used throughout the book.

This chapter starts by examining the general interface of Civil 3D, the various palettes that are part of Civil 3D tasks, and some parts of the interface that are new to 2009 in general. You'll learn how to create a new Civil 3D-based drawing in order to understand the way Civil 3D uses styles to display the various objects that are part of your projects. You'll explore the differences between plan, isometric, and profile styles for various objects, and how these styles and layers work together. The chapter then discusses some general labeling topics, including the relationship between Civil 3D text and drawing scale, how styles determine label accuracy and placement, and how you can share styles of all sorts with the rest of your office. As a last bit, you'll look at the help system, and we'll point you to some great online resources for further exploration.

This chapter includes the following topics:

- **The Toolspace palettes**
- **Object display styles**
- **Object label styles**
- **Navigating in 3D**
- **Creating new Civil 3D drawings**
- **Sharing styles and template creation**

The Civil 3D Interface

As soon as you load Civil 3D for the first time, you'll see some changes afoot. Unlike most versions of AutoCAD, Civil 3D asks you to pick a workspace right off the bat, before you even really know what you're selecting. This section explores the menus and palettes that are unique to Civil 3D.

> Civil 3D is built on AutoCAD, and there are many good texts on learning AutoCAD. *Mastering AutoCAD 2009* by George Omura (Sybex, 2008) is a popular choice. Because this text is focused on learning Civil 3D, issues or customization options that are based on the AutoCAD technologies will generally be mentioned more in passing than in detail.

When you first launch Civil 3D, you're presented with a question about workspaces. The default is Civil 3D Complete, so most users select that. It's also where you'll be working for most of this book.

> **WHAT'S A WORKSPACE?**
>
> Workspaces are Autodesk's answer to having the right tool at the right time for the right job. Workspaces allow you to pick and choose the toolbars, menus, and palettes that make up your screen. By picking different combinations based on the tasks at hand, you can minimize the number of toolbars on your screen, limit the number of options presented to new users, and spend less time in menus and more time working. Civil 3D comes with five workspaces right out of the box: Design, Annotation and Drafting, Survey and Topographical, Visualization and Rendering, and Civil 3D Complete.

When Civil 3D has finished loading (and assuming you've accepted the default Civil 3D Complete workspace), it looks something like Figure 1.1. There are all kinds of new buttons and controls along the bottom of the drawing area—be sure to check out the AutoCAD Help for more information.

Here are a couple of basic definitions:

- **Palette set:** A container for palettes. In Civil 3D, this typically contains the Toolspace, Panorama, and Tool palettes. A palette set can be turned on and off; it can collapse automatically when the mouse moves away, and you can make it semitransparent. Palettes within Palette Sets can be toggled on and off.

- **Palette:** One tab within a palette set. Most AutoCAD users are familiar with the Tool palettes set, and the ability to control which palettes (such as Hatching, Rendering, Blocks, and so on) appear. In Civil 3D, you turn on and off the Survey and Toolbox palettes within the Toolspace palette set by choice, and palettes will come and go from the Panorama palette set as needed to give you feedback.

It's all much more confusing to read than it is to use, so don't worry.

Civil 3D includes a number of different palettes for handling blocks, plotting, Xrefs, layers, and so on. These are great tools, but first let's examine the palette sets that make up the power of Civil 3D: Toolspace and Panorama.

Figure 1.1

Civil 3D in its initial setup form

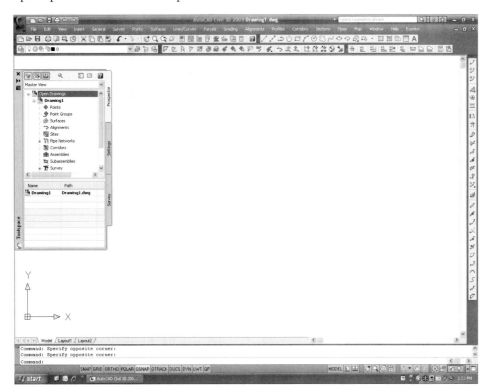

Figure 1.1

Civil 3D in its initial setup form

Toolspace in Civil 3D

In Figure 1.1, the only palette set showing by default is the Toolspace. You'll find that you're in Toolspace almost constantly as you work with Civil 3D, so most users leave it open and docked to one side or another. If you have a second monitor, dragging it to the second screen is a suggested plan as well. Toolspace is where you will spend most of your time interacting with Civil 3D's model and the settings that drive it. Additionally, this is where you'll work with Survey information and generate reports to XML or text formats. Model information, drawing settings, survey, and reporting are each handled by separate palettes: Prospector, Settings, Survey, and Toolbox respectively. This chapter focuses on Prospector and Panorama because they're part of the overall package. Chapter 4, "Survey," deals with the Survey palette, and Chapter 2, "General Tools," covers the Toolbox.

Prospector

Prospector is the main entry to the model you'll build with Civil 3D. This is where you'll dig into the various objects, work with Project Data, and create new drawings. Prospector has some major controls that we want to look at before getting deeper into individual model items. Because there is so much going on, let's start at the top with a couple of buttons that make getting around in Prospector easier.

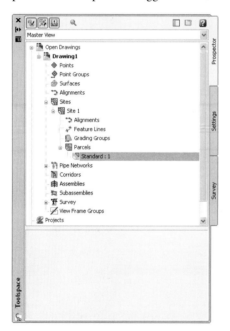

The first button you'll want to know about is the preview toggle that turns on and off the object previews on a global level. As drawing objects are created, they generate previews that can be displayed in Prospector in a preview pane. This button toggles that pane on and off. For example, Figure 1.2 shows the different results when you select a parcel with the preview toggle on versus when it's off.

Figure 1.2

Preview toggled off (left) and on (right) when reviewing a parcel. The preview is a 3D view.

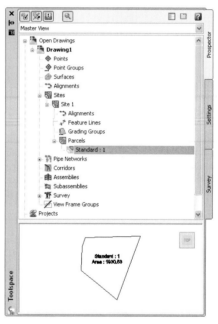

As you are looking at objects in a preview window, it's important to remember two things. First, previews can be toggled on and off for Prospector, as well as for the object branches such as Surfaces, Parcels, and so on. If you don't see the preview when the master toggle is on, check the object branch by right-clicking on the branch and reviewing the menu for Show Preview. Alignments, Surfaces, Networks, Corridors, Assemblies, and Subassemblies can display previews within Prospector. Second, the preview area is a 3D view, so you can use the ViewCube in the upper right to rotate, spin, or twist your perspective. (You'll learn more about this cube in the next chapter, which discusses basic AutoCAD tools that help in Civil 3D modeling.)

The second button you'll want to familiarize yourself with is the Item View Orientation toggle. When using Toolspace as a floating-palette set, this toggles where the Civil 3D list view of various object is oriented, at the right, or at the bottom of the palette. Figures 1.3 and 1.4 show the two options. This toggle can make large amounts of data much more accessible when you're working with list view, so just remember it's there.

The last piece of the main controls you'll want to familiarize yourself with is the drop-down menu for view selection. In this menu, you can select between Master View and Active Drawing View. In Master View, all the branches are presented, including multiple drawings if you have more than one open, the Projects branch, the Data Shortcuts branch, and the Drawing Templates branch. In Active Drawing View, you will see only the data relating to your current drawing. This is handy when you're working with a large number of drawings in general, so you can have them all open but focus on one drawing for the current tasks.

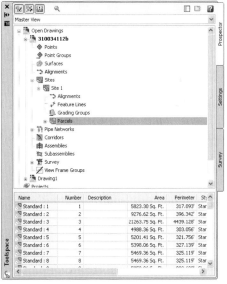

Figure 1.3

List view displayed at the bottom of Prospector

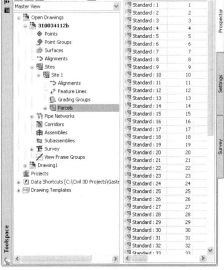

Figure 1.4

List view displayed at the side of Prospector

TEACHING PAINTING OVER THE PHONE

The exercises in this chapter might be more difficult than they should be, simply because you aren't seeing the same things we are. Just to give you a fighting chance, the setup used for the exercises and image captures is the default Civil 3D 2009 Civil 3D Complete workspace, displayed in a 1280×1024 window. Toolspace and Panorama will be floating, and not docked as we use them. We have used the resize handles on some windows to make things easier to read.

Beyond the controls, Prospector has one main pane that never goes away, and an additional pane that shows the list and preview areas when needed. This main pane resembles Windows Explorer's Folder view, with plus symbols designating areas that have deeper objects. These symbols also allow for expansion and contraction as needed to manage the display of various data objects. Let's take some time to review the buttons discussed earlier, and explore the relationships between various objects.

1. Open the Exploring Prospector drawing file. (Remember, all the data for this book can be downloaded from www.sybex.com/go/introducingcivil3d2009.) This drawing shows a typical subdivision layout, with parcels and alignments defined.

2. Within Toolspace, make sure the Prospector palette is selected by clicking its tab.

3. Change the view selection to Active Drawing View to turn off the extraneous information for now. Your Toolspace should look something like Figure 1.5.

4. Expand the Alignments branch, and then select Carson Circle by left-clicking. Note that no preview appears as you might expect.

5. Right-click on the Alignments branch and select Show Preview as in Figure 1.6.

6. Pick Carson Circle again and notice that the preview is now displayed at the bottom of the preview pane.

7. Select the Alignments branch, and note that the full collection of Alignments is now displayed at the bottom of the list area. If your Toolspace is too narrow, you can use the scroll bar to move across all of the columns.

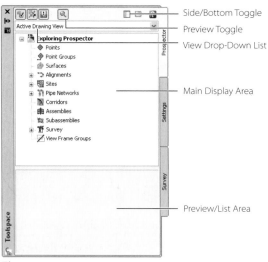

Figure 1.5

Prospector showing the collapsed tree view of the Exploring Prospector drawing file. Note that some branches have plus signs indicating that they contain more subbranches.

Figure 1.6

Turning on Previews for Alignments

8. Click the plus sign next to Sites to expand that branch, and then expand the Site 1 branch as well.

9. Click the Parcels branch to have the parcels in the drawing listed at the bottom of the list area. This list is fairly long, so the short, wider window isn't as efficient at showing the data.

10. Click the Side/Bottom toggle as indicated in Figure 1.5 and note that the list area jumps from the bottom of your palette to the side as shown in Figure 1.7.

Figure 1.7

List view at the side with the palette resized and reproportioned to make more data visible

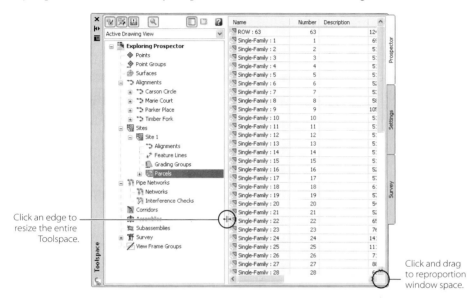

Click an edge to resize the entire Toolspace.

Click and drag to reproportion window space.

You can also customize the columns and data displayed in the list view to make it more concise. Beyond the preview and list views of objects, Panorama can also be used to make quick edits without moving into the drawing space, navigate the drawing, or make easy changes to multiple items. These changes often come when you're trying to change the labels on a series of Parcels, or want to change the style of all your alignments at once. Now you'll work with some of the controls in the preview area to customize the data presented:

1. Continuing with the Exploring Prospector drawing, make sure Parcels are still selected, populating the list view.

2. In the List area, scroll to the right until the Perimeter column is visible.

3. Click and drag the header to rearrange the Perimeter column to the left of the Area column. Any time a list is presented in this view, you can drag the column headers to rearrange the view.

4. Once you've moved Perimeter, scroll a little further to the right to see the Address column.

Figure 1.8

Hiding a column in the list view

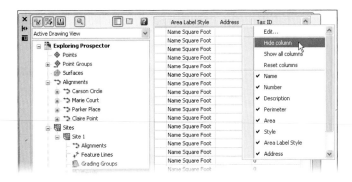

5. Right-click on the Address column header and select Hide Column as in Figure 1.8 to make it disappear. You can use the Hide Column option to make an individual column disappear, or you can move down the list that appears and uncheck columns as you see fit. These changes are persistent, which makes customization worth the seconds it takes.

6. Select the Alignments branch to display the alignments in the list view.

7. In the list view, double-click the Name field for Timber Fork, and notice that the name becomes editable.

8. Change the name to Claire Point and press Enter. Notice that this immediately updates the main Prospector pane as well.

9. In the list view or tree view, right-click the renamed Claire Point, and select Zoom To. The ability to zoom to almost any object using right-click menus makes project and model navigation very easy.

10. Click the Alignments branch one more time to bring back the list view back.

11. Select the first item in the list to highlight it.

12. Hold down the Shift key and click the last item in the list. This will highlight all the items between the two selected. If you need to remove an item from this selection, hold down the Ctrl key as you pick individual items.

13. With all the alignments highlighted, scroll to the right to find the Style column.

14. Right-click the Style column header as shown in Figure 1.9 and select Edit to bring up the Select Style dialog.

15. Select Layout from the Style drop-down list, and click OK to dismiss the dialog. Note the change in the arc portion of Claire Point.

The Prospector and its various views can be invaluable in working with data efficiently. When you're trying to find a short alignment or zoom to the correct profile view, the navigation aids in Prospector can shave a few seconds off every search. The ability to mass-change styles and properties is available only in Prospector.

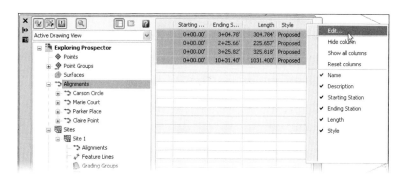

Figure 1.9

Pick the column header, not the cells, to get the Edit option to appear.

The two branches related to Project and Data Shortcuts that appear in the Prospector pane when Master View is selected are discussed in Chapter 14, "Projects." The Drawing Templates branch is merely a list of the files that are included in the default drawing template folder in your installation, and it can be generally ignored. For most people, the power of Prospector is in the Drawings area, which we've already covered, so let's look at the Settings tab.

Settings

Although most of your time making Civil 3D really come alive will be spent using the settings and styles, we won't go in to great detail in this text. The purpose here is to give you a basic understanding of all the things that are going on, letting you know the major controls, and keeping you moving forward. At a basic level, there are three items in this palette you should understand:

Drawing settings control the coordinate system default layer and naming conventions and abbreviations.

Object styles control the display of the Civil 3D model objects (such as alignments, profiles, surfaces, and so on) in Plan, Model, and Profile views.

Label styles control the rotation, layering, text, accuracy, and display of all object labels and tables.

The following sections discuss drawing settings and styles and include some exercises to illustrate how the changes made in this palette ripple through the drawing itself.

DRAWING SETTINGS

When you first create a new blank drawing in AutoCAD or Civil 3D, you'll find yourself hovering around a coordinate of 0,0. This works fine on objects and designs that have no dependence or tied relationship to the real world, such as a house, or a bolt, or a new car design, where the coordinates of the drawing simply don't matter very much. With land development, however, most projects are going to be built in the real world, with real sites and coordinates, and location is precisely determined on both the front and back ends of the project.

To solve this problem, Autodesk has built coordinate systems into the Civil 3D system, you simply have to tell the program which coordinate system you'd like to use. Let's take a quick look at this setting, and some of the other items in the Drawing Settings dialog.

1. Open the Exploring Settings drawing file.

2. Change to the Setting tab in Toolspace. Note that the same view drop-down menu exists as in Prospector with some different options: Active Drawings Settings View, Active Drawings Labels Only View, and Labels Only View. For the purpose of this exercise, you'll stay in Master View.

3. Right-click the Exploring Settings file name and select Edit Drawing Settings, as shown in Figure 1.10, to bring up the Drawing Settings dialog.

   The Units and Zone tab provides options for Units, Conversion Factors, Scale, and Zone. For the most part, you'll use the Zone portion of this dialog to get your drawing into a real coordinate system.

4. On the Categories drop-down list, select Honduras.

5. On the Available Coordinate Systems drop-down list, select Honduras, Norte; Meter. If you know the Coordinate System Code for the area you're working in, you can enter it where indicated in Figure 1.11.

Figure 1.10

Accessing the Drawing Settings dialog

Figure 1.11

Preparing a new Civil 3D drawing for work in La Ceiba, Honduras

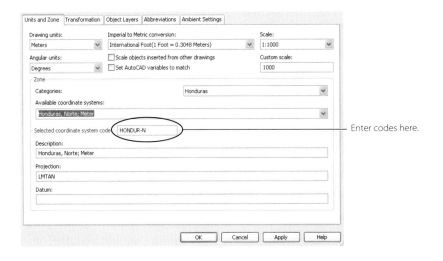

You're now prepared to do survey work in La Ceiba, Honduras, should you ever get a job there. Beyond the coordinates, the most common changes generally relate to abbreviations and terminology, so you'll fix them next.

6. Click on the Abbreviations tab. The settings here are the values that Civil 3D uses when it abbreviates or calls out an option in a label style.

7. Click in the Value column for the Left row and the ellipsis button will appear just to the right. Click the ellipsis button to open the Text Component Editor.

8. Click just to the right of the L and enter **t**. Then click OK to close the dialog.

9. Repeat this process for the Right row to change the value to **Rt.**.

10. Click OK to dismiss the dialog.

These simple changes will tell Civil 3D to use Lt. or Rt. anytime it abbreviates a direction, such as in an offset label. There are also options for Point of Curvature, Reverse Spiral Point, and so on, which can be set however you desire. Now that you've modified a few drawing level settings, let's explore some object settings and styles. This is where the real power of Civil 3D comes to light.

OBJECT STYLES

Working with object styles is where most people begin to see the real changes in Civil 3D versus other drafting or design packages. The ability to change dramatically the display of objects with just a few clicks really makes it easy to repurpose information. You can create new uses for data that were previously more effort to produce than they were worth. Let's look at a surface style to better understand some of the common components of an object style, and some of the power inherent in the applications of style.

1. Open the Exploring Object Styles drawing file. This file has a surface and a preconfigured set of viewports that will help you understand how object styles come into play in various view configurations.

2. Select View → Viewports → Named Viewports to display the Viewports dialog.

3. Select Exploring Styles from the Named viewports list on the left. Click OK to dismiss the dialog, and your screen should look something like Figure 1.12.

4. On the Settings palette, expand the Surface Branch, and then expand Surface Styles.

5. Right-click Contours 2′ and 10′ (Background) and select Copy to bring up the Surface Style dialog shown in Figure 1.13.

6. Click the Name field and change the name to **Exhibits**. Change the description to **A style used for public meeting exhibits**, and click Apply to see the changes. Note that the Last Modified By field now reflects your username.

7. Change to the Contours tab, and expand the Contour Smoothing option by clicking the plus sign next to it.

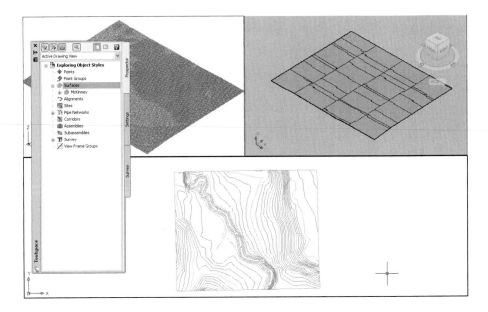

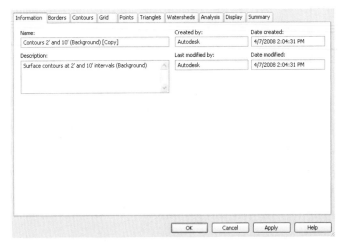

8. Change the Smooth Contours value to True. Remember, this is for meetings, not for plans, so displaying the contours is more about aesthetics than precision. Smoothing in a plan production situation is not generally recommended.

9. Change to the Analysis tab, and expand the Elevations options.

10. Change the Scheme to **Land**, the Number of Ranges to **12**, and the Display Type to **3D Faces**.

11. Change the Elevation Display Mode to **Exaggerate Elevation**, and then change the Exaggerate Elevations by Scale Factor to **5**. The Analysis dialog should now look like Figure 1.14.

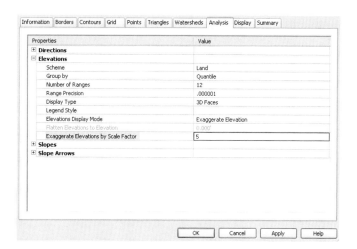

At this point, you've modified the way things will look when they're turned on, but not the objects that are on and off. The Display tab is a common component to all object styles. It controls the display of individual components within an object, and how they are viewed in Civil 3D based on the viewpoint. This level of control allows you to have different representations of a single object in plan views and 3D (or Model as it's used here) views.

12. Change to the Display tab. The View Direction drop-down menu on this tab offers three options for a surface: Plan, Model, and Section. We like the contours as handled in Plan, but let's change what happens in 3D views.

13. Select Model from the list and note that the selections in the Component display area change, most notably in terms of what is visible in a given view. This is indicated by the lightbulb icon being on or off.

14. Click the bulb in the Triangles row and turn it off. Then click the bulb in the Elevations row to turn it on. The Display tab should now look like Figure 1.15.

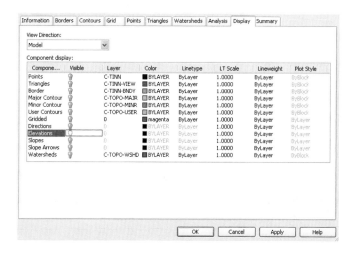

Figure 1.15

Turning on the Elevations display in the Model View Direction. Make sure the View Direction is set when modifying your style.

15. Click OK to close the dialog, and you'll see that Exhibits is now listed under your Surface Styles.

Building a style is all well and good, but until it's applied, it's hard to see any actual changes. Next, you'll modify the surface to use your new style, and you'll see the results of your work.

16. Change to the Prospector palette, and expand the Surfaces branch under the Exploring Object Styles drawing.

17. Right-click McKinney and select Surface Properties to display the Surface Properties dialog.

18. On the Information tab, select Exhibits from the Surface Styles drop-down list.

19. Click OK to close the dialog. Your screen will update to reflect the new colors assigned as part of the Elevations analysis. Each viewport will shift some, because the 5X exaggeration will cause the data to be higher in the z-axis than it was.

20. Click in each viewport and pan to recenter the surface in your view. When complete, it should look like Figure 1.16.

By using styles, you'll be able to change the appearance of your Civil 3D model objects in an instant. Much as you changed the style of the Alignments in a prior section, you can change styles to reflect various modes and display requirements. Now, let's discuss how you can label all these dynamic elements.

Figure 1.16

After assigning a new style, the 3D views have changed dramatically. (We closed Toolspace to make the image cleaner.)

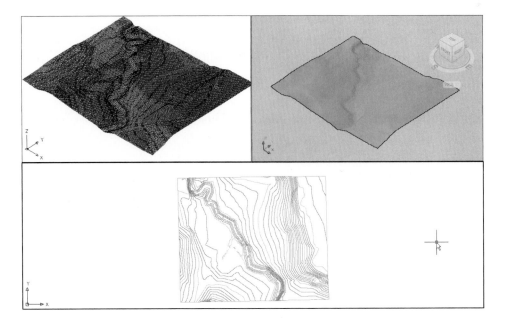

LABEL STYLES

Showing a surface, alignment, pipe, or any number of things in different ways is great. As we work through each chapter, we'll talk about individual labeling requirements, but it's important to look at some common elements here.

1. Open Exploring Label Styles. This drawing contains a surface with both spot labels and contour labels. You'll use both to explore issues within the label settings.

2. Zoom in on some of the contour labels. Notice that they're showing two decimal places. This is a stock style out of the box, but not many people show two decimal places in their contour labels.

3. In Toolspace, switch to the Settings palette, expand the Surface branch, and then expand Label Styles → Contour.

4. Right-click Existing Major Labels and select Edit to display the Label Style Composer dialog shown in Figure 1.17.

5. Open the Layout tab.

   This label is only one bit of text, but some labels are considerably more complicated. Each piece of text, line, or block is called a component, and appears in the drop-down menu near the top left of this dialog. If you get the task of building every label style for your firm, you'll want to explore all the options. For the purpose of this text, you're just going to change the accuracy of this label to something more reasonable.

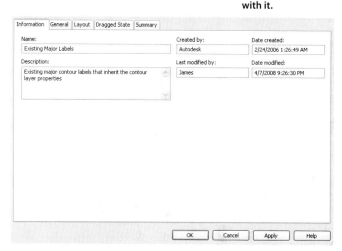

Figure 1.17

The Label Style Composer dialog is the same for almost every label you'll create in Civil 3D. Become familiar with it.

6. Click the Value cell in the Contents row under the Text section. A small button will appear to the right with an ellipsis (…) on it.

7. Click the Ellipsis button (also referred to as the More button) to access the Text Component Editor dialog shown in Figure 1.18.

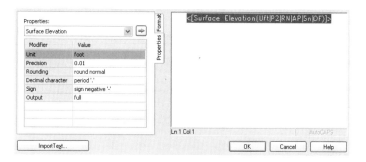

Figure 1.18

The text component editor has two areas: the Properties area on the left and an entry area on the right.

8. Click on the text in the entry area to highlight the value. The less-than and greater-than symbols indicate values that are derived from Civil 3D model information, which in this case are Surface Elevation values.

9. Press the Backspace or Delete key to remove the text.

10. In the Properties drop-down menu, select Surface Elevation.

11. Click the Value field of the Precision row, and change the value to **1**. This indicates a whole number will be used, with no decimal places.

12. Click the blue arrow button to inject this value into the entry area at the right. Your dialog should look like Figure 1.19.

Figure 1.19

Click the blue arrow, or nothing will happen! This will bite you more often than you'd ever expect.

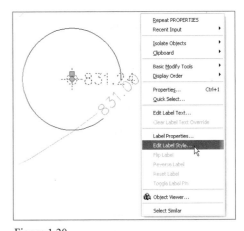

13. Click OK to close the dialog, and note that the preview area has updated to reflect your changes. You may need to zoom in the preview area to see them.

14. Click OK to close the Label Style Composer and update the drawing.

    You'll notice that some of the labels have updated, and some have not. This is because the minor contours are using a different label style than the major contours. If you want, you can repeat this process to update the style called Existing Minor Labels.

In the following exercise, you take a look at that spot label to understand how the Civil 3D labels react to different view orientations:

1. Continuing with the Exploring Label Styles drawing, zoom in on one of the surface spot labels as shown in Figure 1.20.

2. Select the label and then right-click and select Edit Label Style to display the Surface Spot Elevation Label Style dialog.

Figure 1.20

Using right-click menus will make editing much faster, but you have to make sure the correct object is selected first.

On the dialog, to the right of the Style drop-down list is another button with a drop-down menu. This button appears every time you have the option to select a style, and it gives you the ability to create a new style, copy the current style, edit the current style, pick from drawing, or create a child style. The idea is that you don't have to stop the task at hand to dig through the full settings tree to edit or create a style; you can do it on the fly.

3. Click the Edit button to display the Label Style Composer. You looked at the basics of the layout tab earlier, so now you'll look at the view orientation options.

4. Switch to the General tab.

5. In the preview area, click one of the rotation arrows as shown in Figure 1.21.

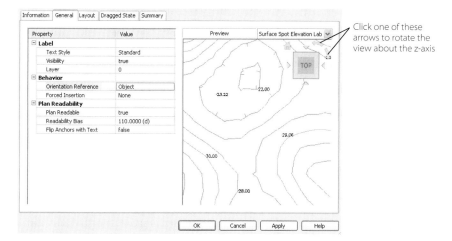

Click one of these arrows to rotate the view about the z-axis

Figure 1.21

Rotating the preview drawing

6. Change the Orientation Reference dropdown list to **View**. Note how the labels adjust to reflect this change. By setting a label's orientation reference to View, they'll be placed in relation to the screen or viewport, regardless of the rotation of your view.

7. Click OK to close the dialog, and click OK to return to your drawing.

   Although there is no obvious change, you can experiment with rotating your view, or moving to paperspace and creating viewports with various rotations. Thanks to the view orientation setting, the labels will update accordingly.

   Before we leave the topic of labels entirely, let's look at one last feature of Civil 3D: the ability of labels to scale with drawing scale.

8. Click the Annotation Scale menu and select 1″ = 100′, as shown in Figure 1.22. The Annotation Scale menu is located in the lower right of your screen by default.

   The size of the drawing labels and text is directly related to the scale of the drawing, so as you work, you can assign a drawing scale, knowing that a change in the scale come plan time won't mean you've wasted all your effort.

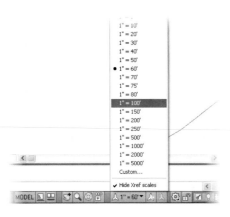

Panorama

The Panorama palette set is Civil 3D's way of talking back to you. The palettes that appear on the Panorama are typically designed for special purposes such as editing pipe or manhole data, viewing the full array of alignment information, or warning you about surface building issues. Take a look at the following quick example so you're familiar with the interface:

1. Open the Exploring Panorama drawing file.

2. In the drawing, select the Parker Place alignment as shown in Figure 1.23. Right-click and select the Edit Geometry option to display the Alignment Layout toolbar.

Figure 1.23

Accessing the Alignment Layout toolbar

3. Within the new toolbar displayed, click the Alignment Grid View button (the third button from the right) to display Panorama with an Alignment Entities palette.

    When Panorama is activated, various palettes will come and go as needed for the task at hand. When alignment is being edited, it's one palette; when a pipe network is being edited, there's one palette for pipes and another for structures. Within the palettes, some interface conventions hold true across the board: gray text cannot be edited, and columns can be turned on and off just as in the list view of Prospector.

4. Click in the Radius column for Row 2, and change the value to **250** as shown in Figure 1.24.

Figure 1.24

Data can often be modified directly in Panorama for instant changes in the model.

5. Right-click on the Chord Length column header, and scroll down to turn on the Chord Direction value. A new column will appear to the right of the Chord Length column, listing the relevant values.

6. Close Alignment Layout Tools by clicking the close button on the top of the palette.

    There aren't many tricks to Panorama, but remember that when it appears, it's generally trying to tell you something important, so be sure to read the messages and information being passed until you're familiar with what will and won't trigger an appearance by Panorama.

Getting Around in 3D

When you're dealing with a 3D model, you should know how to get around in 3D space. Because many Civil 3D users come from a very flat CAD background, this section describes some tools and options for dealing with the model: the ViewCube that's handy for getting around the model and the visual style options.

1. Open the Exploring 3D Space drawing; it contains three viewports showing the same surface in various representations. In the lower view of the screen is your typical Plan view, the top left is a 2D Wireframe view of the surface, the top right is a 3D Conceptual view.

2. Click in the Plan view area to activate the viewport.

Figure 1.25

One surface, three views. The upper left is still considered a 2D view by AutoCAD.

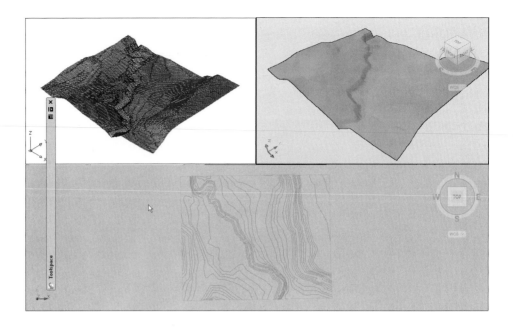

3. From the main menus, select View → Visual Styles → 3D Wireframe, and your screen should look like Figure 1.25. Note the ViewCube in the upper right of the two 3D styled views.

THINKING ABOUT A NEW VIDEO CARD?

Performing this sort of work—where you display multiple view angles of the same objects, with different texture and display options—is a good way to stress out your video card. With older cards, you might get some unpredictable results. We recommend reviewing the Autodesk approved list if you're thinking of upgrading. Visit www.civil3d.com\resources and look for the link to the Autodesk approval list.

4. Still within the Plan view, move your mouse near the ViewCube, and you'll see various arrows appear. Experiment with rotating the model by clicking the arrows and the various edges of the cube to spin the model.

5. Click an edge to rotate the model out of a Planimetric view. Notice that the style display changes to show the color banding that is part of the style.

Feel free to experiment with various visual style combinations with these objects. Most civil engineers and land development professionals don't spend a lot of time working with realistic conceptual styles, but knowing what they look like and having the ability to move about in three dimensions to view your model is crucial to taking advantage of the full product.

Summary

Civil 3D is designed to work in a new way. The pieces from which you build your design are no longer lines arcs and text; they are representations of real world objects you design. This brings the power of dynamic modeling to the desktop, allowing you as a designer to experiment with multiple solutions, looking for a better solution instead of just the first working solution. Accessing the model through palettes such as Panorama, Prospector, and Settings gives you access to the design constraints and information that you'll build the plans from as you work through the process. Finally, because these objects represent real-world items, they have length, width, and depth—which means that you need to understand how to view the model from every conceivable angle. Welcome to the next generation of land-development design.

CHAPTER 2

General Tools

Before getting into the specifics of the modeling tools that make up Civil 3D, it's important to look at some tools that cover all aspects of the model and design. These tools are designed to be part of the overall picture as opposed to any particular function or task. Although this isn't part of the modeling operation per se, these tools cover tasks that many users of the data consider important, such as the generation of inquiries, reports, and spreadsheets.

This chapter discusses the following concepts:

- ▪ **Using the Inquiry tool to understand the model**

- ▪ **Generation and basic customization of data reports**

- ▪ **Tool palettes and catalogs**

Interrogating the Model

As soon as the first piece of a model has been built, users want to know more about it. For example, they may need surface elevations, alignment station and offset information, point inverse information, or other data. Although it's possible to use labels or other model tools as discussed in Chapter 1, "Welcome to the Civil 3D Environment," more commonly, you just need a bit of information and don't want to disturb the drawing file itself. In this situation, you use the Inquiry tool.

The Inquiry tool is part of the general menu, and it has specific tools for finding information about points, surfaces, alignments, profiles, profile views, sections, sections views, and corridor sections. These queries run in the drawing and return information to the Inquiry tool. This returned information can then be copied to other documents, pasted as data to the command line for input, or just noted for later use. Let's look at examples dealing with points, surfaces, and alignments as these tend to be the most commonly used.

Inversing Points

As soon as many users get into Civil 3D, they want to know how to inverse between two points. You could draw a line and list it or label it using the Civil 3D labeling routines, but far simpler is just a basic inquiry. In this exercise, you'll get some point information from survey data in your proposed subdivision.

1. Open the Inquiry Tools.dwg file. (Remember, all data for this text can be downloaded from www.sybex.com/go/introducingcivil3d2009.)

2. Zoom to the southeast portion of the site to review the point data you're interested in, as shown in Figure 2.1. These points represent the centerline of the road according to the survey field data.

Figure 2.1

Surveyed point data

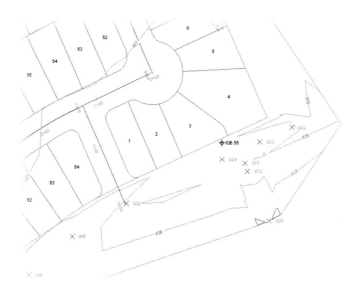

3. From the main menu, select General → Inquiry Tools to display the Inquiry tool palette.

4. On the Inquiry tool, select the Inquiry Type pull-down list and expand the Point branch to select Point Inverse as shown in Figure 2.2.

5. Click the ellipsis button near the top right, and then select the text or point symbol near point number 924 to make your display appear as shown in Figure 2.3.

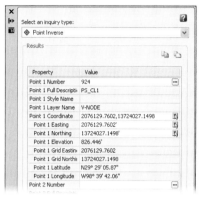

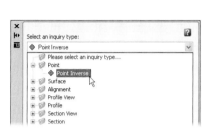

Figure 2.2

Selecting the Point Inverse inquiry type

Figure 2.3

Point 924 selected as part of the Inverse inquiry

There are a few things that you should note about this drawing file and the results so far. When you selected using the ellipsis, the toolbar knew you were looking to pick a Civil 3D point object, so it would not have allowed you to snap to a line endpoint. When you selected that point, the Point 1 coordinate filled in based on the *X* and *Y* of the point, but the Easting, Northing, and other coordinate system information filled in as well. These values are calculated only because this drawing has a coordinate system assigned. If the system had not been assigned, these values would be blank.

6. Click the ellipsis button on the Point 2 Number row, and select point 939 (it's near the entrance road to the subdivision). The palette should look like Figure 2.4.

Figure 2.4

Completed inquiry based on Civil 3D points

The calculated direction and horizontal distance are reported back in the last few lines of the palette, along with an adjusted version based on the grid coordinate system. Although this information can be handy, let's try one more inquiry based on linework, and push that data into a text editor for further reporting or archiving purposes.

1. With the Inquiry tool still open, click the Pick On-Screen button on the Point 1 Coordinate row, and select the southeast corner of Lot 4 as shown in Figure 2.5.

2. Click the Pick On-Screen button on the Point 2 Coordinate row, and select the northeast corner of Lot 11 (pan to the northwest to follow the back of the lots). A tracking line is displayed to show the two points being inversed, and the Point 1 Number and Point 2 Number values are blank because you are not inversing a pair of Civil 3D points.

Figure 2.5

Picking the lot corner of Lot 4

It's great to be able to get this data, but how can you use it? When legal documents are being prepared, one of the most common problems is getting data into the document without a typo, especially with long strings of numbers. Within the Inquiry tool, right-click on any row to get two options: Copy Value to Clipboard and Copy to Clipboard. Copy Value to Clipboard will put the current cell on the clipboard, while Copy to Clipboard puts the entire palette on the clipboard. You can then paste that data into another document, as shown in Figure 2.6.

You can also paste directly into a spreadsheet program, and the cells will be separated as you'd expect. Finally, a single value paste can be valuable when filling in a note or when updating a complex legal description after updating some linework.

Figure 2.6

Pasted values in WordPad

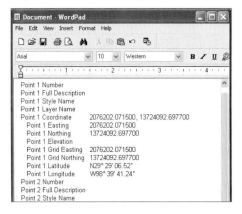

Analyzing a Surface

You'll look at building surfaces in Chapter 7, "Surfaces," but if you want a feel for how they can be analyzed for simple inquiries, stay in the Inquiry toolbox. The Surface inquiry options include Surface Elevation and Grade at Point, and Surface Elevation and Grade Between Points. Here's an exercise that uses the first option:

1. Open or continue using the Inquiry Tools.dwg file.

2. Open the Inquiry Tools palette from General → Inquiry (if it is not already open).

3. Zoom to the middle of the subdivision so that you can see the rough area around Lots 36 and 37.

4. On the Inquiry tool palette, click the Select Inquiry Type pull-down list and select Surface → Surface Elevation and Grade at Point.

5. Click the Select on Screen button in the Point Coordinate row and snap to the endpoint of the Lot 37 lot line as shown in Figure 2.7.

Figure 2.7

Surface inquiry on Lot 37

It's important to realize that the single point grade will reflect a single triangle face in a larger surface, so you'll be getting one point of data. You also have no visual indication of the actual slope direction other than the bearing shown on the inquiry palette. For this reason, many people will use surface labels for handling single-point slope inquiries. Those are covered in Chapter 7.

The more common inquiry of a surface is to look at the difference in elevation and grade across a site or a single lot. These are more general inquiries to give the designer a feel for how drainage issues might be addressed. This is where the second Surface option, Elevation and Grade Between Points, comes in:

1. On the Inquiry tool palette, change the Inquiry Type to Surface Elevation and Grade Between Points.

2. Click the ellipsis button on the Surface Name row to display another Inquiry Tool dialog. Select Existing Ground (1) and click OK to dismiss the dialog.

3. Zoom so that you can see the entire subdivision.

4. Click the Select on Screen button in the Point 1 Coordinate row and select a point near the entrance road to the site.

5. Click the Select on Screen button in the Point 2 Coordinate row and select a point in the middle of the northernmost cul-de-sac. Your screen will show a temporary line indicating the analysis points, and the Inquiry tool should look similar to Figure 2.8.

Figure 2.8

Two-point surface analysis completed

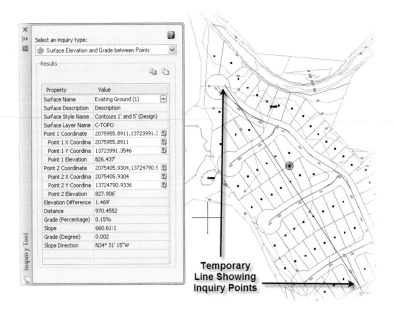

The data in the Inquiry tool reflects a direct line between the two points selected, meaning that the calculated data ignores any troughs or peaks between the points. This data is not an average slope between the points, merely a calculated delta expressed in a percentage slope. With the surface analyzed, let's look at a couple of alignment inquiries, and see how that data can be reviewed.

Finding Alignment Information

Alignments tend to be the main location instruments within transportation or subdivision design. Based on a station and offset from a given alignment, most points on a site can be located. In this case, you'll just be locating some on a property corner along the street. Additionally, you can get surface elevations at these points. This can be handy when looking at design surface information for laying out building pad elevations or drive entrances.

1. Open or continue using the Inquiry Tools.dwg file.

2. Open the Inquiry Tools palette from General → Inquiry (if it is not already open).

3. Zoom to the middle of the subdivision so that you can see the rough area around Lots 38 and 39.

4. Change the Inquiry Type to Alignment → Alignment Station Offset, and Surface Elevation at Point. An Inquiry Tool dialog will appear asking you to select an alignment. Select Carson Circle and click OK to dismiss the dialog. You should be back in

the Inquiry tool palette now. Note that you can change either the reference surface or alignment using the ellipsis buttons on the corresponding rows.

5. Use the Pick on Screen button in the Point Coordinate row to select the front point on the lot line splitting Lots 38 and 39. Your palette should look like Figure 2.9.

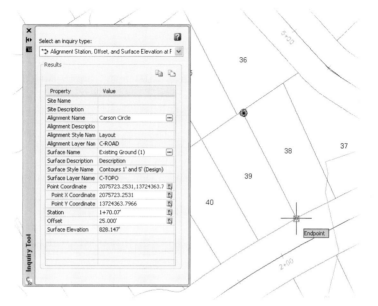

Figure 2.9

Inquiry along the Carson Court alignment

The offset of 25′ also helps verify that the street and lots have been laid out correctly based on the right-of-way requirements. By using the various inquiry tools, you can understand the existing conditions quickly, as well as perform design checks without changing the contents of the drawing in an adverse way. Now it's time to look at generating some reports from within Civil 3D.

Reporting on the Model

Land development projects don't consist simply of construction documents. Many projects require the filing of reports and other documents that relate to the design information on the site, but don't make sense in the construction documentation package. However, much of this data can be extracted from the model in the form of reports that can then be printed or saved for historical purposes.

Civil 3D offers built-in reports covering alignments, corridors, parcels, points, profiles, pipes and surfaces. These reports are accessed from the Toolspace palette set on the Toolbox palette. To open the Toolbox, select General → Toolbox.

There are two types of reports in Civil 3D: XML-based reports that are displayed directly inside Internet Explorer where they can be saved or printed; and .NET-based text reports that are simply saved to your hard drive and then displayed in Internet Explorer (IE). You'll see an example of each in the next section, where you look at a parcel metes and bounds report and a station offset report for some lot corner points.

Generating a Parcel Legal Description

Although you can review the legal metes and bounds of any parcel by exploring that parcel's Properties dialog, it's often required to generate simple reports for each lot for archiving. You can get a basic report almost automatically from Civil 3D's Toolbox.

1. Open the `Generating Reports.dwg` file. This file has the lots and alignments we looked at previously, as well as some Civil 3D points placed along lot corners.

2. Open the Toolbox palette within Toolspace, if it's not already open. (Remember, Toolbox is accessed from General → Toolbox.)

3. Within the Toolbox palette, expand Reports Manager → Parcels.

4. Right-click Metes_and_Bounds and select Execute to display the Export to XML Report dialog.

5. Click the Pick from Drawing button (shown on the bottom left of Figure 2.10), select the lot numbers for 38, 39, and 40, and then press ↵. When you pick from a drawing, only the selected items are exported.

6. IE should launch and display the report shown in Figure 2.11.

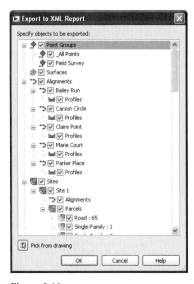

Figure 2.10

Data available for export. Use the Pick from Drawing option to limit the output file.

Figure 2.11

Completed metes and bounds report

When you're running reports, be aware that some reports require an ActiveX control
to be used in IE to complete. If you're running IE7, you should see a warning bar across
the top warning you about ActiveX controls. Right-click on this warning bar and select
Allowed Blocked Content, and then click Yes on the Security Warnings that appear. Be
sure to contact your IT staff if you run into more complex problems! You can close IE
when you're done reviewing the reports.

Although the report and the data created were just fine, it has a generic Your Company
Name heading (as shown in Figure 2.11). So, in the following exercise, you'll make the
quick change required there before moving on to the other report you're going run:

1. Back in Civil 3D, within the Toolbox palette, click the Report Settings button near
   the top left to display the Edit Report Settings dialog.

2. Expand the Owner branch, and fill in appropriate information as shown in Figure 2.12. You are the owner, and the Client branch is typically your client or the
   report recipient. Note that these settings are installation-dependent, meaning they'll
   be used every time you run the report, no matter which drawing file you are in.

3. Rerun the report, picking a new parcel if
   you'd like, and you should see your report
   updated as in Figure 2.12.

Although it's not really a topic that pertains
to Civil 3D per se, you can customize these XSL-
based reports if you have some knowledge of the
XSL language, as well as some level of program-
ming knowledge. Be sure to back up the originals
if you decide to really tweak the output.

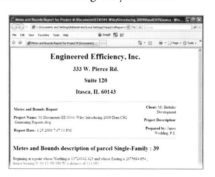

Figure 2.12

**Report settings
for your client
should be reviewed
each time.**

Generating a Point Report for Alignment Station Offset Data

When preparing survey information for stakeout or lot pin placement, being able to use
the alignment as a reference point for geometry is invaluable. In the following exercise,
you set up and run one of the more complicated .NET-based reports available in Civil 3D:

1. Continue with the Generating Reports drawing file and the Toolbox palette open.

2. Within the Toolbox, expand the Point branch.

3. Right-click Station Offset to Points and select Execute to display the dialog shown in Figure 2.13.

4. Click the Select Alignment drop-down list and select Carson Circle.

5. Click the Browse button (circled in Figure 2.13) on the far right of the Save Report To: path to display the Select a HTML file.

6. Navigate to your desktop, enter a file name of your choice, and then click Save to close the dialog.

7. Click the Create Report button to display the information in Figure 2.14.

8. When you are finished viewing the report, dismiss the Internet Explorer screen by clicking the X.

9. Click the Done button on the Create Reports screen to dismiss the dialog.

Figure 2.13

The Create Reports dialog

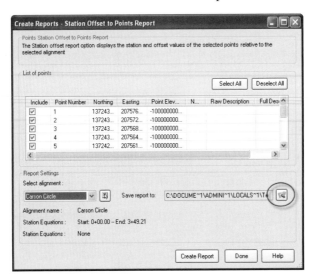

Figure 2.14

Completed station offset report

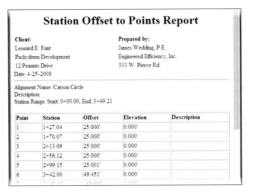

These reports can be printed directly from IE for filing or archival purpose, but modifying the reports that come from .NET sources is not generally possible beyond changing the Client and Owner information as shown here.

Tool Palettes and Catalogs

In AutoCAD, tool palettes are general AutoCAD tools; however, in Civil 3D, there are some great blocks and special functionality that you'll want to understand. Most Civil 3D interaction focuses on using the tool palettes in conjunction with corridors, but there are a lot of great tools and blocks on the tool palettes that are valuable to civil designers. Let's start with exploring these items before we get into the Corridor and Catalog functions.

Built-in Blocks

With every release of Civil 3D, more content has been added to the box to make your design and presentations a bit easier to realize. Too few users recognize these blocks exist, as they're hidden away by default in Civil 3D. Because there are several new blocks included in Civil 3D 2009, it's worth examining a few of them in the following brief exercise:

1. Open the `Tool Palettes` drawing file. The surfaces in this drawing have been set to not display, but they're still available to the model.

2. Open Tool Palettes by selecting General ▸ Tool Palettes, or by pressing Ctrl+3. The default tool palette should look something like Figure 2.15.

Figure 2.15

The default Civil 3D Imperial tool palette

The Tool Palettes feature in Civil 3D can handle an almost unlimited number of individual palettes. These are typically organized into palette sets. The default palette set, Imperial, is focused on Corridors. There is one palette here that you should check out: the Imperial Parking tools palette. You'll put some parking lots in your drawing just to illustrate the use of these tools.

1. Mouse over the tabs or drag the bottom of the tool palette to make the tabs larger and make searching easier. When you see the Imperial Parking tools palette, click its tab to activate it as in Figure 2.16.

2. Use the scroll bar to locate the button labeled 9ft Stall-60(s) and click it.

3. Snap to the front of the lot line dividing Lots 8 and 9 to place the block.

4. Zoom in on the new block placement and select it to activate the grips shown in Figure 2.17.

Figure 2.16

The Imperial Parking tools palette

Because not many Civil 3D users spend a lot of time playing with the dynamic block feature in Civil 3D, let's look at the grips numbered in Figure 2.17 and how to use them.

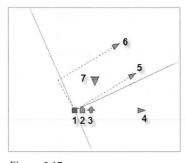

- Grip 1 is the insertion point of the block.

- Grip 2 will allow you to align the block with another.

- Grip 3 will flip the block along a line drawn from the insertion point to this grip.

Figure 2.17

The 9ft Stall-60(s) block in place

- Grip 4 will stretch the block along the x-axis, adding more parking spaces in a dynamic fashion, based on the original definition of the block.

- Grips 5 and 6 will lengthen the legs of the stall.

- Grip 7 will enable an option for a parking stop to be drawn in each parking space.

The construction of dynamic blocks is beyond the scope of this text, but the idea of constrained blocks and other items that size based on their requirements is incredibly powerful. There is very good information in the Help files and in other AutoCAD focused texts.

Next, you'll use this block to lay out the parking stalls.

5. Click grip 2 and then the front line of Lot 9 to align the parking stall.

6. Click grip 3 to flip the stall out into the street.

7. Click grip 4 and drag your mouse southwest. Notice that the length increases in increments related to the distance required to fit in another parking stall.

8. Snap to the front endpoint of the lot line dividing Lots 6 and 7, as shown in Figure 2.18, to finish the parking stall layout.

Although this is more of an illustrative example than a practical one, you can see the speed of layout available with predefined tools. There are over 20 different layout tools on this palettes, including curb islands and handicapped accessible stalls, all built to industry standards.

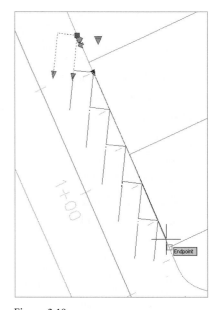

Figure 2.18

Completing the parking stall layout

Beyond the layout tools presented here, there are also hundreds of blocks built and designed to help make basic presentation drawings and renderings. These blocks include street signs, benches, landscape objects, houses, and trees. In this exercise, you'll place some blocks in the drawing using Civil 3D tools to place them at the right elevation and use the visual styles discussed in Chapter 1 to create a quick site illustration.

1. Right-click the Tool Palettes title bar to display a menu of palette sets.

2. Select Civil 3D – MV Blocks.

3. Switch to the Building Footprints palette.

4. Scroll down within the palette to find the Colonial 01 block and click it.

5. Place the block somewhere within Lot 7, and then place another Colonial 01 in Lot 6. If you pick the block just placed, you can right-click and select Object Viewer. Tilted into an isometric view as in Figure 2.19, these blocks gain height and design features, hence the name *multiview* blocks.

6. Place a Colonial 02 in Lots 3, 4, and 5.

7. After placing the blocks, rotate them using standard AutoCAD commands so that each building's outline falls inside the lots.

8. Change to the Landscape palette. There are scores of trees, bushes, and other landscape elements located on this palette.

9. Click a few varied elements and place them in the lots, in front of the house to create some conceptual landscaping design. To make it go fast, place one tree or shrub block from the palette, and then use AutoCAD commands to copy and array more blocks however you like.

10. From the main menu, select Surfaces → Utilities → Move Blocks to Surface.

11. Press Enter to display the Select a Surface dialog. Select Proposed Ground and click OK to dismiss this dialog and bring up the Move Blocks to Surface dialog shown in Figure 2.20.

12. Click the first block listed, and then Shift+click the last block listed, scrolling if necessary. All the blocks should be highlighted (as in Figure 2.20).

13. Click OK to dismiss the dialog.

14. From the main menu, select View → 3D Views → NW Isometric.

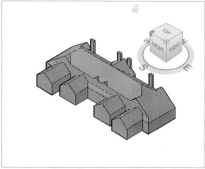

Figure 2.19

An apartment multiview block in the Object Viewer

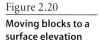

Figure 2.20

Moving blocks to a surface elevation

15. Select View → Visual Styles → Conceptual Style to see these items painted with color.

16. Zoom in on the building and plant blocks just inserted, and your screen should look similar to Figure 2.21. This view has been tilted a bit using the Free Orbit tool found in the AutoCAD Standard toolbar.

Explore the other palettes in the MV Block palette set, and you'll find objects such as fencing, benches, landscape rocks, light posts, and even a golfer with a flag. You're not going for a full-rendered view, but it's amazing what a few buildings and trees can do for the layman trying to understand your site design.

Figure 2.21

Completed conceptual view of the cul-de-sac design

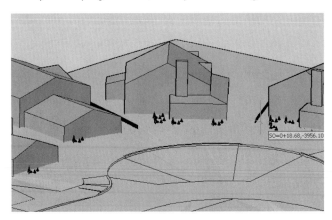

Creating Palettes with Catalogs

While the palettes are populated with a large number of tools, there are also times when you'll want to make your own. One primary example is when you're dealing with corridor design. Corridors are a powerful toolset within Civil 3D for building roads, channels, ponds, or almost anything. Between the myriad of controls and the wide variety of parts available for building design sections, you can program almost any solution within Civil 3D. However, all these parts come with a dizzying array of options. To make things simpler, many users find that building a custom palette from the parts catalog makes their day-to-day design work faster.

Civil 3D comes with preloaded palettes broken down by category. In this exercise, you'll make a new palette and populate it from the stock parts catalogs based on use instead. Because you are modifying the Civil 3D environment instead of a drawing file, you can do this exercise in any drawing file you like, but a drawing does have to be open to modify the tool palettes.

1. Open Tool Palettes (if it's not already open) by selecting General → Tool Palettes, or by pressing Ctrl+3.

2. Right-click the Tool Palette title bar and select the Civil 3D Imperial palette set.

BUILDING PALETTE SETS

You can build your own palette sets to carry the commands, blocks, tools, hatches, subassemblies, or assemblies as you need. To customize the sets, right-click the title bar and select Customize Commands. (There are detailed instructions under Help if you need them.)

3. Right-click the topmost tab and select New Palette from the pop-up menu. A new palette will be created and the name text will be highlighted for entry.

4. Enter **Subdivision** as the name of the new palette and press Enter.

5. From the main menu, select General → Catalog to launch the Autodesk Content Browser shown in Figure 2.22. Civil 3D and some of the other AutoCAD products use these catalogs to carry specific modeling elements. In the architectural world, this can mean doors and windows; in the Civil 3D world, it's section elements such as paving and guardrails.

Figure 2.22

The default Content Browser

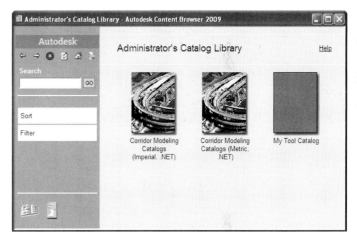

6. Click the Corridor Modeling Catalogs (Imperial, .Net) icon to open the catalog and display the catalogs list.

7. Click the C3D Imperial Subdivision Roads Subassembly catalog to open it.

8. Click Lanes to view the Lanes subassemblies within this catalog.

9. Click the blue icon located over LaneOutsideSuper and hold down your mouse button. You will see the eyedropper tool fill as in Figure 2.23.

10. Still holding the mouse button down, drag your eyedropper to the Subdivision palette you created in the first part of this exercise and let go.

11. Civil 3D will create a new icon on the palette and you'll see the name LaneOutsideSuper next to it. Some users (including your author) have problems getting Civil 3D to display the pictures in the tool palette. (Don't worry, the tool is still there.)

Figure 2.23

Selecting a subassembly for use

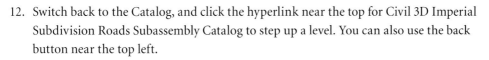

12. Switch back to the Catalog, and click the hyperlink near the top for Civil 3D Imperial Subdivision Roads Subassembly Catalog to step up a level. You can also use the back button near the top left.

Figure 2.24

**Completed
subdivision palette**

13. Click Urban on the lower right to open the sidewalk, curb, and gutter subassemblies.

14. Using the same eyedropper technique, drag the UrbanCurbGutterGeneral and UrbanSidewalk subassemblies to your palette. When complete, your palette should look something like Figure 2.24.

By organizing the subassemblies needed for a given design situation instead of organizing by type, you can reduce the amount of hunting and clicking as you're building your model.

Summary

Within Civil 3D, there are a number of tools available for your use. These include blocks and palettes for making quick conceptual renderings, inquiry tools for project managers and designers to understand the model better, and reports for producing documentation beyond the construction drawings. By using these tools in all phases of your model and plan preparation, you'll be a faster and more efficient designer.

CHAPTER 3

Lines and Curves

In civil engineering, lines and curves are indispensible. Lines and curves "connect the dots" to represent simple things such as fences, walls, and property lines, all the way through complex highway centerlines, wetlands delineations, and more. In Civil 3D, these lines and curves serve as foundation geometry for parcels, alignments, corridors, and pipe networks.

This chapter includes the following topics:

- **Drawing deeds with lines and curves**

- **Creating a property line by best fit**

- **Labeling lines and curves**

- **Creating a segment table**

Drawing Deeds with Lines and Curves

One of the most common tasks at the beginning of any land development project is re-creating deeds. These deeds could represent single family lots, roadway centerlines, easements, or any other legal description. In the following example, you add a missing lot to an existing subdivision plat (Figure 3.1).

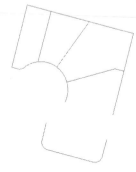

Beginning at a point whose Northing is 13724393.058 and whose Easting is 2076100.598; thence bearing N 14-57-55.122 E a distance of 3.724 feet; thence along a curve to the RIGHT, having a radius of 15.000 feet, a delta angle of 52° 01′ 12.46″, and whose long chord bears N 40-58-31.351 E a distance of 13.156 feet; thence along a curve to the LEFT, having a radius of 50.000 feet, a delta angle of 40° 31′ 52.13″, and whose long chord bears N 46-43-11.516 E a distance of 34.637 feet; thence bearing S 75-2-4.878 E a distance of 91.002 feet; thence bearing S 14-57-55.122 W a distance of 45.000 feet; thence bearing N 75-2-4.878 W a distance of 115.000 feet to the point of beginning.

Figure 3.1

A subdivision plat with a missing lot. You will create the linework for this lot in the next few exercises.

Creating Property Lines Using the Line Creation Tools

There is no one "right" way to re-create a deed in Civil 3D. You may prefer to use the tools under the Lines/Curves menu or a combination of commands found on the Draw and Modify toolbar, such as polyline, arc, circle, trim, and extend. You can also use the transparent commands, which are discussed in the next section. The following exercise shows you some of the tools available under the Lines/Curves menu that you may find useful when drawing legal linework.

1. Open the drawing file `LinesCurves1.dwg`, which you can download from `www.sybex.com/go/introducingcivil3d2009`. Note that there are a few lines and curves representing lot lines. There is a lot missing.

2. Choose Lines/Curves → Create Line → Line by Bearing.

3. At the `Specify First Point:` prompt, use your endpoint osnap to choose the end of the line marked with a red circle.

4. At the `>>Specify quadrant (1-4):` prompt, type **1** and then press Enter.

5. At the `>>Specify bearing:` prompt, type **14.5755122** and then press Enter.

6. At the `>>Specify distance:` prompt, type **3.724** and then press Enter. A short line will be drawn to match these specifications, similar to Figure 3.2.

Figure 3.2

You have drawn a 3.724′ line.

Creating Property Curves Using the Curve Creation Tools

The Lines/Curves menu contains an assortment of commands for curve creation. While the resulting curves are simply AutoCAD arc entities, the Lines/Curves → Create Curves tools provide an interface for data entry that closely matches the way data is presented in a legal description. For example, curves can be created using any meaningful combination of a start point, delta angle, curve length, chord bearing, and several other options that all use surveying language.

The next steps lead you through creating a curve and a reverse curve.

1. If the Line by Bearing command is still active, cancel it by pressing Enter twice.

2. Choose Lines/Curves → Create Curves → Curve from End of Object.

3. At the `Select arc of line object:` prompt, choose the line you just drew in steps 2 through 6.

4. At the `Select entry [Radius/Point] <Radius>:` prompt, press Enter to choose Radius.

5. At the `Specify Radius, or [degreeArc/degreeChord]:` prompt, type **15** and then press Enter.

6. At the `Select entry [Tangent/Chord/Delta/Length/External/Mid-Ordinate] <Length>:` prompt, type **D** for delta and then press Enter.

7. At the `Specify delta angle:` prompt, type **52.011246** and then press Enter. A curve will be drawn to match these specifications, and the command will end. A short report on the curve will also appear in the command line.

8. The next curve builds upon the first curve, but it goes to the left instead of the right. Choose Lines/Curves → Create Curves → Reverse or Compound Curve.

9. At the `Select arc object:` prompt, choose the curve you completed in steps 2 through 7.

10. At the `Select entry [Compound/Reverse} <Compound>:` prompt, type **R** for reverse and then press Enter.

11. At the `Specify Radius, or [degreeArc/degreeChord]:` prompt, type **50** and then press Enter.

12. At the `Select entry [Tangent/Chord/Delta/Length/External/Mid-Ordinate] <Length>:` prompt, type **D** for delta and then press Enter.

13. At the `Specify delta angle:` prompt, type **40.315213** and then press Enter. A curve will be drawn to match these specifications, and the command will end. A short report on the curve will also appear in the command line. Your drawing should now look like Figure 3.3. As in many real-world deeds, there will be a gap of misclosure between the newly created arc and the existing arc.

Figure 3.3

A 15′ radius curve and a 50′ radius curve drawn using the Lines/ Curves menu

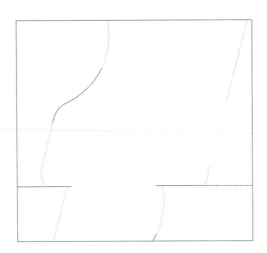

Figure 3.3

A 15′ radius curve and a 50′ radius curve drawn using the Lines/ Curves menu

Creating Property Lines Using Transparent Commands

Additional tools to aid with drawing are provided on the Transparent Commands toolbar (Figure 3.4). Transparent commands can be used within any AutoCAD or Civil 3D geometry creation command much like an object snap. If the Transparent Commands toolbar is not on your screen, you can add it to your workspace or refresh the Civil 3D Complete workspace.

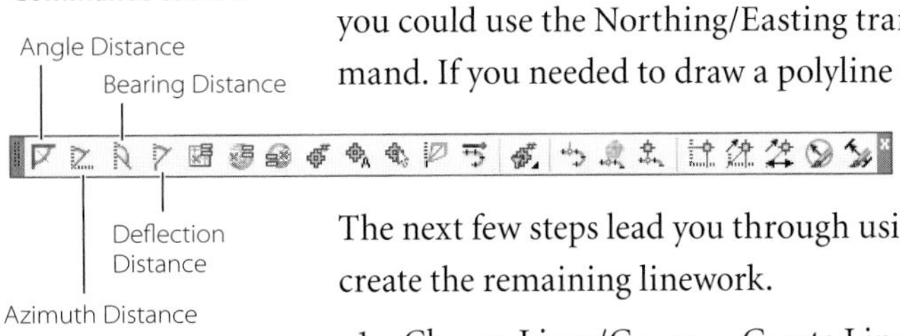

Figure 3.4

The Transparent Commands toolbar

Angle Distance

Bearing Distance

Deflection Distance

Azimuth Distance

For example, if you needed to place an iron pin block at a certain northing and easting, you could use the Northing/Easting transparent command within the Insert → Block command. If you needed to draw a polyline connecting a series of consecutive point numbers, you would start drawing your polyline and then select the Point Number transparent command. The next few steps lead you through using the Bearing Distance transparent command to create the remaining linework.

1. Choose Lines/Curves → Create Lines → Line.

2. At the `Specify first point:` prompt, use your endpoint osnap to snap to the end of the 50 ′ radius curve you just drew.

3. At the `Specify next point or [Undo]:` prompt, press the Bearing Distance button on the Transparent Commands toolbar.

4. At the `>>Specify quadrant (1-4):` prompt, type **2** and then press Enter.

5. At the `>>Specify bearing:` prompt, type **75.0204878** and then press Enter.

6. At the `>>Specify distance:` prompt, type **91.002** and then press Enter. The line will be drawn, and the command will continue.

7. At the `>>Specify quadrant (1-4):` prompt, type **3** and then press Enter.

8. At the >>Specify bearing: prompt, type **14.5755122** and then press Enter.

9. At the >>Specify distance: prompt, type **45** and then press Enter. The line will be drawn, and the command will continue.

10. At the >>Specify quadrant (1-4): prompt, type **4** and then press Enter.

11. At the >>Specify bearing: prompt, type **75.0204878** and then press Enter.

12. At the >>Specify distance: prompt, type **115** and then press Enter. The line will be drawn, and the command will continue. Press Enter twice to exit the command.

    The missing lot is completed, as shown in Figure 3.5. As in many real-world deeds, there will be gaps of misclosure between the newly created linework and the existing linework.

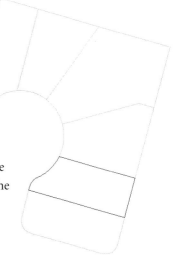

Figure 3.5

The completed deed

Creating a Property Line by Best Fit

Although engineers try to make sure surveying is an exact science, there are often occasions where benchmarks cannot be located or deeds have been lost. An example of this would be a property *line of agreement*. Two land owners will walk the property with a surveyor and agree on a new property line. They will point out features such as trees or fence posts that they mutually agree are on one property or the other. The surveyor collects these points and uses a combination of hard data and anecdotal information to create a new property line. The Line by Best Fit tool would be useful in this circumstance. Other occasions for using Line (or Arc) by Best Fit might be creating an existing road centerline from survey points and approximating stream centerlines from aerial imagery.

The next exercise leads you through creating a Line by Best Fit for use as a property line for the subdivision.

1. Open the drawing file LinesCurves1.dwg (or continue working in it if it's already open). Note that there are Civil 3D points along the rear of the northern lots (see Figure 3.6).

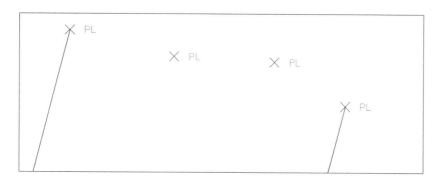

Figure 3.6

Civil 3D points along the proposed line of agreement

2. Choose Lines/Curves → Create Best Fit Entities → Create Line. The Line by Best Fit dialog appears.

3. In the Line by Best Fit dialog, confirm that the radio button next to "From Civil 3D points" is selected. Note that you can also choose AutoCAD points, entities, or locations on the screen. Click OK.

4. At the `Select point objects or [Numbers/Groups]`: prompt, select the 10 Civil 3D points in the drawing. As you select each point, a temporary red, dashed line will appear, marking the proposed line of best fit (see Figure 3.7). After you choose each point, press Enter. Panorama is displayed, and the following message appears in the command line: `Input data selection completed. See the Regression Data tab in Panorama to accept or modify the calculated data and create the best fit entity.`

5. In Panorama, note that you can exclude points, force pass-through points, and choose other options that would refine your line of best fit, as shown in Figure 3.8. Click the green checkbox in the upper-right corner of Panorama to dismiss this window. The line will be drawn and the command will end.

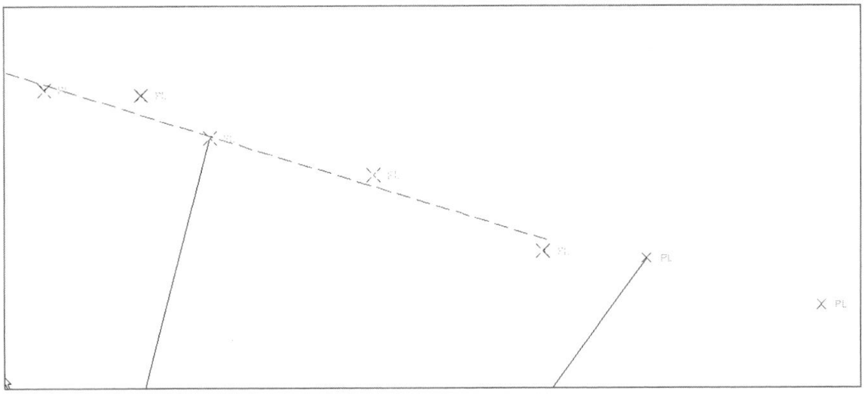

Figure 3.7

As you select the Civil 3D points, a preview of the line of best fit will appear.

Figure 3.8

The Line of Best Fit Panorama

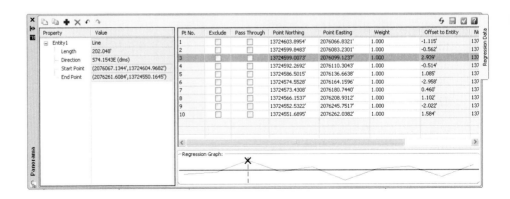

Labeling Property Lines and Curves

After deed linework has been drawn, you will often want to label it. Most commonly, you will label your lines with legal information, such as bearing, distance, curve information, and so on. The standard _AutoCAD Civil 3D (Imperial) NCS Extended.dwt template file includes many typical line and curve labels, as well as others that you might not have thought of, such as labels that read the elevations of the line and calculate grade or slope.

> It is important to note that line and curve labels are limited in their power. Although it is certainly appropriate to leave your linework as lines and arcs as you are checking your work, working with legacy plans, or creating a simple site plan, you should consider using Civil 3D parcels, alignments, survey networks, pipe networks, and other tools for most of your design tasks. For example, in this chapter, you are constructing a subdivision plat. If you would like to perform robust area analysis, or have more powerful editing tools, it would be in your best interest to convert the linework into Civil 3D parcels. If you were using the line/curve tools to create a road centerline, you would need to convert that geometry to a Civil 3D alignment in order to create profiles, design a road corridor, and perform additional design tasks.

The next exercise shows you how to add line and curve labels.

1. Continue working in LinesCurves1.dwg.

2. Choose Lines/Curves → Add Line/Curve Labels → Add Line/Curve Labels. The Add Labels dialog appears.

3. In the Add Labels dialog, change the Label type to Multiple Segment. Confirm that the Line label style is set to Bearing over Distance and the Curve label style is set to Distance Only, as shown in Figure 3.9. Click Add.

4. At the Select Entity: prompt, pick each line and arc in the drawing one at a time. A label will appear at the midpoint of each entity. After you have labeled all of the lines, click Close on the Add Labels dialog. Your result should be similar to Figure 3.10.

Most Civil 3D labels behave much like line and curve labels. They can be moved and dragged using special grips, and they can be edited, changed, and customized. The next

Figure 3.9

The Add Labels dialog

Figure 3.10

The labeled linework

exercise will help you build skills for manipulating not only line and curve labels, but also other labels throughout Civil 3D.

1. Zoom in on any line label. Select the label and right-click. A context-specific shortcut menu appears (Figure 3.11).

2. Select Flip Label. Note that the bearing component and distance components are on opposite sides of the line.

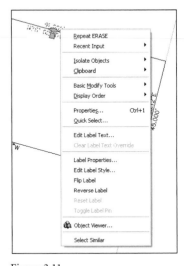

3. Select the label again, and right-click. Select Reverse Label from the shortcut menu. Note that the direction of the label is now reversed. (For example, if it was originally NE, it is now SW.)

   There may be times when you accidentally place a label with the wrong style, or perhaps several labels are crowded together. The next few steps show you how to swap the Distance Only curve label for a label that shows distance, radius, and delta angle, and then how to drag the label out of the way.

Figure 3.11

The context-specific shortcut menu for a line label

4. Zoom in on any curve label. Select the label and right-click. A context-specific shortcut menu appears.

5. Select Label Properties. The AutoCAD Properties dialog appears.

6. Make sure you are on the Design tab of the AutoCAD Properties dialog. You should see a section called Civil 3D on the dialog.

7. In the Civil 3D section, click in the whitespace next to the General Curve Label Style entry. A pull-down menu appears (see Figure 3.12). Choose Distance-Radius and Delta. If you have trouble working with the AutoCAD properties dialog, right-click on the spine of the dialog and disallow Autohide.

8. Dismiss the Properties dialog, or move it away from the drawing space so that you can see the new label.

9. Select the label. Note that there are two grips that appear. Grab the square grip and drag the label off to the side. Note that an arrow appears and the label changes to a stacked formation (Figure 3.13).

10. Select the label and right-click. Choose the Reset Label option from the shortcut menu. Note that the label returns to its original location along the curve.

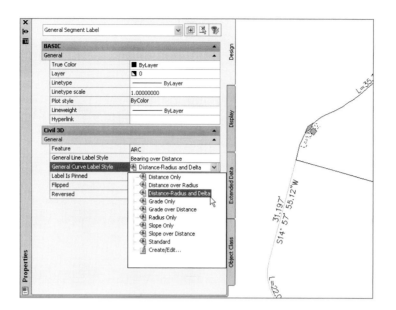

Figure 3.12

The AutoCAD Properties dialog showing the curve label pull-down menu

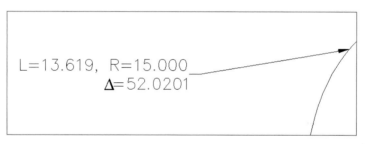

$$L=13.619, \quad R=15.000$$
$$\Delta=52.0201$$

Figure 3.13

A curve label in dragged state

Making a Segment Table

Plans can become cluttered with labels, and there may be times when you want to replace your line or curve labels with numbered tags that are referenced on a table. Figure 3.14 shows a series of curve tags that are referenced on the table shown in Figure 3.15.

1. Choose Lines/Curves → Add Tables → Add Segments. The Table Creation dialog will appear.

Figure 3.14

A series of curves that have been labeled with tags instead of labels

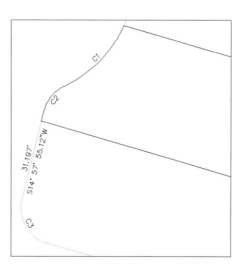

Figure 3.15

A curve table

Curve #	Length	Radius	Delta	Chord Direction	Chord Length
C1	35.37	50.00	40.53	N46° 43' 12"E	34.64
C2	21.95	14.00	89.81	N59° 52' 22"E	19.77
C3	22.04	14.00	90.19	S30° 07' 38"E	19.83
C4	133.96	50.00	153.50	N50° 17' 48"W	97.34
C5	13.62	15.00	52.02	N78° 57' 46"E	13.16

Curve Table

2. In the Select by Label or Style list, check the General Curve: Distance Only box and the General Line: Bearing Over Distance box, as shown in Figure 3.16. It may be helpful to make the window larger by using the resize grip (located in lower-right corner of the window). Click OK to dismiss the dialog.

3. At the Select upper left corner: prompt, pick a location in the drawing to place your table. The table will appear in the drawing and the command will end. Your result should be similar (but unlikely identical) to Figure 3.17. Also note that your labels have changed from their original form to tag form.

Figure 3.16

The Table Creation dialog

Figure 3.17

A segment table

Segment Table			
Line #/Curve #	Length	Direction/Delta	Radius
C2	13.619	52.0201	15.000
C3	22.036	90.1853	14.000
C4	133.955	153.5017	50.000
C5	13.619	52.0201	15.000
C6	21.946	89.8147	14.000
C7	133.955	153.5017	50.000
C8	133.955	153.5017	50.000
L1	45.000	N14° 57' 55.12"E	
L2	31.197	S14° 57' 55.12"W	
L3	149.941	N14° 57' 55.12"E	
L4	17.431	N75° 02' 04.88"W	
L5	91.585	S74° 55' 35.50"W	
L6	100.722	S36° 42' 51.80"W	
L7	202.066	N75° 01' 38.04"W	
L8	93.009	S14° 58' 21.96"W	
L9	115.000	S14° 58' 21.96"W	
L10	10.850	S75° 01' 38.04"E	
L11	87.000	S75° 13' 12.10"E	
L12	30.916	N14° 57' 55.12"E	
L13	115.000	N75° 02' 04.88"W	

Segment Table			
Line #/Curve #	Length	Direction/Delta	Radius
L14	91.002	N75° 02' 04.88"W	
L15	149.941	N14° 57' 55.12"E	
L16	202.066	N75° 01' 38.04"W	

Summary

In this chapter, you became familiar with some of the tools available under the Lines/Curves menu. Although AutoCAD lines and arcs are not the most powerful objects you will create in Civil 3D, they often serve as an important foundation for more sophisticated creations, such as parcels, alignments, survey networks, and more. You also saw that lines and curves can be dynamically labeled using Civil 3D tools, and you learned a few ways to manipulate these labels and create tables from them.

CHAPTER 4

Survey

Although there continues to be new developments in LiDAR, GPS, and aerial photography for basemap information, almost every civil engineering project begins with a ground survey. Surveyors are responsible for locating property boundaries, existing features, utilities, surface elevations, and more.

In previous generations, the surveyors simply picked up data for a collection of points, and the linework was drawn after the data was brought into the drawing, either on paper or in CAD. As survey technology becomes more sophisticated, surveyors now have the option of field-to-finish systems, including automatic linework.

The Civil 3D survey tools are geared toward surveyors who are taking full advantage of this field-to-finish technology. This chapter focuses on the Survey Toolspace and importing a field book. Surveyors will also want to reference Chapter 3, "Lines and Curves," and Chapter 5, "Points." All three chapters combined provide engineers and surveyors with an introduction to the tools they need to import existing information and to prepare points for stakeout.

This chapter includes the following topics:

- Setting equipment properties
- Creating a figure prefix database
- Creating description keys
- Establishing a working folder
- Creating a local survey database
- Creating a new network
- Importing a field book
- Examining points and figures
- Importing additional survey data
- Creating and editing survey figures

Establishing Survey Settings

Figure 4.1

A combination of field standards and Civil 3D survey settings will automatically create properly formatted points and linework.

In the days of running a level or using less-sophisticated survey equipment, it was pretty common to simply dump a batch of generic points into a drawing. A CAD operator in the office would then sort through each point and figure out which dots to connect, as well as manually make adjustments to elevation, style, and so on. The CAD system had no real intelligence to offer for equipment adjustment, nor could it do automatic formatting or draw lines based on point code.

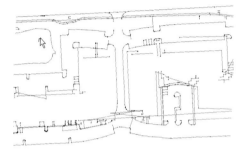

With today's equipment, things are different. There are countless manufacturers, specifications, standard field codes, and other variables, so it is important that you take time in the beginning of the project to customize the Civil 3D survey settings to your requirements.

A combination of well-crafted field standards and survey settings will produce well-formatted points and linework, as shown in Figure 4.1. This data is imported as a field book (with the filename extension .fbk), and will serve as a foundation for surface building, existing conditions plans, parceling, and all other design functions as the project evolves.

Many of the survey settings, such as equipment and prefixes, are not drawing-specific, but instead are kept in a series of external databases. By default, these folders are mapped locally. The paths for these databases, and many other settings, can be changed in the Survey User Settings dialog. (See Figure 4.2.)

Figure 4.2

The Survey User Settings dialog provides an interface to change the default database paths and other options.

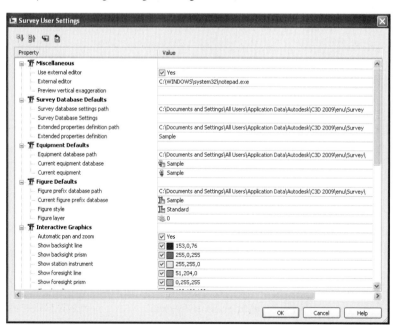

Setting Equipment Properties

Every piece of survey equipment is different. Several tasks, such as traverse adjustment, may require special corrections based on the equipment properties. Civil 3D maintains an equipment database for you to store information about the tools that your crew uses for collecting data in the field. It is important to have the manufacturer's guide to each piece of equipment in hand when creating a new entry in the database.

Figure 4.3

Expand the Sample equipment database to reveal the Sample equipment entry.

The equipment database is not drawing-specific. The database is an external file and will, therefore, be available to any project on which you are working. The storage location for this database can be changed using the Survey User Settings button on the Survey Toolspace.

The following exercise shows you how to access and modify a piece of equipment in the equipment database:

1. Open the Survey.dwg, which you can download from www.sybex .com/go/introducingcivil3d2009. The drawing is empty.

2. If the Toolspace is not already visible, choose General → Toolspace.

3. Choose Survey → Open Survey Toolspace. The Survey tab will be added to the Toolspace. There will now be three tabs: Prospector, Settings, and Survey.

4. Switch to the Survey Toolspace. Click the plus sign (+) button to expand the Equipment Databases entry, and then click + again to expand the Sample equipment database as shown in Figure 4.3.

5. Select the Sample equipment entry, right-click, and choose Properties. The Equipment Properties dialog appears.

6. Change the name of the equipment from Sample to **Introducing Civil 3D Collector** in the Name Value Field.

7. Use the pull-down button in the Value column next to Distance to change the distance units from meters to feet. Your dialog should now look like Figure 4.4.

8. Use the scroll bar to scroll down, and note each equipment option. When you're adding your specific field equipment, be sure to study the manufacturer's manual and make the necessary adjustments in this dialog. Click OK.

    An entry appears under the Sample equipment database for Introducing Civil 3D Collector, as shown in Figure 4.5.

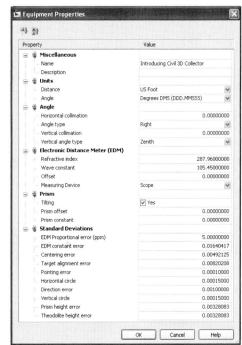

Figure 4.4

The Equipment Properties dialog

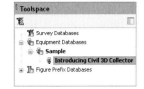

Figure 4.5

The new equipment entry appears in the Sample equipment database.

Creating a Figure Prefix Database

Survey figures are special lines drawn to connect survey data points. For example, a figure may be drawn to connect shots taken along an edge of pavement or around a property boundary. These figures can be foundation linework for exhibits, added to surfaces as breaklines, targeted by corridors, or used to create parcels.

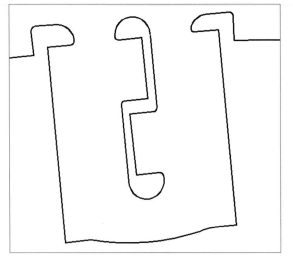

When the crew enters specific codes into the data collector as the points are collected, these codes can be used to automatically create figures in the drawing. It is important to note that your company must have established standards and procedures for field coding before figures can be automatically created upon the import of a field book (.fbk).

The figure prefix database allows you to standardize how these figures appear in the drawing. With the appropriate figure prefix database in place, the figures will be automatically drawn on the correct layer, with the correct style applied, as shown in Figure 4.6.

The following exercise will lead you through creating a figure prefix database to standardize the styles of imported figures.

Figure 4.6

When a field book for a shopping center was imported, these curb figures were automatically created from the field codes. The figure prefix database automatically applied the appropriate style.

1. Continue working in the Survey.dwg file.

2. Right-click the Figure Prefix Databases entry and choose New. The New Figure Prefix Database dialog will appear.

3. Type **Introducing Civil 3D** as the name for the prefix database. An entry for the new database appears.

4. Select the Introducing Civil 3D prefix database, right-click, and choose Edit. The Panorama window appears.

5. Right-click in the first Name cell, and choose New. An entry called Sample appears in the Panorama.

6. Click inside the cell that reads Sample, and change the name of the entry to **EP**. Use the Layer pull-down list to assign the V-SURV-FIGR layer. Use the Style pull-down list to assign the Basic style to the EP entry.

7. Repeat step 5 to create an entry for CL. Use the Layer pull-down list to assign the V-SURV-FIGR layer. Use the Style pull-down list to assign the Road Centerline style to the CL entry.

8. Repeat step 5 to create an entry for BOC. Use the Layer pull-down list to assign the V-SURV-FIGR layer. Use the Style pull-down list to assign the Curb style to the BOC entry. Your Panorama should now look like Figure 4.7.

9. Click the green checkmark in the upper-right corner of Panorama to accept the entries. A dialog will appear asking if you would like to apply changes. Click Yes.

   The database is now set up and will be available when a field book is imported.

Figure 4.7

Create survey prefix entries for EP, CL, and BOC.

Creating Description Keys

There are two different types of points in Civil 3D: coordinate geometry (COGO) points and survey points. Each type of point contains the same basic information. They each have a Number, Northing, Easting, Elevation, and Description specification. They can both be placed into groups and have point styles and label styles applied.

COGO points can be imported from external lists, created manually, moved, erased, and edited. (COGO points are discussed in more detail in Chapter 5.)

Survey points are created from a field book (.fbk) file, and can only be edited by adjusting the data in that field book.

Although the two types of points have their differences, both can be automatically processed using description keys. When a point is imported into the drawing (either through the methods discussed in Chapter 5 or when a field book is imported), it is matched up with the appropriate description key. For example, a description key for a point that is coded TREE will ensure that point has the Tree Point Style applied and is placed on the tree layer, as shown in Figure 4.8.

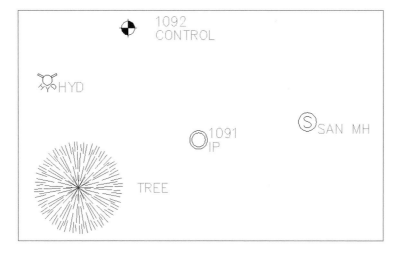

Figure 4.8

A description key automatically assigns the appropriate point style, label style, and layer based on the point code.

It is very common for point codes to consist of letters that identify the type of point followed by a number signifying the figure or series to which it belongs. For example, in the field book you will import later in the chapter, the edge-of-pavement points are coded EP1 and EP2, where all EP1 points are connected to create the figure that represents the north side of the road, and all EP2 points are connected to create the figure that represents the south side of the road. When creating the description key for this type of point, a wildcard (*) can be used to identify which portion of the code may vary. In this example, the code for edge-of-pavement points will be EP*, as shown in Figure 4.9.

Unlike the equipment database and the figure prefix database, description keys are drawing-specific. Once your company has established standard codes for the field crews, you need to create a description key set to match your company standard and save it in your company standard drawing template (.dwt).

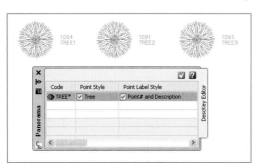

Figure 4.9

Description keys allow for wildcards when part of the standard code may vary.

In the following exercise, you create description keys for the four types of points that will import with the field book. These points are Edge of Pavement (EP), Back of Curb (BOC), Road Centerline (CL), and Control (CONTROL).

1. Continue working in the Survey.dwg file.

2. Switch to the Settings tab of the Toolspace.

3. Locate the Description Key Sets entry under the Point tree.

4. Right-click Description Key Sets and choose New. The Description Key Set dialog appears.

5. In the Name field, change the name to **Introducing Civil 3D Desc Keys**. Click OK.

6. Click the plus sign (+) to expand the Description Key Sets list and expose the new description key that you just made.

7. Select Introducing Civil 3D Desc Keys, right-click, and choose Edit Keys. The Panorama window appears.

8. Change the name of the New Desc Key entry to **EP***.

9. Check the box next to <default> in the Point Style column. The Point Style dialog will appear.

10. In the Point Style dialog, use the pull-down list to assign the Basic point style. Click OK.

11. Check the box next to <default> in the Point Label Style column. The Point Label Style dialog will appear.

12. Use the Point Label Style pull-down list to assign the Point#-Elevation-Description label style. Click OK.

13. Check the box in the Layer column. The Layer Selection dialog will appear.

14. Choose V-NODE and click OK.

15. Right-click the EP* entry, and choose Copy.

16. Change the code of the new description key to **BOC**.

17. Repeat step 15, and change the code of the new description key to **CL**.

18. Right-click over the CL description key and choose New. A new description key will appear.

19. Change the code of the new description key to **CONTROL***. Assign the Benchmark point style, the Description Only Point label style, and the V-CTRL-BMRK layer. The Panorama should now look like Figure 4.10.

20. Click the green checkmark in the upper-right corner to accept the description keys.

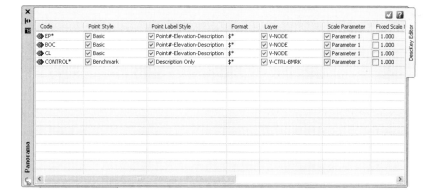

Figure 4.10

Completed description keys for Edge of Pavement, Back of Curb, Centerline, and Control

Importing Survey Data

After the survey settings have been customized for equipment, figures, and point codes, you are ready to bring in the data. The Civil 3D survey tools are designed to accept data input from either SurveyXML or a field book (.fbk) file. For the exercises in this chapter, you will import a field book.

A field book file is not simply a list of points. The field book contains a record of how the data was collected, such as where the instrument was set up, the height of the rod, vertical and horizontal angles, and other critical information. Depending on your equipment, field standards, and procedures, a field book can also contain information about how to draw figures.

When a field book is imported into Civil 3D, the data is converted into an external survey database that will be available for use in other related drawings.

Establishing a Working Folder

The survey database is stored in a working folder. The working folder must be set before you import survey data, and you may want to establish different working folders for different projects.

The following exercise will lead you through setting the working folder to
`C:\Civil 3D Projects`.

1. Continue working in the `Survey.dwg` file.

2. Switch to the Survey tab of the Toolspace.

3. Right-click the Survey Databases entry and choose Set Working Folder (Figure 4.11). The Browse for Folder dialog will appear.

4. Select the Civil 3D Projects folder under your `C:` drive, and click OK. The working folder is now established and all survey databases will be saved to this location.

Figure 4.11

Right-click the Survey Database entry and choose Set Working Folder.

Creating a Local Survey Database

Before you can import survey data, you must create a local survey database. You can create more than one survey database in any given working folder. For example, if a certain project were surveyed in phases, it would make sense to keep the data from those phases separate.

You will create a new survey database in the following exercise:

1. Continue working in the `Survey.dwg` file.

2. Switch to the Survey tab of the Toolspace (if it is not already displayed).

3. Right-click the Survey Databases entry and choose New Local Survey Database. The New Local Survey Database dialog will appear.

4. In the dialog, type **Introducing Civil 3D Survey Database**. Click OK. An entry will appear in the Toolspace for the new database that contains placeholders for Networks, Figures, and Survey Points, as shown in Figure 4.12.

Figure 4.12

Placeholders for Networks, Figures, and Survey Points are created in the Survey Toolspace.

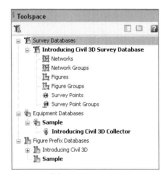

Creating a New Network

A survey network is a collection of connected data from the field. A network can contain any of the following: setups, control points, non-control points, known directions, observations, and traverses. One survey database can contain several networks. For example, if the crew collects data over three days and creates three separate field books, you may want to have three networks in the project survey database.

This exercise teaches you how to create a new network.

1. Continue working in the Survey.dwg file.

2. Switch to the Survey tab of the Toolspace (if it is not already displayed).

3. Right-click the Networks entry under Introducing Civil 3D Survey Database, and choose New. The New Network dialog will appear.

4. In the New Network dialog, name the network **Fieldwork 3-18-08**. Click OK. Placeholders for Control Points, Non-Control Points, and more will appear under Networks in the Toolspace, as shown in Figure 4.13.

Figure 4.13

Placeholders for Control Points, Non-Control Points, Directions, Setups, and Traverses appear under the newly created network.

Importing a Field Book

After the survey database has been created and a network is in place, the field book can be imported. When you import a field book, the setups, points, and figures are drawn on the screen with interactive graphics. Interactive graphics mimic the actions of the survey crew as the data is processed in the drawing. When the import is complete, the data is displayed on-screen, and the survey database is populated.

The next exercise leads you through importing a very simple field book.

1. Continue working in the Survey.dwg file.

2. Right-click on the Fieldwork 3-18-08 network. Choose Import Field Book. The Field Book filename dialog will appear.

3. In the Field Book filename dialog, navigate to the 3-18-08.fbk file (which you can download from www.sybex.com/go/introducingcivil3d2009). Click Open. The Import Field Book dialog will appear.

4. Use the pull-down list to set the Introducing Civil 3D prefix database.

5. Confirm that all of the Yes boxes are checked except Display Tolerance, as shown in Figure 4.14. Click OK.

Figure 4.14

The Import Field Book dialog

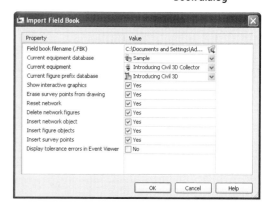

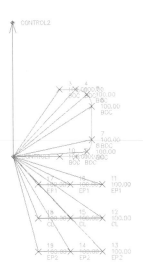

Figure 4.15

The data from the field book is drawn on-screen.

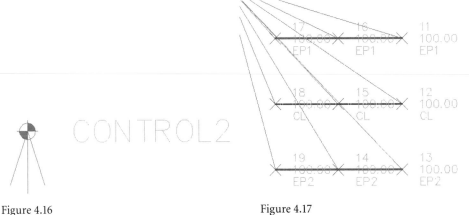

Figure 4.16

The points appear with the appropriate symbols as specified in the description key.

Figure 4.17

The figures appear with the appropriate style as specified in the figure prefix database.

6. Wait as the interactive graphics draw the field book elements on the screen. When they have finished, you will see the points and linework in the drawing as shown in Figure 4.15.

7. Zoom in on the northernmost control point. Note that the description key automatically assigned the benchmark symbol to this point based on its code of CONTROL*, as shown in Figure 4.16.

8. Zoom in on the edge-of-pavement and road-centerline figures. Note that the figure prefix database assigned the appropriate figure style based on the EP and CL codes, as shown in Figure 4.17.

Examining Points and Figures

A survey network has two fundamental components: points and figures.

Survey points, as introduced in the description key section earlier in this chapter, cannot be edited within the drawing environment. To edit a survey point, you must change the observations and data that created that point in the survey database. This may seem tedious at first glance, but it ensures that the original survey data remains intact. Survey points can be examined in Prospector, on the Survey tab under Networks, and in the drawing through tooltips and the right-click shortcut menu.

Figures are the linework created by codes and commands entered into the raw data during field collection. Figures can be edited and adjusted within the drawing environment. Figure properties can be examined on the Survey tab under Networks, and in the drawing through the right-click shortcut menu.

The following exercise will lead you through some methods for inspecting survey points and figures:

Figure 4.18

1. Continue working in the Survey.dwg file.

2. Move your mouse over any point, and note that a tooltip appears with information about that point.

Information regarding the setup appears in the item view.

3. On the Survey tab of the Toolspace, click the plus sign (+) to expand the Control Points tree. Select one of the control points, right-click, and choose Zoom To. Note that the drawing zooms in on the selected point.

Property	Value
Station Point	1
Backsight Point	2
Backsight Direction	0.0000
Backsight Orientation	0.0000
Backsight Face1	
Backsight Face2	
Instrument Height	5.000
Instrument Elevation	105.000
Easting	5000.0100
Northing	5000.0100
Elevation	100.000
Longitude	
Latitude	
Setup Equipment Properties	Introducing Civil 3D Collector

4. Click + to expand the Setups tree. Note that information regarding each setup appears in the item view (Figure 4.18).

5. Click + to expand the Figures tree. An entry for each figure—BOC, CL, EP1, and EP2—is listed.

6. Select BOC and note that the BOC figure becomes high-lighted in the drawing, as shown in Figure 4.19. Also note that figure information appears in the item view at the bottom of the Survey tab.

7. Select the Survey Points entry. Note that each survey point is listed in the item view.

Figure 4.19

When you select a figure in the Survey Toolspace, the figure is highlighted in the drawing.

Refining Survey Data

You will rarely find that the first trip to the field for a project is the only fieldwork you will do for that project. Often, the first batch of data creates more questions than it answers. Once some idea of site features and topography is established, the designer will often request additional shots taken (for example, along a bordering road or to locate upstream manholes). Perhaps the first day of fieldwork alerted the crew to possible wetlands, and a few weeks later, they return to pick up the flag locations placed by the wetlands specialist.

After this new data is imported, there is always work to be done to tie the two sets of information together. Figures may need to be extended to accommodate extra points, or new figures may need to be drawn.

Importing Additional Data

Survey crews will commonly return to the field to collect more data. One of the most common requests from designers is to gather more information about an existing road so that more entrance locations can be explored, or to make sure drainage has been accommodated. If the in-house crews are busy, an outside surveyor may be contracted. This surveyor may not use the same equipment as your company, or they may not be as well trained in figure creation.

The following exercise leads you through importing a field book that contains only points.

1. Continue working in the `Survey.dwg` file.

2. Right-click the Networks entry, and choose New. The New Network dialog appears.

3. Name the network **Fieldwork 9-18-08**. Enter a network description of **From outside surveyor - no linework**. Click OK. A new entry appears under the Networks tree.

4. Right-click the Fieldwork 9-18-08 entry, and select Import Field Book. The Field book filename dialog appears.

5. Navigate to `AdditionalSurvey.fbk.`, and click Open. The Import Field Book dialog appears.

6. Confirm that the Introducing Civil 3D prefix database is selected, and that all of the Yes boxes are checked except the one for tolerance errors. Click OK.

7. A collection of survey points appears in the drawing representing EP and CL, as shown in Figure 4.20.

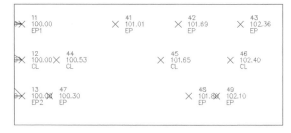

Figure 4.20

Additional survey points are added for EP and CL.

Creating and Editing Survey Figures

There are often occasions where you need to draw new figures. Perhaps you have legacy projects where the data was collected before your crew learned how to draw figures in the field, or before your standards were in place. Maybe you receive a batch of data from an outside surveyor who doesn't use your codes. Sometimes you might find it useful to draw a figure that doesn't follow your company standards and, therefore, must be hand-drawn.

Survey figures can be created using interactive tools under the Survey menu, or by right-clicking the figure name in the Toolspace. You can also draw lines, polylines, or feature lines and convert them to figures using Survey → Create Figure from Object.

If you find an error in a figure, it might be best to make the adjustments to the field book data. If that isn't possible, figures can be edited using many of the Feature Line tools, which can be found on the Feature Line toolbar as well as under Survey → Edit Figure Geometry.

In the following exercise, you create figures (lines) to connect the new survey points that represent the edge of pavement and road centerline:

1. Continue working in the Survey.dwg file.

2. Click the plus sign (+) to expand the Figures tree.

3. Right-click Figures and choose Modify Figure → Begin New Figure.

4. At the Enter Figure Name: prompt, type **EP3** and then press ↵.

5. At the Specify first vertex or [Point]: prompt, type **P** and then press ↵.

6. At the Enter Point Identifier: prompt, type **43** and then press ↵.

7. At the Specify vertex or [Point]: prompt, type **P** and then press ↵.

8. At the Enter Point Identifier: prompt, type **42** and then press ↵. A preview of the EP3 figure is drawn between points 43 and 42, as shown in Figure 4.21.

9. Repeat steps 7 and 8 for points 41 and 11. Press ↵ to leave the point entry portion of the command.

10. At the Select entry[Point/Angle/Azimuth/Bearing/DEflection/Right-turn/CUrve/CLose/DOne>: prompt, type **DO** and then press ↵. While the figure has been created in the survey database, it has not yet been drawn in the drawing.

11. On the Survey tab of the Toolspace, right-click Figures and choose Update Figures. The new EP3 figure is drawn, as shown in Figure 4.22. Note that the figure prefix database ensured that this EP figure was drawn with the correct style.

Figure 4.21

A new figure segment is drawn between points 43 and 42.

✕ 41 101.01 EP	✕ 42 101.65 EP	✕ 43 102.36 EP

Figure 4.22

The new figure is completed, connecting the three new survey points to point number 11.

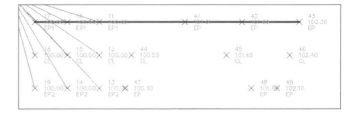

12. In the drawing, select the EP3 figure. Right-click and choose Elevation Editor. The Panorama window will appear.

13. Note in Panorama that each vertex of the figure is assigned an elevation that corresponds to the appropriate survey point. (See Figure 4.23.)

14. Repeat steps 3 through 8 to create new figures for the additional CL and EP points. The end result will look like Figure 4.24

Figure 4.23

The elevation editor can be used to view each vertex in detail.

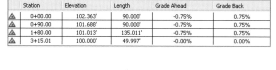

	Station	Elevation	Length	Grade Ahead	Grade Back
△	0+00.00	102.363'	90.000'	-0.75%	0.75%
△	0+90.00	101.688'	90.000'	-0.75%	0.75%
△	1+80.00	101.013'	135.011'	-0.75%	0.75%
△	3+15.01	100.000'	49.997'	-0.00%	0.00%

Figure 4.24

Three new figures are drawn to connect the new points.

Summary

In this chapter, you were introduced to a just a few of the tools available for surveyors. First, settings must be established for equipment and field codes. Next, a file location for the survey database is chosen so that the field book can be imported to populate the database with information from the survey crew. After this data has been brought into Civil 3D, the data can be adjusted, refined, and used as a basis to launch the balance of the project.

It is important to remember that tools such as figure prefixes and description keys cannot be used until your company has well-established standards. The survey crew must use standard field codes and be well-versed in using their equipment to collect data properly for figure creation.

Inside the office, your company must also have established a Civil 3D template that contains the appropriate layers, blocks, point styles, figure styles, label styles, description keys, and other fundamental elements. An equipment database and a figure prefix database are also critical.

Although it may seem overwhelming at first, after the standards are in place, much of the tedious manual drafting that was once necessary to draw survey linework is minimized.

CHAPTER 5

Points

In civil engineering, points are the foundation of all geometry—both existing and design. When a project is started, points are often used to represent ground elevations, feature locations, property corners, and other critical elements. When working through a project, a designer might set points to assist with grading or to mark special areas. Finally, the project cannot be built in the field without a survey crew marking out the design through a list of points from the engineer.

This chapter includes the following topics:

- Importing points from a text file
- Creating point groups
- Changing a point elevation
- Creating points at parcel corners
- Creating points at alignment and profile geometry points
- Creating tree points along an alignment
- Organizing stakeout points with point groups
- Creating a point table
- Exporting stakeout points

Working with Ground Points

At the beginning of a project, you are often presented with a text file listing point numbers, northings, eastings, elevations, and descriptions (see Figure 5.1). This file may come from an outside surveyor or GPS, or perhaps your own crew doesn't take advantage of the survey tools discussed in Chapter 4, "Survey." Civil 3D provides tools for working with these coordinate geometry (COGO) points. The next few exercises focus on giving you hands-on practice with importing, manipulating, organizing, and stylizing points from a text file.

```
1,13723761.0154,2075725.6882,823.9807,GS
2,13723761.0154,2075775.6882,824.4762,GS
3,13723811.0154,2075725.6882,824.5473,GS
4,13723811.0154,2075775.6882,824.8232,GS
5,13723811.0154,2075825.6882,825.3147,GS
6,13723861.0154,2075725.6882,826.1577,GS
7,13723861.0154,2075775.6882,826.1891,GS
8,13723861.0154,2075825.6882,825.4544,GS
9,13723861.0154,2075875.6882,825.6364,GS
10,13723861.0154,2075925.6882,825.6495,GS
11,13723861.0154,2075975.6882,825.3934,GS
12,13723911.0154,2075675.6882,824.6068,GS
13,13723911.0154,2075725.6882,826.8439,GS
14,13723911.0154,2075775.6882,826.6489,GS
15,13723911.0154,2075825.6882,826.0783,GS
16,13723911.0154,2075875.6882,825.5154,GS
17,13723911.0154,2075925.6882,825.9581,GS
18,13723911.0154,2075975.6882,826.2310,GS
19,13723911.0154,2076025.6882,825.9749,GS
20,13723911.0154,2076075.6882,825.7188,GS
21,13723911.0154,2076125.6882,825.4627,GS
22,13723961.0154,2075675.6882,824.9813,GS
23,13723961.0154,2075725.6882,827.8400,GS
```

Figure 5.1

A typical text file of point locations in Point Number, Northing, Easting, Elevation, Description (PNEZD) format

Importing Points from a Text File

Although most firms are striving to make their survey processes more automatic, starting a project with a text file of points downloaded from a data collector is still the most common way to begin a project. These points will be the foundation for linework—such as curbs, centerlines, and property boundaries—as well as for building surfaces. The following exercise leads you through importing a PNEZD file of points:

1. Open the drawing file `Points1.dwg`, which you can download from www.sybex.com/go/introducingcivil3d2009. It is an empty drawing.

2. Choose Points ▸ Import/Export Points ▸ Import Points. The Import Points dialog will appear.

3. In the Import Points dialog, confirm that the PNEZD (comma delimited) format is selected.

4. Click the blue plus sign (+). The Select Source File dialog will appear.

5. In the Select Source File dialog, navigate to the `IntroducingPoints.txt` file. Select the file and click Open.

6. Back in the Import Points dialog, uncheck the Do Elevation Adjustment If Possible box. The dialog should look like Figure 5.2.

7. Click OK. The points will appear in the drawing as red *X*s without labels, as shown in Figure 5.3.

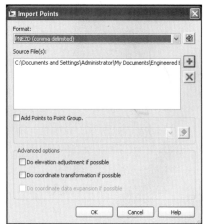

Figure 5.2

The Import Points dialog

8. Locate the Points entry on the Prospector tab of the Toolspace, as shown in Figure 5.4. Select the Points entry.

9. Look at the bottom half of the Prospector and locate the item view that lists all of the points in the drawing.

10. Scroll down to the entry for point number 408, as shown in Figure 5.5. Select the entry, and right-click. A context-specific shortcut menu will appear. Choose Zoom To. The drawing will zoom in on point 408.

11. Hover your cursor over the point on the screen. Note that a tooltip appears with point information, as shown in Figure 5.6.

Creating Point Groups

After the points are imported, they must be organized and annotated. Although it may occasionally be useful to have points simply marked with an X, most designers will want some labeling to help identify the points. The following exercise leads you through using the _All Points group to assign a label style to the newly imported points:

1. Continue working in the drawing from the previous exercise, or open the Points2 .dwg (which you can download from www .sybex.com/go/introducingcivil3d2009).

2. Locate the Point Groups entry on the Prospector tab of the Toolspace. Expand the entry. The _All Points group will appear in the tree.

3. Right-click the _All Points group, and choose Properties. The Point Group Properties dialog appears.

4. In the Point Group Properties dialog, use the Point Label Style pull-down list to choose Point#-Elevation-Description.

5. Click OK.

   All of the points in the drawing now have the Point#-Elevation-Description label style assigned.

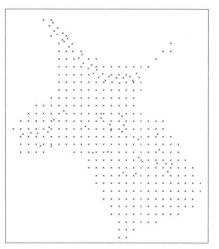

Figure 5.3

The points will appear as red *X*s with no labels upon import.

Figure 5.4

The Points entry in Prospector

Point Number	Northing	Easting	Point Elevation	N
397	13725146.2224'	2075286.8067'	827.995'	
398	13725112.0571'	2075319.0827'	827.419'	
399	13725077.8918'	2075351.3586'	826.313'	
400	13725043.7266'	2075383.6345'	825.897'	
401	13725009.5613'	2075415.9104'	825.632'	
403	13724941.2307'	2075480.4622'	824.932'	
405	13724872.9002'	2075545.0140'	824.116'	
406	13724840.6887'	2075579.1620'	823.669'	
407	13724815.4567'	2075618.7278'	823.339'	
408	13724798.3072'	2075662.4086'	823.814'	
409	13724789.8811'	2075708.5725'	823.784'	
410	13724790.4929'	2075755.4952'	823.636'	
411	13724800.1198'	2075801.4237'	823.674'	
412	13724818.4023'	2075844.6425'	823.578'	

Figure 5.5

Use the item view in Prospector to examine individual point information.

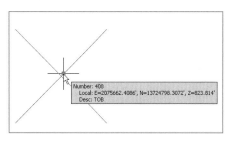

Figure 5.6

When near a point object, tooltips display point information.

Labeling is a great way to display the information that was captured during the field work, but it is often not enough. Special points representing hydrants, shrubs, manholes, guy poles, and other features require an appropriate symbol.

In the following exercise, you use point groups to assign a point style to points based on their descriptions:

1. Continue working in `Points2.dwg`.

2. Locate the Point Groups entry on the Prospector. Right-click the Point Groups entry and choose New. The Point Group Properties dialog appears.

3. Change the Name of the point group from the default to **Trees**.

4. Use the Point Style pull-down list to choose Tree, and use the Point Label Style pull-down list to choose Elevation and Description. The dialog should now look like Figure 5.7.

5. Switch to the Include tab. Check the With Raw Description Matching box, and type **TREE** in the empty field as shown in Figure 5.8.

6. Click OK.

All of the points in the Trees group will now have the tree style and the Elevation and Description label style applied, as shown in Figure 5.9.

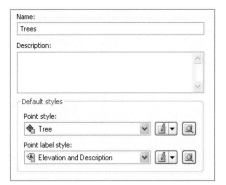

Figure 5.7

Set the style to Tree and the label style to Elevation and Description.

Figure 5.8

Include all of the points having the raw description of TREE.

Figure 5.9

All of the points in the Trees group appear with the tree symbol.

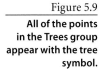

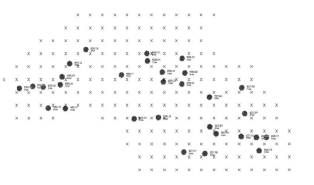

In addition to organizing points into groups to assist with their visual appearance, it is a good idea to create groups to sort points that will be edited together or perhaps used for certain linework. This could include creating points for edge-of-pavement shots, stream-course centerlines, property corners, or other similar, meaningful groups. The following example sorts some ditch top-of-bank points into their own group so that they can be visually isolated from the other drawing points to make linework creation easier.

1. Continue working in the Points2.dwg file.

2. Locate the Point Groups entry on the Prospector. Right-click the Point Groups entry and choose New.

3. Change the Name of the point group from Point the default to **Top of Bank**.

4. Use the Point Style pull-down list to choose Basic. Use the Point Label Style pull-down list to choose Elevation and Description.

5. Switch to the Include tab. Check the With Raw Description Matching box, and type **TOB** in the empty field.

6. Click OK.

   All of the TOB points in the northeast portion of the site are now in the Top of Bank point group.

A point can belong to multiple point groups, which at first glance might seem confusing. How does the point know which style to use if the two groups have different styles assigned? In the previous exercise, how did the tree points know they should appear as trees and not the style assigned to the _All Points group? Figure 5.10 illustrates the point group appearance hierarchy that will be used several times in the next few exercises. The groups that are higher on the list control the appearance over point groups that are lower on the list.

Figure 5.10

Point groups can be moved up or down the hierarchy to determine which group controls the visual appearance of points.

The following exercise will lead you through changing the Point Group hierarchy for controlling point group visibility:

1. Continue working in the Points2.dwg file.

2. Locate the _All Points group on the Prospector. Right-click and choose Properties. The Point Group Properties dialog will appear.

3. In the Point Group Properties dialog, use the pull-down lists to change the Point Style to <none> and the Point Label style to <none>. Click OK. Most of the points in

the drawing become invisible, except the Trees group and the Top of Bank group, as shown in Figure 5.11.

4. Locate the Point Groups entry on the Prospector. Right-click and choose Properties. The Point Groups dialog appears.

5. Use the up arrow to move the _All Points group to the top of the list that appears in the Point Groups dialog, as shown in Figure 5.12. Click OK. All of the points in the drawing become invisible.

6. Repeat step 4 to bring up the Point Groups dialog. Use the up arrow to move the Top of Bank group above the _All Points group. Click OK. The Top of Bank group appears in the drawing. This would be handy for creating linework for the Top of Bank points without having to sort through all of the rest of the ground shots.

Figure 5.11

When the _All Points group is set to not display, only the trees and top-of-bank shots remain visible.

Figure 5.12

Move the _All Points group to the top of the hierarchy.

Changing a Point Elevation

After points have been imported, it is fairly common to find a mistake. Perhaps the surveyors miskeyed a description in the field, or an elevation got an extra digit. Civil 3D makes it easy to edit points. Any changes made to the point will immediately be reflected in the point labeling and Prospector information.

Points can be moved, copied, erased, or aligned using standard AutoCAD commands. Points can also be rotated using a special grip that appears when the point is selected, as shown in Figure 5.13.

Point information such as elevation and raw description can also be edited in the Item View in Prospector and in the AutoCAD Properties window.

Figure 5.13

Points can be rotated by dragging the rotation grip.

The following exercise shows you how to use Panorama to edit a point elevation.

1. Continue working in the drawing from the previous exercise, or open the `Points3.dwg` file (which you can download from `www.sybex.com/go/introducingcivil3d2009`).

2. Locate the Points entry on the Prospector. Use the item view at the bottom of Prospector to scroll down to point number 412. Right-click the entry for 412, and choose Zoom To. The drawing will zoom in on point 412, which has an elevation of 823.58 as shown in Figure 5.14. (The point number is not visible in the label.)

Figure 5.14

Zoom in on point number 412.

3. Select the point, right-click, and choose Edit Points. The Panorama window appears with the point information displayed.

4. Click inside the Point Elevation field, and change the point elevation from 823.578′ to **824′**, as shown in Figure 5.15. Dismiss the Panorama. Note that the point label has adjusted to match the value entered in Panorama.

Figure 5.15

Change the point elevation in Panorama.

Setting Points for Stakeout

Points often serve as the foundation for a project's beginnings, but they are also critical for taking a drawing from being an abstract idea on the computer to being actively created in the field.

After the plan is complete, there are many point creation tools for creating the stakeout locations required by the field crew. This section describes several of the most common stakeout requirements.

Creating Points at Parcel Corners

One of the elements of a site plan that requires staking is property corners. It is incredibly important to accurately set property corners to avoid potential disputes between homeowners, easement issues, or other costly confusion. Often, these points are set without elevation information—they are simply a horizontal location.

The following exercise leads you through using point tools and the finished parcels to create stakeout information:

1. Open the `Points4.dwg` file (which you can download from `www.sybex.com/go/introducingcivil3d2009`). This drawing contains parcels, alignments, profiles, a

surface, and more for a subdivision plan, as shown in Figure 5.16. Also note that although there are no points in the drawing, there is already a Trees point group.

2. Choose Points → Create Points. The Create Points dialog will appear.

3. Click the chevrons button on the far-right side of the Create Points dialog to expand the parameter options, as shown in Figure 5.17.

4. Click the plus sign (+) sign next to Points Creation to expose additional options.

Figure 5.17

Use the chevrons to reveal additional options.

5. Click inside the field next to Prompt for Elevations. Use the pull-down list to change the setting from Manual to None.

6. Click inside the field next to Prompt for Descriptions. Use the pull-down list to change the setting from the default to Automatic.

7. Click inside the field next to Default Description. Change the default description by typing **LOT**.

8. Click the chevrons button on the far-right side of the Create Points dialog to roll up the parameter options.

9. Click the arrow on the leftmost button on the Create Points dialog and choose Automatic. The parameters should appear similar to Figure 5.18.

Points Creation	
Local Coordinates	Northing - Easting
Grid Coordinates	Grid Northing - Grid Easting
Geographic Coordinates	Latitude - Longitude
Prompt For Elevations	Automatic
Prompt For Point Names	None
Prompt For Descriptions	Automatic
Default Elevation	0.000'
Default Description	LOT
Match On Description Parameters...	true
Disable Description Keys	false
Echo Coordinates to Command Line	true

Figure 5.18

Set the parameters to create LOT points with no elevation.

10. At the Select arcs, lines, lot lines, or feature lines: prompt, zoom in on the any of the right-of-way segments in the drawing and select it. Press Enter.

   Points will appear at each parcel corner and vertex along the right-of-way parcel segments.

11. Repeat steps 9 and 10, except this time choose a rear parcel segment instead of the right-of-way.

   Points will appear at each parcel corner and vertex along the rear lot lines, as shown in Figure 5.19.

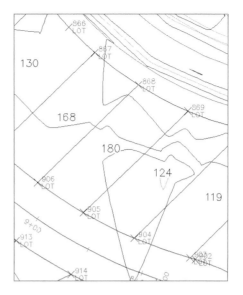

Figure 5.19

Property corners and vertices are automatically set with the Point Creation tool.

Creating Points at Alignment and Profile Geometry Points

There are several points along a road centerline that must be carefully noted. From a horizontal design perspective, the northings and eastings of points of curvature, tangency, and intersection are required to properly create curves in the field. For vertical curves, the locations and elevations of points of vertical curvature, tangency, and intersection are necessary. After an alignment and its associated finished grade profile have been created, this information is easy to access.

The following exercise leads you through setting points that mark the locations of horizontal curve points as well as the location of vertical curve points and their elevations:

1. Continue working in the Points4.dwg file.

2. If the Create Points dialog is not already on the screen, choose Points → Create Points. The Create Points dialog will appear.

3. Click the chevrons button on the far-right side of the Create Points dialog to expand the parameter options.

4. Click the plus sign (+) next to Points Creation to expose additional options.

5. Confirm that Prompt for Elevations is set as None.

6. Confirm that Prompt for Descriptions is set as Automatic. If necessary, use the pulldown list to change the setting from Manual to Automatic.

7. Click inside the field next to Default Description. Change the default description by typing **ROAD**.

8. Click the chevrons button on the far-right side of the Create Points dialog to roll up the parameter options.

9. Click the arrow on the third button from the left in the Create Points dialog and choose At Geometry Points.

10. At the Select alignment: prompt, select the alignment that runs down the main road (Timber Haven). The Select a Profile dialog will appear.

11. Leave the selection as <none> in the Select a Profile dialog, and click OK.

12. At the Starting station <0+00>: prompt, press ↵.

13. At the Starting station <10+31.40>: prompt, press ↵.

    Points will appear at the PC, PI, PT, and other alignment geometry points, as shown in Figure 5.20.

14. Click the arrow on the third button from the left in the Create Points dialog and choose Profile Geometry Points.

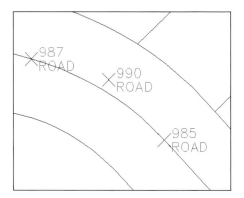

Figure 5.20

Points are placed at horizontal geometry points.

15. At the Select alignment: prompt, select the alignment that runs down the main road (Timber Haven). The Select a Profile dialog will appear.

16. Use the pull-down list to choose Timber Haven FG. Click OK.

17. At the Starting station <0+00>: prompt, press ↵.

18. At the Starting station <10+31.40>: prompt, press ↵.

    Points will appear in the drawing at PVC, PVT, PVI, and other profile geometry points. The elevation information was extracted from the finished ground profile, which can be inspected on the right side of the site plan.

Creating Tree Points Along an Alignment

Special features (such as trees, light posts, hydrants, poles, and fencing) also need to be staked. These types of points may also include elevation information from a design surface.

You can use several different tools to create points along an alignment task, including the Measure Alignment Points command, which places points at a set interval along an alignment. The following exercise uses the Divide Alignment command, which prompts for a number of segments and determines out how far apart the points need to be:

1. Continue working in the `Points4.dwg` file.

2. If the Create Points dialog is not already on the screen, Choose Points → Create Points. The Create Points dialog will appear.

3. Click the chevrons button on the far-right side of the Create Points dialog to expand the parameter options.

4. Use the plus sign (+) next to Points Creation to expose additional options.

5. Confirm that Prompt for Elevations is set as None.

6. Confirm that Prompt for Descriptions is set as Automatic.

7. Click inside the field next to Default Description. Change the default description by typing **TREE**.

8. Click the chevrons on the far-right side of the Create Points dialog to roll up the parameter options.

9. Click the arrow on the third button from the left in the Create Points dialog and choose Divide Alignment.

10. At the `Select alignment:` prompt, select the alignment that runs down the main road (Timber Haven). The Select a Profile for Timber Haven dialog will appear.

11. In the Select a Profile dialog, leave the selection as <none> and click OK.

12. At the `Enter the number of segments <1>:` prompt, type **25** and press ↵.

13. At the `Specify an offset <0.00>:` prompt, type **15** and press ↵.

14. Points with the description of TREE will appear at regular intervals along the alignment. If desired, you can repeat steps 9 through 13 for the other side of the road, using a –15 offset.

15. If the tree points do not automatically appear as trees, locate the Trees point group on the Prospector. Note that there is a yellow exclamation point next to the group, as shown in Figure 5.21.

16. Select the Trees point group, right-click, and choose Update.

    The tree points will now use the style assigned in the Trees point group, as shown in Figure 5.22.

17. Choose Points → Edit Points → Elevations from Surface. The Select surface dialog will appear.

Figure 5.21

When the point group is out of date, an exclamation point appears next to the group in Prospector.

Figure 5.22

After the point group is updated, the trees will appear with the proper symbol.

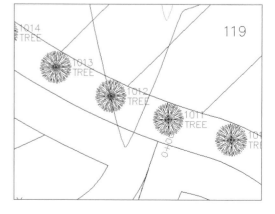

18. In the Select Surface dialog, use the pull-down list to choose the Existing Ground surface. Click OK.

19. At the `Points [All/Numbers/Group/Selection]<All>:` prompt, type **G** for group. The Point Groups dialog will appear.

20. In the Point Groups dialog, choose the Trees group. Click OK.

    The tree points in the drawing now have an elevation assigned from the surface, as shown in Figure 5.23.

Figure 5.23

The points are moved up to the surface elevation.

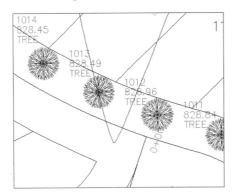

Organizing Stakeout Points with Point Groups

You will probably create many points during a project. There are existing points, proposed points, points used in grading, points used for reference, and finally, the stakeout points. It wouldn't make sense to export the entire list of points from the drawing when some of them weren't created with stakeout in mind.

Throughout this chapter, many uses for point groups have been discussed from both an aesthetic and organizational standpoint. In the following exercise, you will build a point group to contain all of the different types of stakeout points created so far in this chapter:

1. Continue working in the Points4.dwg file, or open Points5.dwg (which you can download from www.sybex.com/go/introducingcivil3d2009).

2. Locate the Point Groups entry on the Prospector. Right-click the Point Groups entry and choose New. The Point Group Properties dialog appears.

3. Change the Name of the point group from the default to **Lot Corners**.

4. Confirm that the Point Style is set to Basic, and the Label Style is set to choose Elevation and Description.

5. Switch to the Include tab. Check the With Raw Description Matching box, and type **LOT** in the empty field.

6. Click OK. All of the Parcel corner points are grouped together.

7. Repeat steps 2 through 6 to create a point group for the Road Points, using **ROAD** in the Raw Description Matching field.

8. Locate the Point Groups entry on the Prospector. Right-click the Point Groups entry and choose New. The Point Group Properties dialog appears.

9. Change the Name of the point group from the default to **Stakeout Points**.

10. Switch to the Point Groups tab. Check the boxes next to the Road, Trees, and Lot point groups, as shown in Figure 5.24.

Figure 5.24

A new point group can be created by combining existing point groups.

11. Click OK. A new point group is created that contains the points from all three types of stakeout points you created.

Creating a Point Table

Sometimes it is appropriate to create a point table to list certain points in the drawing. Perhaps the local municipality requires a detailed list of hydrant placements or a breakdown of wetlands flags locations. In the following example, you create a dynamic point table for the stakeout points you've created so far:

1. Continue working in Points5.dwg.

2. Choose Points → Add Tables. The Point Table Creation dialog appears.

3. Click the Select Point Group button. The Point Groups dialog appears.

4. Choose the Stakeout Points group. Click OK.

5. In the Point Table Creation dialog, click OK.

6. At the Select upper left corner: prompt, select a location on the right of the site plan.

Point tables appear in the drawing, similar to Figure 5.25. These tables will dynamically update if the points are edited, or if more points are added to the stakeout group.

Figure 5.25

An example of a dynamic point table

Point Table				
Point #	Elevation	Northing	Easting	Description
992	826.10	13724029.14	2076083.89	TREE
993	826.71	13724066.74	2076066.91	TREE
994	826.67	13724104.33	2076049.92	TREE
995	826.68	13724141.93	2076032.93	TREE
996	826.85	13724179.52	2076015.94	TREE
997	827.00	13724217.12	2075998.95	TREE
998	827.15	13724254.72	2075981.96	TREE
999	827.32	13724293.15	2075959.74	TREE
1000	827.49	13724325.25	2075931.17	TREE
1001	827.64	13724355.24	2075902.84	TREE
1002	827.77	13724385.23	2075874.51	TREE
1003	827.94	13724415.22	2075846.18	TREE
1004	828.02	13724445.21	2075817.85	TREE
1005	828.20	13724475.20	2075789.52	TREE
1006	828.37	13724505.19	2075761.18	TREE
1007	828.43	13724535.18	2075732.85	TREE
1008	828.47	13724585.17	2075704.52	TREE
1009	828.52	13724595.76	2075674.61	TREE
1010	828.66	13724619.63	2075635.29	TREE
1011	828.64	13724632.10	2075594.96	TREE

Exporting Stakeout Points

After points have been set at all of the necessary locations, the information can be exported for use by the survey crew, or perhaps to be imported into a new project or sent out to a subcontractor.

The following exercise shows you how to quickly create a text file to export the stake-out point group:

1. Continue working in Points5.dwg.

2. Locate the Stakeout point group. Right-click the Stakeout entry and choose Export Points. The Export Points dialog appears.

3. In the Export Points dialog, confirm that the Format is set to PNEZD (comma delimited).

4. Click the File button. The Select Destination File dialog appears.

5. Navigate to any folder on your computer that can receive the text file. Type **Stakeout** in the File Name field, and click Open.

6. Back in the Export Points dialog, note that the box next to Limit to Points in Point Group is checked. Confirm that the Advanced Options are all unchecked. Click OK.

   A text file is created in the folder of your choosing. This file can be imported into another drawing, or other software that supports text imports.

Summary

In this chapter, you learned about some of the tools available for working with points. You learned how to import points from a text file, edit their elevations, and then use point groups to organize and control visibility. You also learned several methods for creating common stakeout points after the design is complete, and practiced the skills necessary to create dynamic point tables and export a text file of critical points.

CHAPTER 6

Parcels

After the surveyors have finished their work and determined a property boundary, the next task is often to create a subdivision plan. Before Civil 3D, the designers would spend a few days sketching on paper, or working through scenarios by trial and error with AutoCAD linework. With Civil 3D, the designer can work directly in the drawing with tools that automatically size parcels, as well as create dynamic labels and tables. Civil 3D makes it easy to go through more iterations of a subdivision plan in less time than traditional methods.

This chapter includes the following topics:

- Converting a boundary to a parcel
- Creating internal boundary segments
- Creating lots at the end of a cul-de-sac
- Creating evenly sized subdivision lots
- Renumbering parcels
- Labeling parcel segments
- Analyzing parcels with an area table
- Working through and finalizing a site plan

Converting a Boundary to a Parcel

All land development projects begin with a boundary. Perhaps this boundary was created from field information and brought in using the survey tools discussed in Chapter 4, "Survey;" or maybe this boundary was created from deed research using techniques described in Chapter 3, "Lines and Curves."

Before you can take advantage of the dynamic nature of parcels for labeling, and before you can subdivide your boundary using the automatic parceling tools, you must convert the boundary into a parcel. It is best to use a closed polyline for this outer parcel boundary.

The following exercise leads you through converting a closed polyline into a Civil 3D parcel:

1. Open the drawing file `Parcels1.dwg`, which you can download from `www.sybex.com/go/introducingcivil3d2009`.

2. Choose Parcels → Create Parcel from Objects.

3. At the `Select lines, arcs, or polylines to convert into parcels or [XREF]:` prompt, select the blue colored polyline that represents the outer site boundary, as shown in Figure 6.1.

4. Press ↵. The Create Parcels - From Objects dialog will appear. Confirm that the Parcel Style is set to Property, the Area label style is set to Parcel Name, and the Erase Existing Entities box is checked, as shown in Figure 6.2. Click OK. Note that a parcel called Property: 1 is formed.

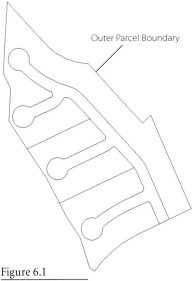

Figure 6.1

Choose the polyline that represents the outer boundary.

Figure 6.2

Establish settings for newly formed parcels using the pull-down menus in the Create Parcels - From Object dialog.

5. Zoom in on the Property: 1 label. Select the label and right-click. Choose Parcel Properties from the shortcut menu. The Parcel Properties dialog will appear.

6. Open the Composition tab of the Parcel Properties dialog, as shown in Figure 6.3. Note that the area and perimeter of Property: 1 are shown. Use the pull-down list under Area Selection Label Style to change the area label from Parcel Name to Name Square Foot & Acres. Explore the Analysis and User Defined Properties tabs of the Parcel Properties dialog, if desired. Click OK. Note that Property: 1 is now shown with the Name Square Foot & Acres label.

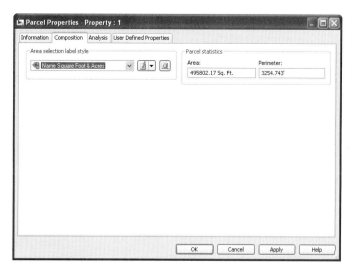

Figure 6.3

The Parcel Properties dialog can be used to gather information about a parcel. The pull-down on the Composition tab can also be used to change the parcel area label.

Creating Internal Boundary Segments

When working on a land development plan in Civil 3D, it is best to map out key locations on the site before you begin creating residential lots. You would use regular Auto-CAD linework to sketch out areas for easements, dedications, open space, and utility lots, and then convert the linework to parcel segments. Although there is a tool to create simple right-of-way parcels based on an alignment, it is often better to create a polyline using AutoCAD tools (such as offset, fillet, circle, and more) that represents your road right-of-way.

The following exercise leads you through converting some internal boundaries into Civil 3D parcels to prepare for subdivision:

1. Continue working in the drawing from the previous exercise or open Parcels2.dwg (which you can download from www.sybex.com/go/introducingcivil3d2009).

2. Zoom in on the southern portion of the site where the road right-of-way polyline intersects with the boundary parcel. Use tools such as Trim, Extend, and Join to

ensure that the road right-of-way polyline touches the boundary without gap or overhang, as shown in Figure 6.4.

3. Choose Parcels → Create Parcel from Objects.

4. At the Select lines, arcs, or polylines to convert into parcels or [XREF]: prompt, select the green polyline that represents the roadway right-of-way, and the two magenta lines that represent some internal lot lines, as shown in Figure 6.5.

5. Press ↵. The Create Parcels - From Objects dialog will appear. Confirm that Parcel Style is set to Property. Change the Area Label Style to Name Square Foot & Acres. Confirm that the Erase Existing Entities box is checked. Click OK. Three new parcels are formed in the drawing.

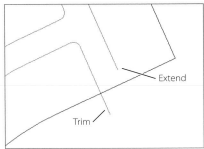

Figure 6.4

All linework that will be used for internal lot lines must be properly cleaned up before being turned into parcels.

Figure 6.5

Use the road right-of-way polyline and the internal lot lines to form new parcels.

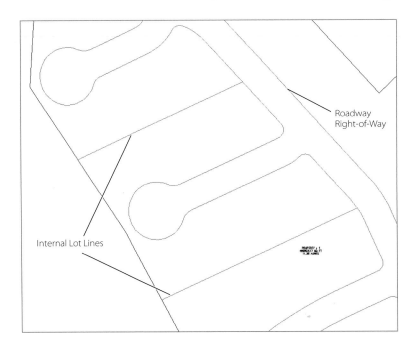

Creating Lots at the End of a Cul-de-Sac

When you're first learning Civil 3D, it is often tempting to rely on AutoCAD linework, and then convert those lines, arcs, and polylines into parcels. Although there is nothing wrong with this approach for things like an outer boundary and some key internal lot lines, you will be missing out on some powerful functionality if you don't take time to learn and apply tools like the Free Form Create tool. The Free Form Create tool can be used before you begin working with the details of your site plan, or as a tool to refine and improve your plan once the bulk of the residential lots has been created. Once you learn how it works, you will find many other uses for it.

The following exercise introduces you to using the Free Form Create tool by leading you through making an open space lot at the end of a cul-de-sac:

1. Continue working in the drawing from the previous exercise or open `Parcels3.dwg` (which you can download from www.sybex.com/go/introducingcivil3d2009).

2. Choose Parcels → Create Parcel by Layout. The Parcel Layout tools dialog will appear.

3. Use the Parcel Sizing tools pull-down list to choose the Free Form Create tool, as shown in Figure 6.6. The Create Parcels - Layout dialog will appear.

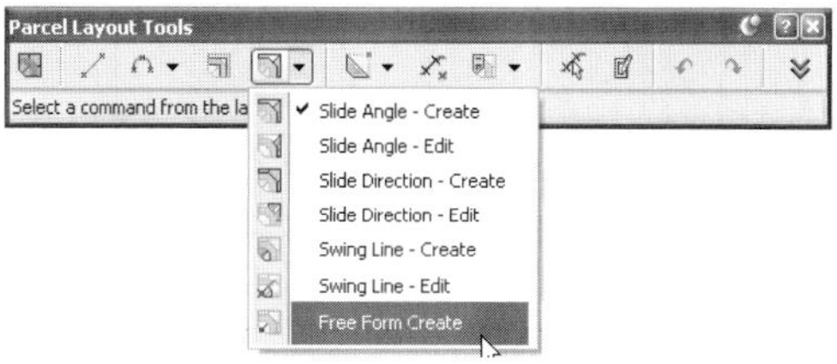

Figure 6.6

Use the pull-down list to choose the Free Form Create Tool.

4. In the Create Parcels - Layout dialog, change the Parcel Style to Single Family, and the Area label style to Name Square Foot & Acres. Leave the Automatically Add Segment Labels box unchecked. Click OK.

5. At the `Select attachment point:` prompt, use your endpoint osnap to select the beginning of the first arc on the northern cul-de-sac, as shown in Figure 6.7. A parcel segment glyph will appear.

6. At the `Specify lot line direction (ENTER for perpendicular) or [Bearing/aZimuth]:` prompt, press ↵ to choose perpendicular. A lot line will be created from the right-of-way parcel line extending to the boundary parcel line.

Figure 6.7

Select the beginning of the first arc on the northern cul-de-sac as your attachment point for the parcel jig.

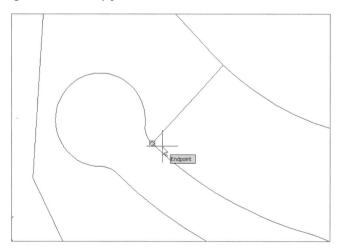

7. Repeat steps 5 and 6 for the other side of this cul-de-sac.

8. When you're finished creating lot lines, press ↵. At the Select from the layout tools or [eXit]: prompt, type **X** and press ↵ to exit.

9. Note that new parcels have been formed, as shown in Figure 6.8.

Figure 6.8

Two new parcel segments created using the Free Form Create tool

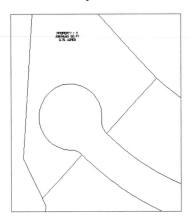

Creating Evenly Sized Subdivision Lots

Everyone working on land development plans for a subdivision wants the best design possible. The designer wants to ensure a quality layout that will meet code requirements and be livable, aesthetically appealing, and cost effective to construct. Within those constraints, the designer often struggles to maximize the number of subdivision lots. Before Civil 3D, there were no real tools to assist with this task.

The automatic parcel creation tools, such as Create Parcel by Layout, allow the designer to establish parameters and run through many iterations and configurations quickly. The more iterations that are performed, the more likely the designers will be to produce a site plan that they feel truly captures their design intent.

The next exercise has you create evenly sized subdivision lots using Create Parcel by Layout.

1. Continue working in the drawing from the previous exercise or open Parcels4.dwg (which you can download from www.sybex.com/go/introducingcivil3d2009).

2. Choose Parcels → Create Parcel by Layout. The Parcel Layout tools dialog will appear.

3. Click the chevrons button at the far right end of the dialog to expand the Parameters.

4. Change the Default Area value to **5175.00 Sq. Ft.** and the Minimum Frontage value to **45.000′** as shown in Figure 6.9.

5. Click inside the Automatic Mode field to activate the drop-down list. Use the drop-down list to change the Automatic Mode to On.

6. Click inside the Remainder Distribution field to activate the drop-down list. Use the drop-down list to set the Remainder Distribution to Create Parcel from Remainder.

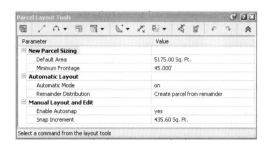

Figure 6.9

Change the parameters to match your design constraints.

7. Use the Parcel Sizing tools pull-down list to choose the Slide Angle Create tool, as shown in Figure 6.10. The Create Parcels - Layout dialog will appear.

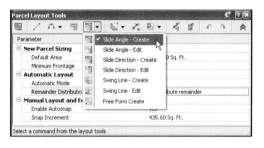

Figure 6.10

Select the Slide Angle Create tool.

8. In the Create Parcels - Layout dialog, change the Parcel Style to Single Family, and the Area Label Style to Name Square Foot & Acres. Leave the Automatically Add Segment Labels box unchecked. Click OK.

9. At the `Pick a point within the parcel to be subdivided:` prompt, click anywhere inside the large parcel on the north side of the main road.

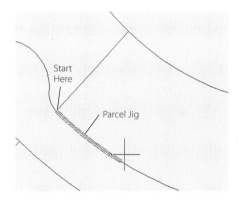

Figure 6.11

Select the lot line created in the last exercise as the starting point of your frontage.

10. At the `Select start point on frontage:` prompt, use your endpoint osnap to select the end of the lot line that you created in the last exercise, as shown in Figure 6.11. The parcel jig will appear along the road frontage.

11. At the `Select end point on frontage:` prompt, use your endpoint osnap to select the intersection of the boundary parcel and the right-of-way parcel on the south side of the site, as shown in Figure 6.12.

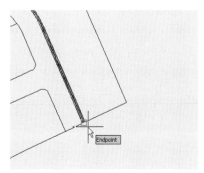

Figure 6.12

Choose the intersection of the right-of-way and the parcel boundary as the end point on the frontage.

12. At the `Specify angle at frontage:` prompt, press ↵. This specifies an angle of 90 degrees.

13. At the `Specify area <5175.00 Sq. Ft.>:` prompt, press ↵. This specifies accepts the area setting.

Figure 6.13

**Evenly sized sub-
division lots and a
remainder parcel**

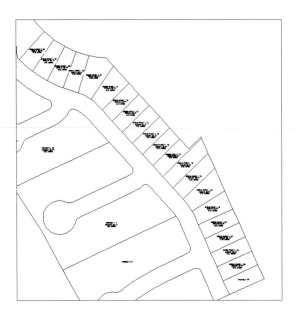

14. Your evenly sized subdivision lots will appear as shown in Figure 6.13. Notice that a small remainder lot was created on the southern part of the site. Press Esc.

15. When you're finished creating lot lines, press ↵. At the Select from the layout tools or [eXit]: prompt, type **X** and press ↵ to exit.

16. The remainder parcel still has the original parcel area label style. Change the label to Name Area & Perimeter using the technique shown in the first exercise of this chapter.

17. The remainder parcel also still has the original parcel style. Select the parcel, right-click, and choose Parcel Properties. Switch to the Information tab. Use the Object Style pull-down list to choose Single-Family. Click OK.

Renumbering Parcels

Civil 3D numbers parcels as they are created, so after a few iterations you can find yourself with some pretty odd number combinations. Also, because Civil 3D assigns numbers to your road right-of-way and open space areas, you may find yourself wondering how to make the numbers in your drawing match the numbers on an existing plat or to please the review agency.

Renumbering parcels in Civil 3D is extremely easy. It is recommended that you wait until you have most of your site plan done before you renumber your lots so that you save yourself from having to do it over and over again. The next exercise will show you how.

1. Continue working in the drawing from the previous exercise or open Parcels5.dwg (which you can download from www.sybex.com/go/introducingcivil3d2009).

2. Choose Parcels → Edit Parcel → Renumber/Rename Parcels. The Reumber/Rename Parcels dialog will appear.

3. Confirm that the radio button next to Renumber is selected. Confirm that the Starting Number is set to 1; if not, change the Starting Number to 1. Click OK.

4. At the `Specify start point or [Polylines/Site]:` prompt, click anywhere inside the southernmost subdivision lot. The renumbering jig will appear as shown in Figure 6.14.

5. At the `End point or [Undo]:` prompt, click along anywhere inside the lots on the northern side of the road right-of-way, as if you were drawing a polyline through the lots. Click inside the last lot near the cul-de-sac, and then press ↵. Your lots should now be renumbered with Property: 1 at the southernmost point.

Labeling Parcel Segments

Although you may be able to submit a preliminary site plan without a full set of labels, most final plats require detailed labeling of parcel segments to confirm that lengths and radii meet code specifications, to assist with stakeout, and for writing legal descriptions for deeds.

It is recommended that you wait until you have most of your site plan done before you proceed with detailed labeling. The next exercise will lead you through adding labels to parcel segments.

1. Continue working in the drawing from the previous exercise or open `Parcels6.dwg` (which you can download from `www.sybex.com/go/introducingcivil3d2009`).

2. Choose Parcels → Add Parcel Labels → Add Parcel Labels. The Add Labels dialog will appear as shown in Figure 6.15.

3. Use the Label Type pull-down menu to choose Multiple Segment.

4. Use the Line Label Style pull-down menu to select Bearing over Distance, if it's not already selected.

5. Use the Curve label Style pull-down menu to select Distance Only.

6. Click Add.

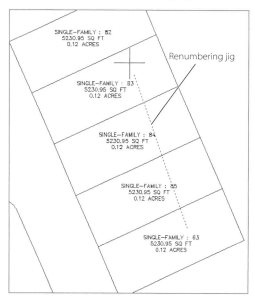

Figure 6.14

Draw an imaginary line that passes through the parcels you would like to renumber.

Figure 6.15

The Add Labels dialog

7. At the Select parcel to be labeled by click on the area label: prompt, click the area label for Property: 1.

8. At the Label direction [CLockwise/COunterclockwise] <CLOckwise>: prompt, press ↵. Labels will appear along each parcel segment.

9. Repeat steps 7 and 8 for all of the subdivision lot parcels created in the previous exercise. The labels will appear as shown in Figure 6.16.

10. Click the close button to dismiss the Add Labels dialog.

Figure 6.16

Parcel segment labels

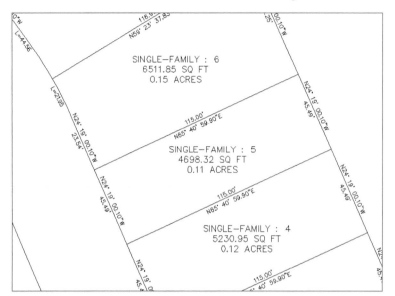

Analyzing Parcels with an Area Table

Most land planners are required to bring site plans to hearings or through some kind of review process. The review agency typically wants to know if the site plan meets minimum lot size requirements and other data that is best presented in table form. Civil 3D parcel area tables provide a great way to present much of this data. The following exercise leads you through a simple example, but you should also explore ways to add more information to your parcels through user-defined properties.

1. Continue working in the drawing from the previous exercise or open Parcels7.dwg (which you can download from www.sybex.com/go/introducingcivil3d2009).

2. Choose Parcels → Add Tables → Add Area. The Table Creation dialog will appear.

3. Select Area Table from the Table Style: pull-down list.

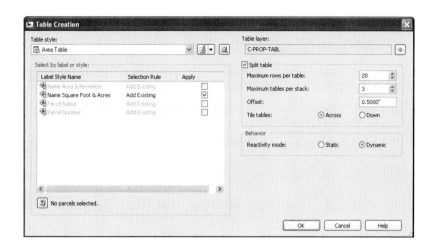

Figure 6.17

Check the Apply box for Name Square Foot & Acres in the Table Creation dialog.

4. Check the box next to Name Square Foot & Acres. This will select all parcels labeled with the Name Square Foot & Acres label for the area table, as shown in Figure 6.17. Click OK.

5. At the `Select upper left corner:` prompt, place the area table somewhere in the open space to the right of the site plan. The area table will appear. The table should look similar to Figure 6.18 (although the parcel numbers and areas may be different in your table).

6. Save your drawing—you will use it to finalize your plan.

Working Through the Plan

So far in this chapter, you have managed to put together one iteration of one side of the road, but what about the rest of the plan? Use the next section as a reference to help you experiment with this site plan and later work through your own plans.

Working with Parcels in Prospector

As you learn more about Civil 3D, you will begin to use the Prospector tab of the Civil 3D Toolspace as your master control center. As Civil 3D objects are created, they populate Prospector. Parcels are no exception. You will find your parcels in the Sites collection in Prospector, as shown in Figure 6.19. Use the item view to sort parcels, examine them, and make batch changes to parcel styles, label styles, and more. Right-click a parcel entry to zoom to that specific parcel.

Figure 6.18

A parcel area table

Parcel Area Table	
Parcel #	Area
1	5230.95
2	5230.95
3	5230.95
4	5230.95
5	4698.32
6	6511.85
7	7336.25
8	6433.93
9	7146.58
10	5503.60
11	5230.94
12	5230.94
13	5230.94
14	5230.94
15	5230.94
16	6700.84
17	7845.54
18	5252.71
19	5252.71
20	5252.71

Figure 6.19

An item view of parcels appears under the Site collection in Prospector.

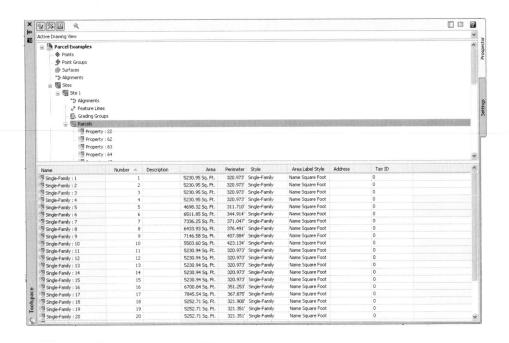

Editing and Refining Parcels

Your first iteration using the automatic parcel creation tools usually will not give you a final product. More often than not, you will need to make refinements and adjustments to parcel size, or perhaps start over completely. This section shows you some of the most useful options.

UNDO YOUR UNDO HABIT

In Civil 3D, especially when working with parcels, avoid using the Undo command to prevent segment overshoots and other unexpected results. If you are unhappy with your automatic parcel creation outcome, use the Erase command to remove the offending segments and try the tool again.

Grip Edits

Parcels created from objects, such as the boundary and internal segments will have standard grips, like a polyline. These grips can be used just as you would expect—you can drag and move your parcel boundary as necessary. Segments created using Parcel Layout tools such as Free Form Create and Slide Angle Create will have a special diamond shaped grip that can slide along the frontage and will respect the original angle setting, as shown in Figure 6.20.

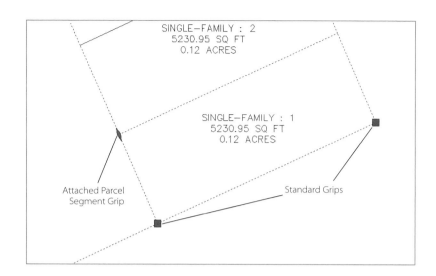

Figure 6.20

Both attached segment grips and standard grips can be used to edit the size and shape of parcels.

Removing Segments

You will want to remove segments to make some parcels larger, refine their shape, or to perhaps go through more iteration with the automatic layout tools.

For example, say you have four lots that share a common internal segment, as in Figure 6.21.

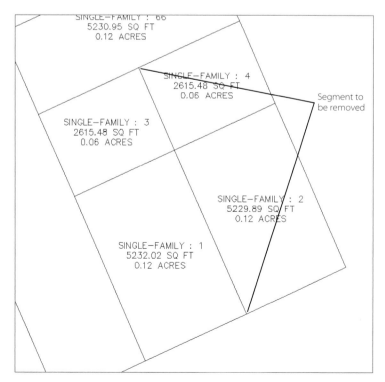

Figure 6.21

Four parcels that share a common segment

If you use the AutoCAD Erase command, the entire length will be removed, and two parcels will remain, as shown in Figure 6.22.

The Parcel Layout Tools dialog also has a Delete Sub-entity button. Clicking this button will delete the length of the segment between other parcel segments, as shown in Figure 6.23.

Figure 6.22

The Erase command removes the entire length of the segment, leaving two parcels.

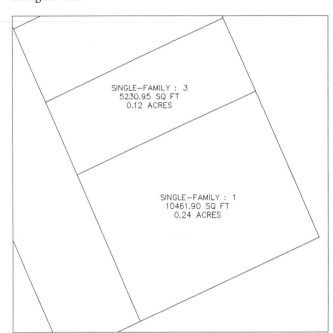

Figure 6.23

When the Delete Sub-entity was used, only the portion of the segment within Single-Family: 3 was removed, eliminating Single-Family: 4.

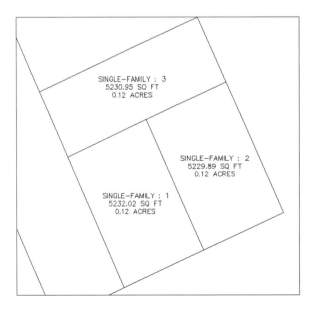

Parcel Layout Editing Tools

You can also make intelligent edits to attached parcel segments using the Slide Angle, Slide Direction, and Swing Line Edit tools from the Parcel Layout Tools dialog (shown in Figure 6.24). These commands will lead you through making changes to an angle, area, and more.

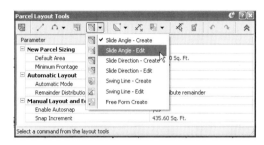

Figure 6.24

Additional editing options on the Parcel Layout Tools dialog

Adding More Internal Segments

If there are no automatic tools to fit your design intent, you can always draw AutoCAD linework to convert to parcel segments, or use Free Form Create. Just be sure to trim or extend your linework as necessary before converting it to a parcel segment. This is especially useful when capping off the rear lot lines so that they are straight instead of curved, creating segments with odd angles, or adding open space, wetlands parcels, or utility lots. An example of a finished lot created from AutoCAD linework is shown in Figure 6.25.

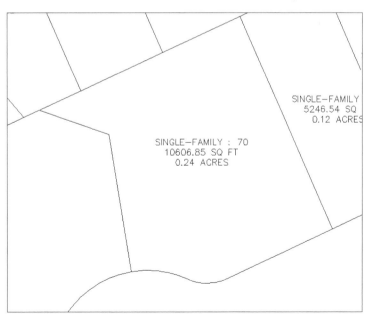

Figure 6.25

Create odd angles using AutoCAD linework converted to parcel segments.

Using the previous editing techniques and all of the tools shown in this chapter, work through the rest of the site so that you get a feel for creating parcels in a real-world situation. One possibility for a final design is shown in Figure 6.26.

Figure 6.26

One possibility for a finished site plan

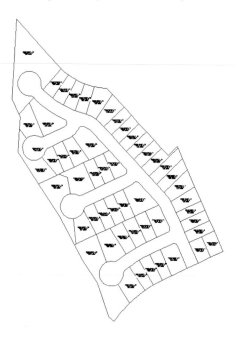

Summary

In this chapter, you were introduced to some of the many tools available for working with parcels. Parcels are incredibly powerful tools that provide ways to automatically label areas and segment information, and stylize linework. Most importantly, parcels give you the power to go through many more design iterations in far less time, which will lead to better-quality site plans that truly meet your design intent and form the foundation for better neighborhoods everywhere.

Surfaces

This chapter is about working with surfaces in Civil 3D. Most land development and civil engineering projects wind up as surfaces eventually. This surface can be a water surface, the top of a new landfill, a rock layer, or airspace above an airport. Surfaces help engineers understand the relationships between the horizontal control data and the vertical elevation data.

In Civil 3D, you have a myriad of ways to interact with surfaces. In this chapter, you'll explore using surfaces as preliminary design tools and performing some basic land analysis. You'll then look at building surfaces from Google Earth, survey, and point information. You'll take this information and edit it for accuracy and clarity, including some labeling concepts. Then you'll look at how to use the analysis tools for preliminary engineering and earthworks.

This chapter includes the following topics:

- **Building surfaces from Google Earth**
- **Building surfaces from point and contour data**
- **Editing boundaries, breaklines, and bad data**
- **Labeling surfaces for clear understanding**
- **Analyzing surfaces for flood analysis and earthworks**

Surface Building Blocks

When you're building a surface in Civil 3D or any other program, it's important to understand the limitations of most surface-based designs. When a program uses a surface, it's not the same as using a solid object. A *surface* is the skin of the object. Imagine if you could peel the color of an orange peel. You could look at and understand by the shape and color that it represents the orange, but you couldn't unwrap it and eat it. A solid has mass and thickness; a surface has neither. In addition, surfaces in Civil 3D recognize only a single elevation for any point in the coordinate system. This means you cannot model caves or overhangs with a single surface. Now that you're aware of the limits, let's look at all you can do with the surface object in Civil 3D.

At its core, Civil 3D builds surfaces from triangles. The exact methodology is based on the Delaunay algorithms, but Civil 3D then attempts to refine that triangulation based on user input and constraints. There are a number of essential building blocks that can be used to build and modify a surface:

- Boundaries
- Breaklines
- Contours
- DEM files
- Points

In addition to these building blocks, you can also edit surfaces after they've been built by modifying the surface points, removing or rearranging triangles, thinning data, or moving the surface datum. We'll explore the most common methods in this chapter, but not all of them.

In this chapter, you'll look specifically at building surfaces from three main sources: Google Earth, surveyed point data, and drawing contour information. Each of them is valuable and has its place in the land-development process.

Building Surfaces from Google Earth

When Google Earth showed up on the scene, a lot of people reacted with, "Cool, but what do we do with it?" The original link between Civil 3D and Google Earth was nice for the demo shows, but there wasn't much meat to it. With the ability to create a surface directly from Google Earth data in Civil 3D, there's a real tool with a real purpose than can be used for real work.

Before you can import data from Google Earth (or any real-world coordinate system for that matter), you have to assign a coordinate system to your drawing. You'll walk through this process in the following short exercise.

1. Open the `Importing GE Surface.dwg` file (which can be downloaded from `www.sybex.com/go/introducingcivil3d2009`).

2. In Toolspace, switch to the Settings tab.

3. Right-click the drawing name and select Edit Drawing Settings to open the Drawing Settings dialog.

4. If necessary, change to the Units and Zone tab.

5. In the Zone area, make the following changes:

   • Change the Zone to **USA, Texas**.

   • Change the Coordinate System to **NAD83 Texas State Planes, South Central Zone, US Foot**.

   Your settings should now look like Figure 7.1.

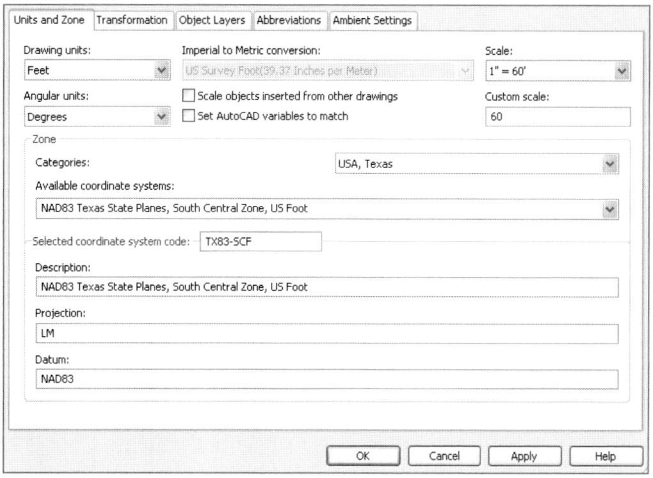

6. Click OK to close the dialog.

Figure 7.1

Drawing Settings dialog for importing the Google Earth surface information

This sets the zone and coordinates for your new file. (For more information on these drawing settings, see Chapter 1, "Welcome to the Civil 3D Environment.") Now you need to find your site in Google Earth.

GOT GOOGLE EARTH?

Google Earth is not included on the Civil 3D DVD. You'll need to visit the Google Earth site (earth.google.com) to download and install the latest version. If you've got it already, we'd still suggest hitting the site to see if you're up-to-date. This book was written on version 4.2.0205.5730, and it will probably change by publishing time. Sometimes even the smallest change in versions will make the software act differently.

7. Launch Google Earth on your computer (but leave Civil 3D open in the background).

8. Once Google Earth has loaded, open the Introducing Civil 3D.kmz file by selecting File → Open and browsing to the Introducing Civil 3D dataset.

9. Switch back to Civil 3D once the file is open.

10. Select File Import Import Google Earth Surface.

11. Press Enter to accept the command line option to use the coordinate system already in place in the drawing. This opens the Create Surface dialog.

12. Click OK to close the dialog, accepting the defaults and completing the exercise.

13. Switch back to Google Earth and exit that program.

Your screen should look like Figure 7.2. Note that the contours seem a bit rough in places. Look particularly at the northwest corner, where the staggered and rough contours would seem to indicate some surface refinement would be in order. These sorts of surface anomalies are quite common when using Google Earth data.

Figure 7.2

Completed Google Earth import

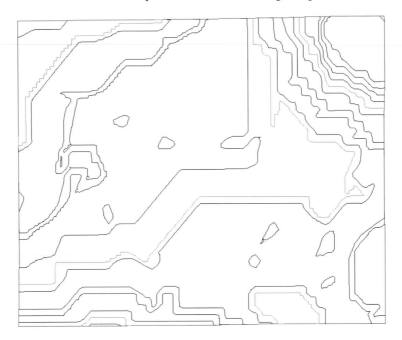

Although this data is accurate enough for most preliminary engineering or large-scale hydrology work, it should not be used for construction or bidding purposes. During informal testing, Google Earth data has been found to be as much as 15′ different from on the ground survey points in spots, while being dead-on in others. If you think of Google Earth data as similar to the topography maps provided by many governments, you'll have the right frame of mind toward its application.

Once you've moved beyond preliminary steps, it's time to get a bit more accurate and look at some other surface sources.

Building Surfaces from CAD Files

Because Google Earth is essentially free, using its data for most projects will become second nature, especially during due-diligence and preliminary design stages. As you move forward with your project though, you'll commonly run into drawing files that represent surface and survey data as a collection of lines, polylines, blocks, and text. Although these files look nice on-screen, converting the information contained in them to a Civil 3D surface is a crucial step in the design process and the subject of this section.

We'll look at this as a two-step process. First, converting lines and polylines that describe contour information to Civil 3D surface data, and then fleshing that data out with points and text that describes a collection of specific point shots throughout the site. This type of drawing can be commonly found on city and county websites, in archived projects, or coming from other software packages.

You begin this process by creating the empty surface object, and then adding in the pieces that are present in the drawing.

1. Open the file `Converting Linework.dwg`.

2. In Prospector, right-click the Surfaces branch and select Create Surface to display the Create Surface dialog.

3. Change the name to **Existing Ground**.

4. Verify that the style selected is Contours 1′ and 5′ (Background). You can also add a description during the surface creation, giving other users an idea of what that surface is representing. Your dialog should look like Figure 7.3. Click OK to close the dialog.

Figure 7.3

The Create Surface dialog settings

At this point, you've simply created the Existing Ground surface, but have not placed data in that surface definition. Remember that objects in and of themselves can be empty in Civil 3D, and it's the defining data that makes them powerful and dynamic.

5. Within Prospector, expand Surfaces → Existing Ground → Definition as shown in Figure 7.4.

6. Right-click the Contours branch and select Add to display the Add Contour Data dialog.

7. Click OK to accept the default values and dismiss the dialog.

8. Using a crossing window, select all of the entities in the drawing. The initial selection will include text and blocks as well as the intended polylines, but these will be weeded out.

Figure 7.4

Adding contour data to a surface via Prospector

9. Press Enter or right-click to complete the selection process, and the Existing Ground Surface will be built.

At this point, the surface is built purely from the polylines that described the contours in the original drawing. By adding the blocks representing items found by the survey crew, you can refine the surface and complete the topographic information for your site.

10. Under the Definition branch, right-click Drawing Objects and select Add to display the Add Points from Drawing Objects dialog.

11. Select Blocks from the drop-down menu in the dialog, and click OK.

12. Use a crossing window to again select the entire screen (there should be 32 objects selected).

13. Press Enter or right-click to complete the selection process. The surface will rebuild, taking into account the new data, and your results should look similar to Figure 7.5. This is a good method for reproducing existing drawing files.

Figure 7.5

The surface built from polylines and points is complete.

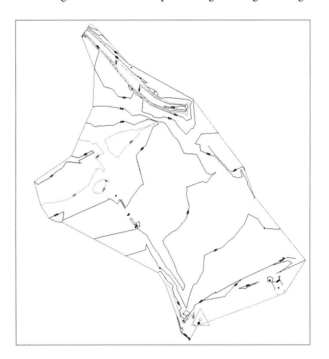

Because the blocks added to this surface were already quite close to the contour-generated surface, there's not much visual change reflected back to the display screen, but there has been a change in the underlying object. Although this method generally reflects the input data very well, it still is not as accurate as a surface built from field data. The next section deals with that issue.

Building Surfaces from Field Linework and Points

The best way to understand existing conditions on a site is to visit it with a survey crew. This allows for human inspection of all the conditions and allows a trained professional to pick up all the data to represent the site correctly in a computer model. Based on points and often field-created linework, this type of surface is the ideal starting point for engineering work, and should be a requirement whenever practical. In the following exercise, you'll walk through adding surveyed points into a surface definition, and then adding breakline data to force the surface triangulation along certain lines:

1. Open the `Building from Points.dwg` file.

2. Expand the Surfaces → Existing Ground → Definition branch.

3. Right-click the Point Groups branch and select Add to display the Add Point group dialog.

4. Select Field Survey from the list, and then click OK to close the dialog and build the surface.

    At this point, the data is correct in general, but there are still some pretty significant errors you can fix by simply using the linework provided to create breaklines.

WHAT'S A BREAKLINE?

Remember, Civil 3D builds surfaces from triangles. If you consider four given points on a surface, there's only one way you can draw the outside boundary, but there are two ways to draw the inside leg that completes the triangles. *Breaklines* force the direction of that interior line, and make the surface behave the way you want it to behave. These breaklines often violate the rules of the Delaunay triangulation model, but they show the surface as it really should be modeled.

---

5. Within the drawing window, select one of the polylines running along the edges of your site. These are lines created by the survey crew during their data-import process to define some site definition lines.

6. Right-click and select Select Similar to highlight the rest of the polylines on your site.

7. Without deselecting, right-click the Breaklines branch under the Existing Ground definition and select Add to display the Add Breaklines dialog.

8. Type **Field Data** into the Description blank, and click OK to complete the data addition and rebuild the surface.

9. The Panorama palette appears, giving a list of points that are duplicates. Because the vertices on the polylines just added match the point data, this is expected. Click the green checkbox to close Panorama and review the surface. It should look like Figure 7.6.

Figure 7.6

Completed surface based on field data consisting of points and linework

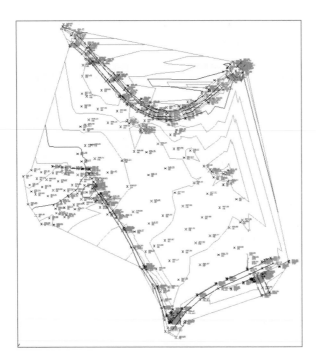

Figure 7.6

Completed surface based on field data consisting of points and linework

You've now built the same site in a number of different ways. Each method adds a level of accuracy, but each method adds a level of cost as well. When working with surface information, it's important to weigh the benefits of field survey information against the cost of a crew and decide accordingly on how you'll be building your site surfaces. Now that we've built a good surface, let's use a few more surface tools and edits to refine your existing ground model.

Refining and Editing Surface Data

If you stop working with your surface after adding points and breaklines, you've probably left some inaccuracies in the model. There are a number of things you can do to refine a surface in Civil 3D, but because this book is introductory, we're going to examine only the two most common edits. First, you'll use a boundary to control triangulation across areas where you have little data, and then you'll tell Civil 3D to ignore the occasional blown shot.

Working with Surface Boundaries

There are a number of reasons to use boundaries when building surfaces. The obvious use (and the one covered in this section) is to limit the location of data and the triangles that connect the surface. Other uses can be to divide a surface along a phase line, to hide a building pad from surface analysis, or to show interior surface data that might be considered an island (such as the landscape inside a courtyard). Because the most common use is to limit data based on location, that's what you do in the following exercise:

1. Open the Surface Boundary.dwg file. This is the same surface you just built, but the point labels and breaklines have been turned off for clarity. Look at the areas indicated in Figure 7.7 and notice how contours appear in areas where you have very little point information.

2. Select Surfaces → Utilities → Extract Objects from Surface to display the Extract Objects from Surface dialog.

3. Uncheck the Major Contour and Minor Contour checkboxes and click OK to close the dialog. This utility creates a 3D polyline around the existing surface definition that you can use to refine and reapply a boundary.

4. Select the outside edge of the surface, and you should see a polyline highlight as in Figure 7.8.

5. Use AutoCAD editing techniques to manipulate this polyline until it looks similar to Figure 7.9. This indicates the desired outer limits of your surface. Notice that the polyline dips into the surface in the problem areas indicated in Figure 7.7.

Figure 7.7

The surface prior to editing

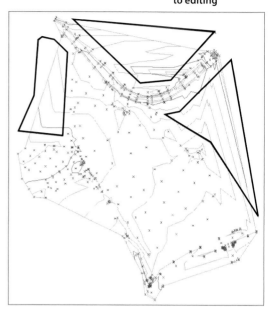

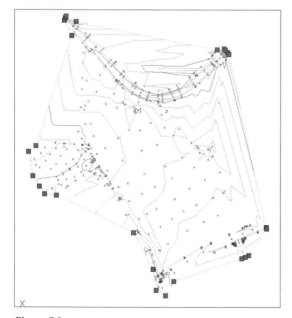

Figure 7.8

A polyline has been extracted from the surface boundary, and its grips are displayed.

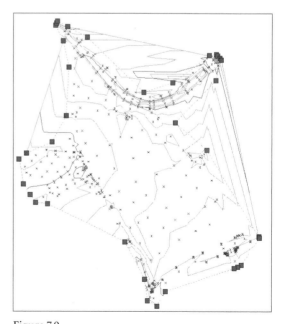

Figure 7.9

Modified polyline to desired limits

6. In Prospector, expand the Surface Boundary drawing and the Surfaces Existing Ground-Definition branch.

7. Right-click the Boundaries branch and select Add to display the Add Boundaries dialog.

8. Uncheck the option for Non-destructive Breakline, and then click OK to accept the other values and dismiss the dialog.

9. Select the polyline you just modified, and Civil 3D will rebuild the surface, limiting the surface as specified.

Your surface should look something like Figure 7.10. Note that the surface boundary does not follow your polyline. The option you unchecked created a *destructive* breakline, ensuring that only data wholly contained in the boundary is part of the surface.

Figure 7.10

Complete boundary addition to the Existing Ground surface

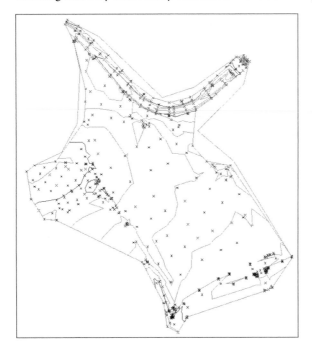

Modifying the Surface Definition Parameters

With a boundary in place, we'll now look at weeding out some bogus data. It's very common for surveyors to place points in a file that lay out the metes and bounds of a site, but have no vertical data. If you're not careful, those points sometimes slip into the surface definition and cause the surface to shoot down to a zero elevation at those locations. In the following exercise, you'll look at some easy options you can use as part of the surface properties to make filtering out bad data an automatic process:

1. Open the `Edit Surface` drawing file. It's important to open this one instead of continuing with the previous file, because we've put some of the bad data back in the file for learning purposes. Notice that there seem to be some deep holes along the boundary, indicated by the large cluster of contours at those locations.

2. Expand the drawing and the surface branch.

3. Right-click the Existing Ground surface and select Surface Properties.

4. Switch to the Definition tab as shown in Figure 7.11.

5. Expand the Build options as shown in Figure 7.11 and change the Exclude Elevations Less Than value to Yes.

6. Change the Elevation < value to **100** and click OK to close the dialog. Civil 3D displays a warning that the surface needs to be rebuilt.

7. Click the Rebuild the Surface option to close the warning. Civil 3D updates the surface, recontouring the areas where zero elevations were affecting the model.

Figure 7.11

Build options within the Existing Ground Surface Properties dialog

Although this simple edit handles a lot of situations, there are also tools for handling points that are too high, triangulating legs that are too long to be accurate, and reordering the build operations within the surface definition itself. As you work with surfaces and want to refine your output to a higher level, you should look at the automated tools in the Surface Properties Definition tab to make your job easier and faster.

You've created a number of different surfaces. Now let's consider the wide variety of display and labeling options.

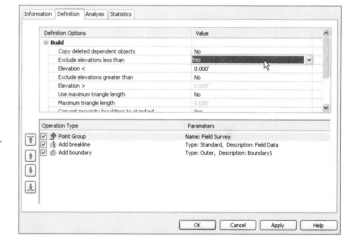

Displaying and Labeling Surfaces

Building surface models is one of the more satisfying tasks in Civil 3D. It's quick, it's easy to see an immediate return, and there are lots of interesting tools and settings. After you're done playing though, you need to share your model, and in most cases, that means printing. A good printout needs good labels, and because you have different print requirements, you'll wind up creating a number of different contours and a bunch of different labels to match—and that means a lot of work. Or does it?

Civil 3D's dynamic model makes it extremely easy to label contours, critical spots, and slopes along a surface model. In this section, we'll look at all three tasks.

Labeling Contours

As discussed in Chapter 1, all labels in Civil 3D are based on styles, and contours are no different. Remember that labels reflect the object itself, and are dynamically related, so as you lay out your labeling, you can do so with confidence knowing that any future change will be accommodated by the label with no work on your part. Let's first look at labeling the ground surface you've been working with so far.

1. Open the Contour Labels.dwg file.

2. Select Surfaces → Add Surface Labels → Contour Multiple at Interval.

3. Using a center osnap, draw a line between the two circles on the screen, as shown in Figure 7.12.

4. Enter **300**↵ at the command line to set the interval value of 300′. This will create a label 300′ along every contour, measured along the contour from the point of contour and the contour label line just drawn.

Figure 7.12

First pass at multiple contour labels

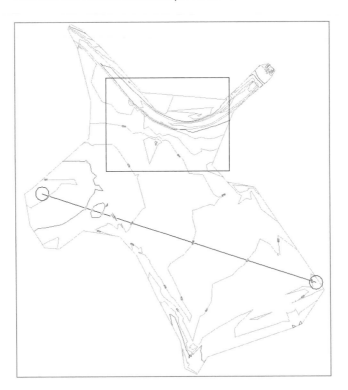

Although this labels a large portion of the site, it only labels the contours that the original line crosses, leaving some areas unlabeled. You could repeat the process, but it's often more efficient to use the labels placed by the first pass to create labels for the other areas.

5. Zoom in on the area indicated by the rectangle in the drawing and in Figure 7.12.

6. Select the 829 label. Notice that three grips appear, not one as you might expect. The label is actually a function of a contour label line. Every place this line crosses a contour, a label will be inserted.

7. Grab the northeastern-most grip of the three, and drag it to an approximate position as shown in Figure 7.13. Note the shadow box areas indicating where new labels will be placed on the surface.

8. Click to finalize the placement, and press Esc to deselect the label line.

9. Repeat steps 6, 7, and 8 with the other labels in the rectangle (828 elevations) and adjust them as desired. After a little grip editing, you should wind up with something similar to Figure 7.14.

10. Select one of the lines to highlight it, and then right-click and select Select Similar. This will select all of the contour label lines in the drawing file.

11. Right-click again and select Properties to display the AutoCAD Properties palette.

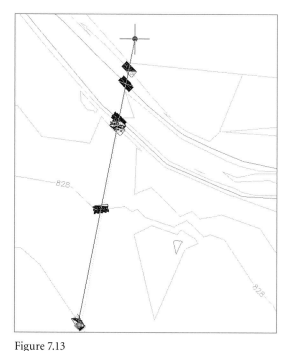

Figure 7.13

Dragging a contour label line to add more contour labels

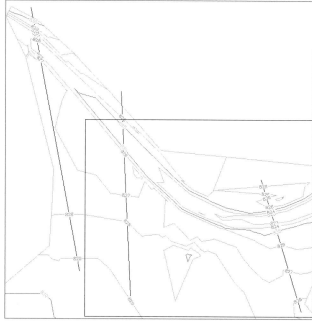

Figure 7.14

Completed Contour Label Line manipulation

12. Within the Properties palette, change the Display Contour Label Line value to False as shown in Figure 7.15. Close the palette if you like.

13. Press Esc again to deselect the Contour Label Lines, and notice that the linework disappears but the labels do not.

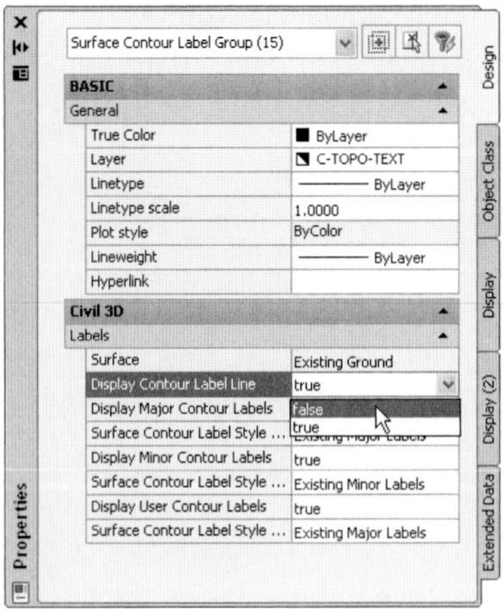

With the labels in place, and the linework gone, you can plot or present this data as needed in other drawing files. Remember that you can get the contour label line grips back by selecting any label. With the label selected, a visit to the Properties window will allow you to modify, change, or toggle the display of the labels and styles. Now that you have labeled the contours, you'll label some critical points on your surface.

Figure 7.15

Turning off the display of the contour label line

Labeling Critical Surface Points

The contours themselves are handy for getting a general feel for site information, but when you get down to it, there are critical points on every site where you must know the precise elevation. This could be a tie-in point, the top of a wall, or the elevation at a loading dock. In every case, this was generally considered tedious work, as any change to the design necessitated removing all those labels and starting over. Thankfully, Civil 3D's dynamic model lets you label once and update many times. In the following exercise, you'll quickly place a number of labels just to get a feel for the process and how these labels can be moved but retain the dynamic link to the surface being labeled:

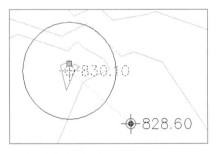

Figure 7.16

Dragging a surface label gives instant feedback without adding more labels.

1. Open the Spot Labels.dwg file.

2. Select Surfaces → Add Surface Labels → Spot Elevations.

3. Turn on your center osnap and place labels in the four circles found in the drawing. Press the spacebar or Enter to exit the command.

4. Zoom in on the northernmost circle and its label.

5. Select the label to show the two grips available for surface spot labels.

6. Click the diamond grip to relocate the label and begin dragging it as shown in Figure 7.16. Note that the label is updated on the fly as the label is dragged.

7. Press Esc to deselect the label and return it to its prior position.

Placing spot labels is quick, easy, and convenient. Now that you know about contours and specific locations, you'll use labels to get some more information about the site in general by labeling slopes in areas of interest.

Labeling Surface Slopes

When labeling slopes on a surface, it's important to remember that there are two ways of measuring the slope: at a single point based on the slope of the TIN triangle beneath that point, or between two points based on the distance and difference in elevation between those two points. Let's look at both methods of labeling.

1. Open the Slope Labels.dwg file.

2. Select Surfaces → Add Surface Labels → Slope Labels.

3. Press Enter at the command line to accept the default slope label type of one-point.

4. Using a center snap, place labels at the center of the four larger circles in the drawing. Press the spacebar or Enter to exit the command.

5. Zoom in on the red circle in the northeast portion of the site and the nearby label as shown in Figure 7.17. Note that because of the nature of the one-point label, the slope label and arrow are pointing in a direction that really doesn't make sense, parallel to the contours. One-point slope labels reflect the instant grade of a TIN triangle, sometimes leading to labeling anomalies like this one.

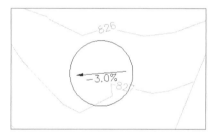

Figure 7.17

A one-point slope label in action

6. Select the label to display its one grip. Select the grip and begin to drag it away as shown in Figure 7.18. Note that the rotation and label text change as the insertion point moves across the surface.

7. Place the label in the center of the green circle just to the northwest. Move or replace the other labels as necessary.

   This type of review is crucial in both methods of labeling slope. The main issue with the two-point label style is that it is possible to miss high or low points.

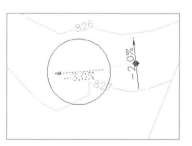

Figure 7.18

Grip editing a single-point slope label allows you to pick a point that makes sense and shows the true nature of the surface.

8. Zoom extents to bring the entire site back on-screen.

9. Select Surface Add Surface Labels Slope again.

10. Enter **T** at the command line to choose a two-point label style.

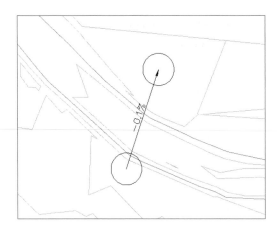

11. Using a center snap, pick one of the smaller circles on the north end of the site, and then pick the other small circle to the south, as shown in Figure 7.19.

12. Using the same center snap, connect the final two smaller circles with one more slope label. Using the longer span between points can help you understand the overall site conditions and prepare for drainage design.

With the surface labeled in a number of different ways, you have a good surface model that you can share with the team and use in plans or further analysis. In the next section, we'll look at analysis tools—reviewing the site on the front end for use suitability, and then performing an earthwork analysis with color-coded areas and soil adjustments.

Analyzing Surfaces

A good model makes for easy plans, but being able to do more than just create nice linework is what makes Civil 3D so powerful. Two common tasks in land development are reviewing the interaction of a flood plain with a site, and understanding how much soil volume exists between existing and proposed conditions. Let's look at those tasks now.

Performing an Elevation Analysis

Quite commonly, a consultant will be engaged to review a site for the suitability of a design based on site conditions. As metropolitan areas become more and more developed, the number of sites with floodplain areas increases. Understanding the interaction of this floodplain water elevation with the existing conditions helps engineers and developers make good site selection choices. In the following exercise, you'll take a look at coloring the surface based on elevation data:

1. Open the Elevation Analysis.dwg drawing file.

2. Select the surface and right-click to display the shortcut menu.

3. Select Surface Properties to display the Surface Properties dialog.

4. On the Information tab, click the Surface Style drop-down button and change the style to Elevation Banding (2D) as shown in Figure 7.20.

5. Switch to the Analysis tab.

6. In the middle of the dialog, change the number of ranges to **4**, as shown in Figure 7.21, and then click the blue Run Analysis button.

When you run the analysis with the stock values, Civil 3D will divide the range of surface elevation into a number of ranges, and assign colors based on a scheme determined by the style—Elevation Banding (2D) in this case. Because you need a more specific answer, you'll now manually tweak the ranges and colors to make more sense.

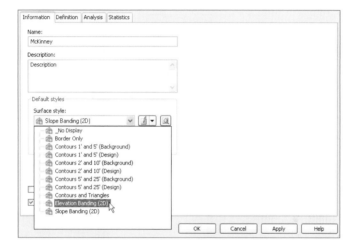

Figure 7.20

Selecting the Elevation Banding (2D) style turns on the display component for Elevations in plan view.

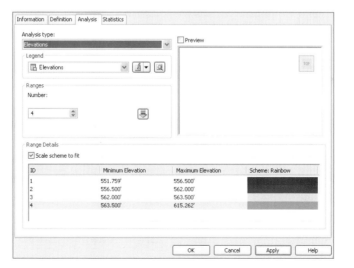

Figure 7.21

Completed elevation analysis setup

Based on information from your flood-plain expert, the creek in this area has the following range of elevations:

- Normal Creek Surface: 556.5
- Flood Surface: 562
- Minimum Freeboard Surface: 563.5

You'll use these elevations to drive your elevation analysis.

7. In the Range Details area of the dialog, click in the column of Maximum Elevation for the row marked 1 and enter **556.5** for a value.

8. Double-click the color block on row 1 to display the Select Color dialog. Select blue and click OK to close the dialog.

9. Continue working through the Minimum and Maximum elevations as shown in Figure 7.21, assigning colors as you go. The colors from top to bottom should be 160, Red, Yellow, and Green.

10. Click OK to close the dialog, and your screen should look a rainbow of colors as shown (approximately) in Figure 7.22.

Although the colors are great, and give a very good visual feel for the land available for development, a legend table will complete the presentation, and is simple to add.

Figure 7.22

The completed surface analysis. Blue indicates the normal channel area, red is the floodplain, yellow is the freeboard, and green is available land.

11. Select Surfaces → Add Legend Table.

12. Press Enter at the command line to accept the default Elevations table type.

13. Press Enter to accept the default behavior of a dynamic table.

14. Select a location for the upper-left corner of your table and click.

Your table should look like Figure 7.23, and you're done with your analysis of the floodplain.

This type of cursory analysis tool, combined with the information available from Google Earth and local government data, means you can do site analysis in almost no time. Now, lets look at the other end of the project, and run some earthwork calculations.

Figure 7.23

Elevations legend table indicating the range, area in acres of each range, and the color

Elevations Table				
Number	Minimum Elevation	Maximum Elevation	Area (Ac.)	Color
1	551.76	556.50	13.0	
2	556.50	562.00	44.8	
3	562.00	563.50	19.5	
4	563.50	615.26	213.6	

Performing an Earthwork Analysis

As land-development projects near their final design stages, the amount of earthmoving always becomes a major design constraint. With Civil 3D's built-in analysis tool and volume surface tool, it's easy to review the design as it is and prepare earthworks calculations.

1. Open the `Earthwork Analysis.dwg` file. This drawing contains both the existing and proposed grade surfaces for the purpose of our sample.

2. Select Surfaces → Utilities → Volumes to display the Composite Volumes palette in Panorama.

3. Click the Create New Volume Entry button to generate a new row in the palette.

4. Click the the <Select Surface> dropdown list under Base Surface and select Existing Ground from the drop-down menu.

5. Click the <Select Surface> dropdown list under Comparison Surface and select Proposed Ground. As soon as you select the second surface, Civil 3D will complete a volume calculation and display the results within the palette as shown in Figure 7.24.

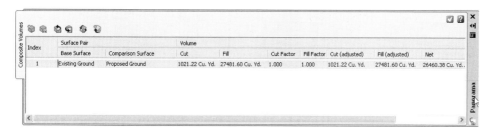

Figure 7.24

The completed earthwork analysis with no adjustment applied

If you have information from a soils professional, you can also apply Cut and Fill factors by entering them manually here. You then need to reprocess the analysis to get updated results, which you'll do in a later step. But first, because the current result is approximately 26,000 yards of fill, you'll adjust the surface, and see how easy it is to get a new number.

6. Without closing Panorama, expand the Surfaces → Proposed Ground → Definition branch in Prospector.

7. Right-click the Edits option and select Raise/Lower Surface.

8. Enter **-1** at the command line and press Enter. This moves the entire surface down one foot. Remember that this type of adjustment works while in the rough grading stages, but would be impractical later in the design.

9. Move back to Panorama, and click the Recompute Volumes button (the second button from the right). Your Composite Volumes should now resemble Figure 7.25, with a net volume near 8,000 cubic yards of fill.

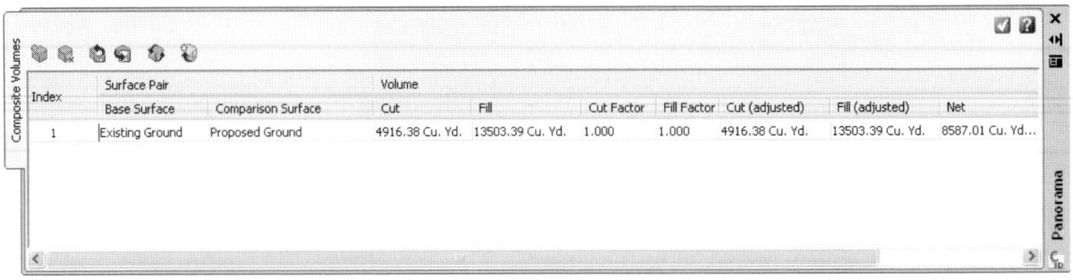

Figure 7.25

The earthwork analysis after a rough surface adjustment

Index	Surface Pair		Volume		Cut Factor	Fill Factor	Cut (adjusted)	Fill (adjusted)	Net
	Base Surface	Comparison Surface	Cut	Fill					
1	Existing Ground	Proposed Ground	4916.38 Cu. Yd.	13503.39 Cu. Yd.	1.000	1.000	4916.38 Cu. Yd.	13503.39 Cu. Yd.	8587.01 Cu. Yd...

Although the calculation here is quick and easy, it's unfortunately limited in that it disappears as soon as you close the Panorama palette. To create a more permanent volume calculation, it's necessary to create a TIN Volume Surface.

1. Close Panorama if you have not already done so.

2. Right-click Surfaces in Prospector, and select Create Surface to display the Create Surface dialog.

3. In the upper-left corner, click the Type: drop-down button and select the TIN Volume Surface option.

4. Change the Name value to **Prelim Volume**.

5. Verify that the Style is set to Contours 1′ and 5′ (Design).

6. Click the <Base Surface> cell, and then click the ellipsis button to display the Select Base Surface dialog.

7. Select Existing Ground, and click OK to dismiss the Select Base Surface dialog.

8. Click the <Comparison Surface> cell, and then click the ellipsis button to display the Select Comparison Surface dialog.

9. Select Proposed Ground and then click OK to dismiss the Select Comparison Surface dialog. Your Create Surface dialog should now look like Figure 7.26. If you have Cut and Fill factors, input them here to use those factors in your analysis.

10. Click OK to close the Create Surface dialog and run the volume analysis.

11. Back in the Surfaces branch, right-click on the Prelim Volume surface that has now appeared and select Surface Properties to display the Surface Properties dialog.

12. Change to the Statistics tab and expand the Volume section as shown in Figure 7.27. Note that the Net Volume value is approximately 8,600 yards, exactly the same as with the other method.

13. Click OK to close the dialog.

With a TIN surface, you can now use the myriad of surface tools and labeling techniques to present the volume information in a concise manner. Think about using the elevation analysis to find the areas of most cut and fill, or the Spot Elevations on Grid option to create a map of cut-fill ticks.

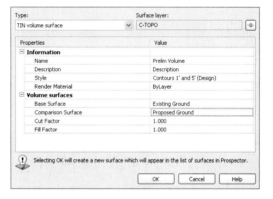

Figure 7.26

Creating a volume surface

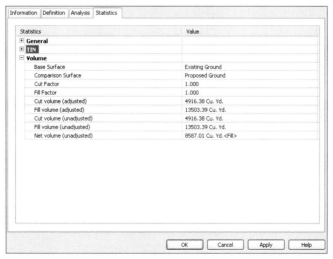

Figure 7.27

Statistics tab of a TIN Volume surface.

Summary

Surfaces are major underlying components of a land development model. Creating them from a myriad of data sources allows you to represent most situations found in practice as a digital model with all the advantages that brings. Digital models and dynamic labels enable you to minimize rework during the plan production stage. Dynamic models and powerful analysis tools enable you to explore design alternatives and paths with less time spent going backwards. By using even the basic portion of the Civil 3D surface modeling suite of tools, you're bound to cut hours from some of the most tedious tasks in land-development projects.

CHAPTER 8

Alignments

For thousands of years, engineers have laid out plans for construction. From the aqueducts of Rome to the Big Dig project in Boston, construction projects have been shown as flat lines on paper illustrating some horizontal placement of the project being designed. In Civil 3D, this planar element of the design is handled by the Alignments feature.

You can use alignments in Civil 3D to determine road centerlines, pipe layouts, curb returns, parking island curbs, pond berms, and any number of things where you've used a polyline in the past. The ability to use the vertical design elements of feature lines, profiles, and corridor design make alignments an integral part of the process like never before. Combined with the ability to reference across drawings and use the benefits of dynamic labeling, alignments are an important tool in the Civil 3D user arsenal.

In this chapter, you'll learn to:

- ▪ **Convert polylines to alignments**

- ▪ **Draw simple alignments by layout**

- ▪ **Edit alignments with grips and tabular tools**

- ▪ **Label station and geometry data with alignment label sets**

- ▪ **Label critical plan points using station-offset labels**

Creating Alignments

The horizontal control of an alignment has some benefits beyond the simple geometry and labeling. The main benefit is that the alignment object has the ability to understand the whole piece instead of just being individual arcs and lines tied together. Alignments can be constructed with relationships between the adjoining segments, so that a change in the properties of an arc changes the length of a line tied to it or the direction of a spiral segment. These powerful relationships are known as *fixed*, *float*, and *free*.

Fixed entities are independent of other segments in the alignment, fixed to the coordinate plane. A fixed entity is typically a line based on a start point and distance and bearing, or an arc based on three known points. This type of segment will not maintain tangency if the segments on either side are moved or edited.

Float entities have some measure of independence but are tied to one other segment in a tangential relationship. This can be a line extending from the end of an arc in a tangent direction for a given distance, or an arc coming from a line and passing through a given point. If the attachment entity is edited in some way, a floating entity will adjust to maintain tangency if at all possible.

Free entities are dependent on the segments before and after for their location. Think of a fillet curve between two line pieces, or a tangent connecting two curves in an S-shape. These segments will adjust and change as required to maintain the tangency on both connection points.

There are two main methods of creating alignments: converting from polylines and creating from scratch, known as creating by layout. In the next sections, you'll practice using both methods.

Converting from Polylines

For many users of Civil 3D, it's easiest to learn the conversion method and then work into the layout method as familiarity with the layout toolset increases. There are some gotchas with using the polyline method of creation, but as long as you are aware of them, you can plan in advance and handle them easily. In this exercise, you'll convert a number of polylines to alignments using different settings and options to understand the options involved.

1. Open the `Converting Alignments.dwg` file. (Remember, all the data for this book can be downloaded from www.sybex.com/introducingcivil3d2009.) Figure 8.1 shows the layout and the street names you'll be referring to in this series of exercises.

2. From the main menu, select Alignments → Create Alignment from Polyline.

3. Select the polyline representing Parker Place somewhere near the southern end to display the Create Alignment – From Polyline dialog shown in Figure 8.2. When converting a polyline to an alignment, the nearest end point becomes the beginning of the alignment.

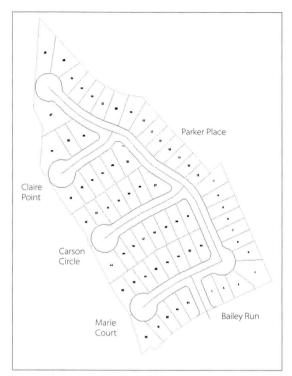

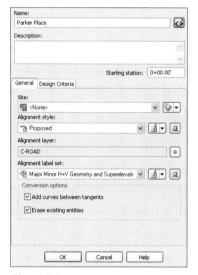

Figure 8.1
Site layout with proposed street names

Figure 8.2
The Create Alignments – From Polyline dialog

4. In the Name area, enter **Parker Place**, but leave the rest of the options alone so your dialog looks like Figure 8.2.

5. Click OK to dismiss the dialog.

Congratulations, you've made your first Civil 3D alignment! Now, let's look back at Figure 8.2 and discuss the options skipped over so rapidly in the exercise.

• The Name and Description fields should be fairly self-explanatory. Descriptions become more important as you begin modeling complex sites and have more align-ments to manage. The Description field can be displayed as part of a label, so some-times it can be used for ancillary information such as road type, channel lining, or other information that could be accessed handily.

• The Starting Station field allows you to set the beginning stationing of the alignment to be created. Most users will leave this value at 0+00, but many sewer systems are laid out with 1+00 as the starting point to allow for some modifications later without a change in the stationing through the line.

There are two tabs on the Create Alignment dialog: General and Design Criteria. The General tab handles alignment properties that are general to all alignments, and the Design Criteria tab is focused on transportation- and infrastructure-based uses.

The General tab includes the following settings:

- Site controls which Civil 3D site an alignment will be contained within. You can refer to Chapter 6, "Parcels," for a full explanation of the Civil 3D sites, but most alignments are best stored in the <None> site as shown in Figure 8.2.

- Alignment Style controls the display of the actual alignment object in Plan, Model, and Section views. This style also controls the appearance of any markers at the beginning, end, or intermittent geometry points along the alignment.

- Alignment Layer controls what layer the alignment object itself will be placed on. If you think of alignments as nested blocks, it's easier. The object will reside on this layer, but the subcomponents (lines, arc, spirals, and so on) will be display-controlled by the style settings.

- An Alignment Label Set is a collection of label styles that are applied to an alignment at creation. These can include labels at the beginning and end, at PC or PT points, and at vertical data points such as a High Point or a Superelevation Critical point.

- The Add Curves between Tangents option enables you to add filleted arcs between lines when the polyline has not had arcs placed in it. These arcs are free arcs per the preceding definition, dependent on the tangent lines before and after for their location.

- Erase Existing Entities simply erases the polyline being converted from the drawing when the conversion is complete.

On the Design Criteria tab, there are essentially two options in play: Criteria-Based Design and Design Check Sets. Criteria-Based Design takes the user input of a design speed, compares it with a design criteria file based on AASHTO 2001 specifications, and sets some design parameters for the alignment to be created. Design Check Sets allow you to specify design values such as Minimum Radius or Minimum Tangent Length and will warn you when these values are violated. Again, this tab is focused heavily on the large transportation market, and many Civil 3D users are happy to ignore it entirely.

To practice converting this method a few more times, convert the three other major streets in the subdivision using the same commands and settings. Be sure to change the names as previously shown in Figure 8.1. When you're done, your drawing should look something like Figure 8.3.

After polylines have been converted to alignments, the segments in the alignment have relationships based on the way the polyline was originally created. In some cases, this means that editing an individual segment or grip breaks the tangency as shown in Figure 8.4.

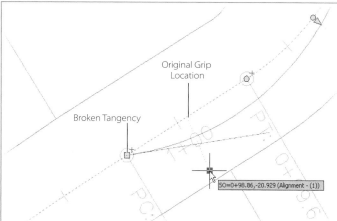

Figure 8.3
Complete alignment conversion

Figure 8.4
Grip editing a converted polyline often breaks tangency.

Experiment with this by selecting the new alignments and grip editing. You will look at editing in a later section, but it's important to note that this quirk of the conversion process is one reason many people advocate simply redrawing alignments using the method in the next section.

Creating Alignments by Layout

When creating alignments by layout, there are many more options to consider. Spirals cannot be drawn at all with polylines, and laying out an alignment piece by piece gives you the ability to control and drive the tangencies of your design. In this first exercise, you'll create the simplest alignment, using typical Point of Intersection (PI)–based design with curves filleted in between the tangents.

1. Open the Layout Alignments.dwg file. This is the same site as in the prior section; the street is drawn without any arcs so that finding PIs is easier.

2. From the main menu, select Alignments → Create Alignment by Layout.

3. Change the name to **Parker Place**, but leave the other options as they are. Notice that the options for Add Curve between Tangents and Erase Existing Entities were part of the conversion process.

4. Click OK and the Alignment Layout Tools toolbar will appear. This toolbar is divided into six sections, as shown in Figure 8.5.

Figure 8.5
The Alignment Layout Tools toolbar

Most users work from left to right across this toolbar. The basic tools for creation are on the left. The PI tools are designed to work with the most basic method of laying out an alignment, working from PI to PI with curves optionally inserted based on a radius, and with or without spirals in and out. The Segment tools allow the user to place individual lines, arcs, and spiral segments, tying them together with the tangent relationships as appropriate. The Conversion tools are handy for converting existing linework into segments, and the Delete Segment tool will remove a single piece of an alignment without erasing the whole object. Finally, the Edit tools allow for detailed, grid-based editing of the alignment components.

Now that you're familiar with the toolbar, you'll make a simple, PI-based alignment.

4. Click the drop-down arrow on the far-left button and select Tangent – Tangent (with Curves) to begin the layout process.

5. Use an end osnap, and click the southern end of the polyline that describes Parker Place.

6. Use an end osnap and click the first PI to the north. A jig will appear showing where the next tangent will be created, as in Figure 8.6. Also, if there is enough room as you move your cursor about, you will see a blue arc indicating the curve that Civil 3D will place in the alignment based on your settings.

7. Use an end osnap and click the successive PIs, working your way to the north end of the cul-de-sac.

8. After selecting the last point, right-click to exit the command, and your alignment will be complete.

The curves created by the program are based on a simple fillet with a given radius. You can set this radius by clicking the same drop-down arrow within the Alignment Layout Tools toolbar and selecting Curve and Spiral Settings. The dialog that appears in this case allows you to set the radius of the fillet curves, along with turning on and off spiral in and out options.

Figure 8.6

Creating the second tangent

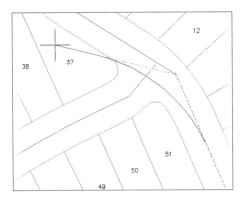

Now that you've created a basic alignment using simple fillets, you'll explore a basic alignment with a fixed and floating component in this next exercise.

1. Within the same `Layout Alignments.dwg` file, select Alignments → Create Alignment by Layout from the main menu to display the Create Alignment-Layout dialog.

2. Change the Name to **Marie Court**, and then click OK to close the dialog.

3. On the Alignment Layout toolbar, click the Fixed Line (Two Points) button.

4. Click the endpoint of Parker Place alignment to begin, and then snap to the end of the tangent line heading west.

5. Right-click to exit the Fixed Line command. Your screen should look like Figure 8.7.

6. On the toolbar, select the Floating Curve (From Entity End, Through Point) command as shown in Figure 8.7.

7. Ctrl+click the western end of the fixed segment just drawn.

8. Using a center snap, end the floating curve at the middle of the cul-de-sac, and then right-click to exit the curve command. Your alignment should look like Figure 8.8. Notice that the tooltip on the cursor also reflects the stationing of this new alignment.

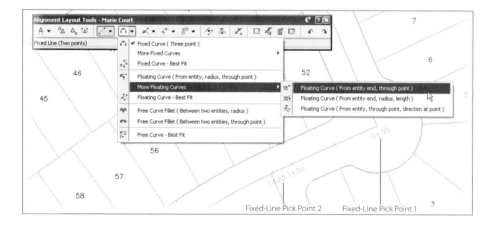

Figure 8.7

A fixed line segment, and selecting the floating curve command

Figure 8.8

Completed Marie Court alignment

9. Click the X on the Alignment Layout Tools toolbar to close it.

10. Select the new alignment to activate the grips. Make sure to pick an alignment segments, not the labels!

11. Select the easternmost grip, where Marie Court and Parker Place intersect, and drag it away. Notice how the curve portion continues to maintain both tangency and the end point in the cul-de-sac as shown in Figure 8.9.

Figure 8.9

Grip editing forces the floating curve to update.

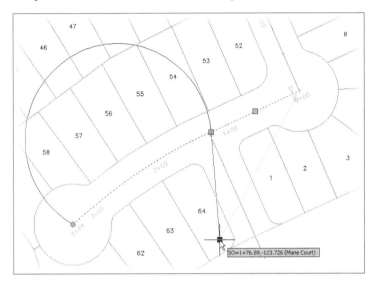

The ability to create and maintain relationships between pieces of your alignments means you can rest easier knowing that your streets are always in tangent, your channels always flow smoothly, and your sidewalks meander gracefully throughout their lengths. Now that you've explored creating alignments, you'll look at grip and tabular editing in the next section.

Editing Alignments

One of the catchphrases used when describing the work process with Civil 3D is, "Design then Refine." The idea here is that your design does not have to be set in stone before you can begin making use of the ideas and information you have. As you've seen, it's pick-and-click simple to make a basic road alignment from polylines or from parameters, designing by simply picking points on the screen and letting Civil 3D handle the fitting and labeling. In this section, you'll look at the refine part of the phrase. You'll learn how to use both grip and tabular editors to modify alignments.

Grip Editing of Alignments

Grip editing is a part of every AutoCAD user's toolbox, allowing for quick and easy edits. This process is no different with Civil 3D alignments, except that some grip edits can't be done based on the relationships between segments. In those cases, Civil 3D simply won't allow you to make the change, reverting to the initial position. In this exercise, you perform a basic grip edit.

1. Open the `Editing Alignments.dwg` file. This is basically the same site as you used in earlier exercises; however, there have been some more alignments created, and some have been inadvertently modified. Zoom in on the northern cul-de-sac and notice that the alignment no longer follows the road centerline sketched in with a line.

2. Select the alignment to activate its grips.

3. Select the triangle grip pointing vertically to select the PI point of the alignment. The triangle pointing radially near the same point is the radius grip for the curve. Figure 8.10 shows the grips with short descriptions. Note that the three pass-through grips on the arc simply change the radius to meet a new pass-through point.

4. Using an end osnap, move the PI to the southern end of the sketched line. Civil 3D will update the alignment, curve, and stationing for you.

This basic grip edit will solve a large number of problems for you. You can also now experiment with various alignments of your object to handle different scenarios. When you're trying to avoid a large specimen tree in a site design, or flirting with the edge of a wetlands area, being able to quickly iterate through options and knowing that your curves and labeling are all intact make the process much less daunting. If you want to experiment some more, use a center snap to fix the Claire Point western arc, which is out of place. Grips work well for approximate work, but for fine-tuning you might need to modify parameters. You'll explore that next.

Figure 8.10

Activated alignment curve grips

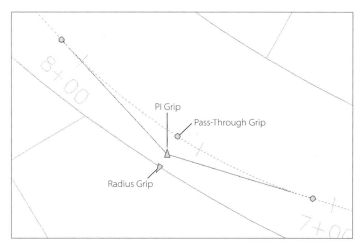

Parameter Editing of Alignments

Sometimes you need a higher level of control within the design. Grip edits are good for placement, but there's no easy way to grip edit the radius on a curve. For this process, Civil 3D offers two main methods of data editing: the Component Editor and the Panorama Editor. You'll use both in this exercise, and you can decide which is better for your everyday toolset.

1. Still using the Editing Alignments.dwg file, select the Parker Place alignment to activate it.

2. Right-click and select Edit Alignment Geometry from the context menu to display the Alignment Layout Toolbar. Refer back to Figure 8.5, and you'll see that the right third of this toolbar is all about editing.

3. Click the Pick Sub-Entity button, and the Alignment Layout Parameters palette shown in Figure 8.11 will appear. Figure 8.11 shows two versions of the same dialog. Note the button in the upper right with multiple horizontal lines. This is the Show Less/More toggle that will alter the amount of information shown in the palette. Set your toggle to Show Less.

4. Click the arc segment of the alignment near station 7+50 to populate the data as in Figure 8.11.

Figure 8.11

Alignment Layout Parameters palette in Show More and Show Less modes

5. Click the Radius cell to highlight the 150′ value. Enter a new value of **200′** and press Enter. The curve immediately reflects the change.

6. Close the Alignment Layout Parameters palette using the red X in the upper-right corner and press Esc to exit the command.

   Note that you can also use this palette to copy values to another program such as Excel by right-clicking in the empty space within the palette and selecting Copy to Clipboard. Editing values one at a time is tedious though, so in this exercise, you'll use Panorama to display the entire alignment in a tabular format.

7. On the Alignment Layout Tools toolbar, click the Alignment Grid View as shown in Figure 8.12 to display Panorama with an Alignment Entities tab active. Note that black values are editable, and grey values are derived values, so they cannot be modified.

8. Click the Radius cell for any of the curves and change the value to **200′**, Repeat this for all of the curve entities. As mentioned in Chapter 1, the columns in this view can be rearranged and resized as necessary.

9. Close Panorama by clicking the X, or by clicking the Alignment Grid View in the Alignment Layout Tools toolbar again.

10. Close the Alignment Layout Tools toolbar to complete your edits.

By using the component editor and the grid view in conjunction, editing to precise values for curves, spirals, and lines can be accomplished simply and quickly. Once your alignment is in place, labeling becomes a critical task.

Figure 8.12

The Alignment Grid View button and Panorama

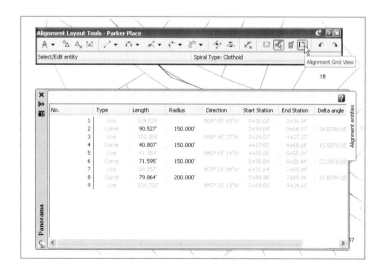

Labeling Alignments

Unlike many design applications, the labels in Civil 3D are inherently tied to the objects they label. This means that the changes and edits you explored previously are all reflected in the alignment labeling. In this section, you'll learn about the three major label types related to alignments: stationing, segment, and station-offset. Each of these is dependent on a myriad of styles, but you'll focus more on the use of these labels in the following exercises as opposed to building a bunch of label styles.

Stationing

Almost every designer has stationed a road or pipeline. With Civil 3D, stationing refers not only to the station values, but also to other labels that are dependent on the alignment (and associated profile) geometry. The options for labeling points in an alignment are as follows:

- Major Station
- Minor Station
- Geometry Point
- Profile Geometry Point
- Station Equation
- Design Speed
- Superelevation Critical Points

Each of these label options is driven by a style, and the whole process can seem a bit overwhelming. Remember, 75 percent of the time, you'll be labeling alignments in exactly the same way, and to that end, you'll have label sets that pull together all of the options. In this exercise, you explore changing individual labels, and then creating and using a label set.

1. Open the Stationing Alignments.dwg file.

2. Select the Carson Circle alignment to activate it. The alignment labels have been removed for this exercise.

3. Right-click and select Edit Alignment Labels from the pop-up menu to display the Alignment Labels dialog in Figure 8.13.

4. Select EE Major on the Major Station Label Style drop-down list, and then click the Add>> button to add that label to the alignment.

5. Select Minor Stations on the Type drop-down list.

6. Select Tick from the Minor Station Label Style drop-down list, and then click Add>>.

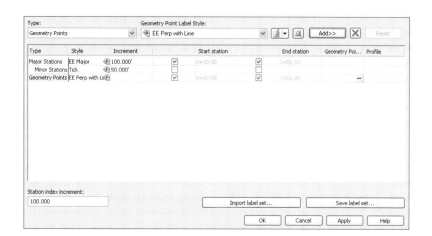

Figure 8.13

The completed Alignment Labels dialog

7. Select Geometry Points from the Type drop-down list.

8. Select EE Perp with Line from the Geometry Point Label Style drop-down list, and then click Add>> one more time. This time, the Geometry Points dialog in Figure 8.14 will appear.

9. This dialog lets you apply different label styles to different geometry point types if desired. Leave them all turned on for now and click OK to dismiss the dialog. Your Alignment Labels dialog should look like Figure 8.13 now.

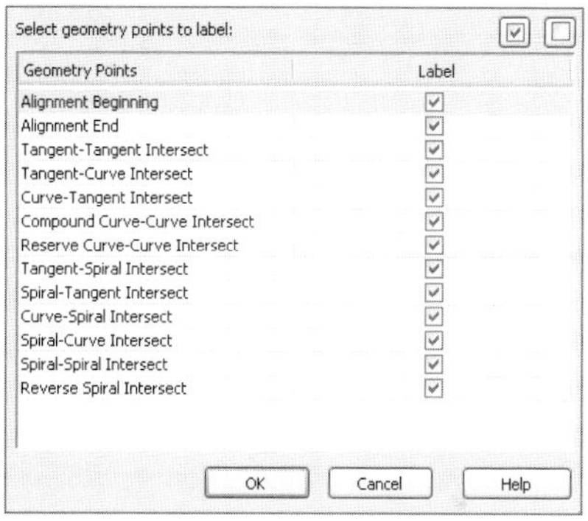

Figure 8.14

The Geometry Points dialog when adding labels

10. Click OK to dismiss the dialog and update the Carson Circle alignment.

    The station is labeled, but you do have a few minor clean up issues to take care of. Individual labels aren't editable unless you use Ctrl+click to pick them. To finish this exercise, you'll remove the Station labels at the beginning and end of the alignment because you already have geometry labels at those points.

11. Press Esc to make sure no objects are selected in Civil 3D.

12. Ctrl+click the 3 label at the end of the Carson Circle alignment. This is a major station label that you don't want to see. Note that this selection picks only the individual label, not the full range of major station labels as a typical click would.

13. Press the Delete key on your keyboard (not the Backspace key) to erase the single label from your drawing.

14. Repeat the process on the 0 at the beginning of the alignment.

It's worth noting that the BP and EP abbreviations used in the beginning and ending labels are abbreviations picked up from the drawing settings. Revisit Chapter 1 if you'd like to see how you can go about making those changes. Also, if you delete an individual label but then decide you want it back, select one of the other major station labels, right-click, and select Reset All Group Labels.

Although this process isn't overly long for a simple setup, it still could be tedious to remove all the labels and reapply the new ones based on your desired settings. To that end, you'll create a Label Set in this exercise and apply it to another alignment.

1. Select the Carson Circle alignment again.

2. Right-click and select Edit Alignments Labels to display the Alignment Labels dialog.

3. Click the Save Label Set button near the lower right to display the Alignment Label Set dialog. This dialog is the same as the individual Alignment Labels dialog in that you can pick labels types and styles to build up a collection of typical labels.

4. Change to the Information tab in the dialog.

5. Click in the Name field and enter **EE Streets** as a name. You can enter a description as shown in Figure 8.15 if you like. Descriptions make it easier to pick a label set later on when you're trying to remember what labels are in each set.

6. Click the OK button to dismiss this dialog, and click OK again to close the Alignment Labels dialog.

7. Press Esc to make sure no objects are selected in Civil 3D, and then select one of the other alignments.

8. Right-click and select Edit Alignment Labels to display the Alignment Labels dialog.

9. Click the Import Label Set on the lower right to display the Select Style Set dialog.

Figure 8.15

Assigning a name to an alignment label set

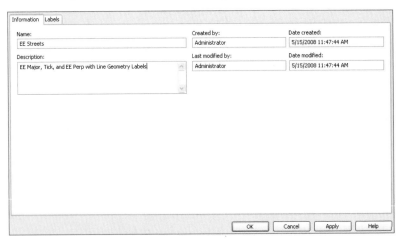

10. Select the EE Streets option from the drop-down list. Note the description entered previously is displayed here to make selection easier.

11. Click OK to close the dialog, and click OK again to return to the drawing window. You have replicated the labeling from Carson Circle in just a few clicks.

12. Repeat this process on the other two alignments. When complete, your drawing should look similar to Figure 8.16.

You will need to make the same edits to the beginning and ending station labels, but in general, using a label set is a fast and easy way of making a whole host of alignments look as desired. Now that the stationing is handled, it's time to explore segment labels.

Segment Labeling

It's a common requirement that labels on alignments assist in the layout of the alignment geometry in the field. To that end, individual segments can be labeled with the necessary information such as distance and bearing, or chord bearing, radius, and other curve information. Many Civil 3D users also use segment labels to place street names in their drawings. You'll do both in this exercise.

1. Open the Labeling Alignments.dwg file.

2. From the main menu, select Alignments → Add Alignment Labels → Add Alignment Labels to display the Add Labels dialog shown in Figure 8.17.

3. Change the Label Type drop-down list to Multiple Segment.

4. Change the Line Label Style drop-down list to EE Bearing over Distance.

5. Change the Curve Label Style to EE Curve. Your dialog should now look like Figure 8.17.

6. Click Add and select the Maries Court Alignment to apply your labels. If you zoom in on the alignment, your drawing will look something like Figure 8.18.

Figure 8.16

All alignments stationed using the EE Streets label set

Figure 8.17

Complete Add Labels dialog

Figure 8.18

**Marie Court seg-
ments labeled**

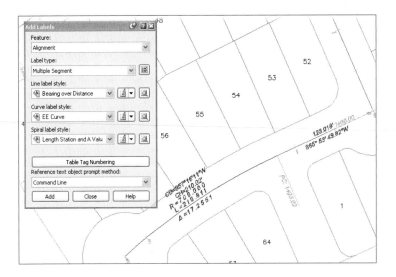

7. The command is still active, so pick each of your alignments to label them as you've configured in this dialog.

8. Move back to the Add Labels dialog and change the Label Type drop-down list to Single Segment.

9. Change the Line Label Style and the Curve Label Style to EE Street Name. Both of these label styles simply add the Alignment name, but you do have to set up both so that you are not limited to only putting the street name label along tangent segments.

10. Click Add, and then zoom in on the Marie Court alignment again.

11. Click the Carson Court alignment near the 2+00 station to place the street name label, and then repeat this on the other alignments at suitable locations. Your drawing should look something like Figure 8.19.

12. Right-click to exit the command, and then close the Add Labels dialog by clicking the Close button.

The first pass of labeling often creates a number of conflicts. Clicking any label will reveal two grips. Moving the square grip will move the label to a more suitable location and make the plan more readable. Also, with a single label selected, the right-click menu will offer the option to flip the label. Experiment with dragging and flipping to clear up any labeling conflicts. With the alignments labeled as needed, it's time to look at labeling some property lines with station-offset labels.

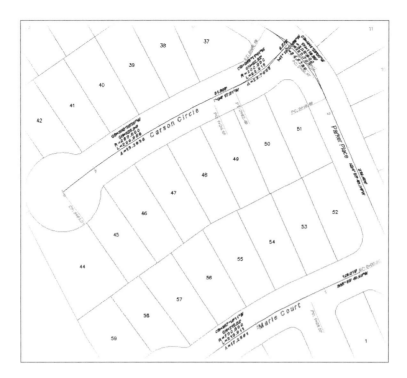

Figure 8.19

**Street names
applied after
segment labels**

Using Station-Offset Labels

The last major type of label in the alignment family is a station-offset label. Some examples of these labels are calling out curb returns, the locations of curb inlets, and street lights, or for placing trees along a path. In the following exercise, you'll use station-offset labels to mark curve points along the street right-of-way.

1. Open the Offset Labels.dwg file.

2. From the main menu, select Alignments → Add Alignment Labels → Add Alignment Labels to display the Add Labels dialog.

3. Change the Station Offset Label Style drop-down list to Station and Offset.

4. Change the Marker Style to Basic X.

5. Click Add, and Civil 3D will prompt you at the command line to select an alignment.

6. Pick the Marie Court alignment to activate it.

7. Using an end osnap, select the ends of the three arcs that make up the cul-de-sac area. When complete, your drawing should look like Figure 8.20.

8. Click Close on the Add Labels dialog to close it.

9. Select any of the labels just created, and you will be presented with two grips. One is to slide the label moving the point being labeled as well, the other is to drag the label moving only the text. Pause near each grip and a tooltip will be displayed to help in selecting the correct grip for your intended use.

10. Drag the four labels to make the labeling clearer, and your drawing will look something like Figure 8.21.

Figure 8.20

Adding station-offset labels on a cul-de-sac

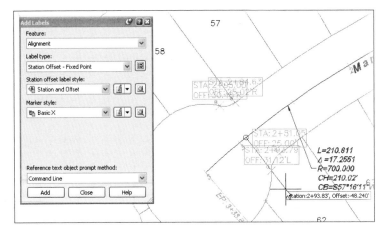

Figure 8.21

Completed label dragging for the Marie Court cul-de-sac

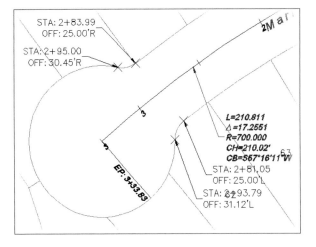

Although a simple station offset is useful, it's important to note that more complex labeling can be accomplished within all of the labels throughout Civil 3D. In this exercise, you'll label a point in space based on two different alignments to understand how that point relates to each.

1. Pan your drawing so the intersection of the Parker Place and Marie Court alignments is on your screen. The exercise is to label the imaginary point in space where the right-of-way lines would intersect.

2. From the main menu, select Alignments → Add Alignment Labels → Add Alignment Labels to display the Add Labels dialog.

3. Change the Station Offset Label Style to EE Intersection.

4. Change the Marker Style to Basic Circle with Cross, and then click Add.

5. Select the Marie Court alignment.

6. Use an intersection osnap, but pick the line on the front of lot 52 as shown in Figure 8.22. Note the ellipsis on the glyph—this indicates an extended intersection, allowing you to pick an imaginary intersection instead of a real one.

7. Mouse over the side lot line of lot 52 and notice the glyph jumps to the point in space where the two lines would cross. Civil 3D will prompt for a Crossing Street at the command line.

8. Pick the Parker Place alignment to complete the label.

9. Drag the label to a more suitable location as shown in Figure 8.23, and then click Close on the Add labels dialog to dismiss it.

This particular label style was built just for labeling plan data, but information can be pulled from profiles as well. The ability to label points in space can be incredibly useful during the design stage to help verify that your geometry is set up correctly and that your vertical design will come together without large leaps between intersecting streets.

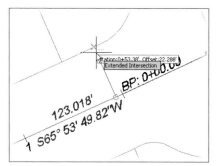

Figure 8.22

Extended intersection to pick the ROW intersection point

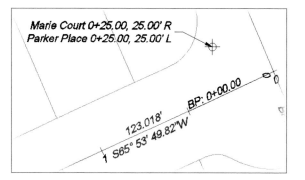

Figure 8.23

Completed intersection label

Summary

Because of its power to maintain geometric relationships, the alignment object in Civil 3D is used for more than just roads. Creating alignments is easily done by converting from existing linework in the form of polylines or by laying out completely new objects. Manipulation of these design elements while adhering to rules about tangency makes the exploration of design alternatives easier than ever.

Labeling functions are straightforward but powerful. By tying to the object instead of simply creating text in the drawing file, Civil 3D makes the tedious tasks of updating stationing, street names, or offset calls a thing of the past. Additionally, the use of label sets makes it easy to standardize how labels appear across a set of plans or within a firm, making standards adherence more straightforward. Finally, by using dynamic labeling for both plan production and design purposes, you can reduce errors and review problems.

CHAPTER 9

Profiles and Profile Views

The vertical component of land developments is generally controlled by one of two Civil 3D features: surfaces or profiles. Surfaces cover the land-like sheets, defining vertical data as connections between points. (See Chapter 5, "Points.") Profiles handle vertical data as linear functions: a pair of station and elevation coordinates. Profiles define the model by providing the z-value, and an alignment provides the x- and y-values. In Civil 3D, profiles are tied to this relationship (with one pseudo-exception, the quick profile). In this chapter, you'll explore the profile as part of the road alignment layout and design.

In this chapter, you'll learn how to:

- ■ **Cut a dynamic surface profile**

- ■ **Layout and edit a design profile**

- ■ **Create profile views for showing the profile data**

- ■ **Superimpose profiles for design review**

- ■ **Label profiles along the profile and along the edges of the profile view grid**

Creating and Editing Profiles

This chapter is titled "Profiles and Profile Views" because to Civil 3D, these are distinct things. To Civil 3D, a *profile* is simply a list of coordinates—a station and elevation pair that make up vertical data along some alignment. The *profile view* comprises the grid, titles, labels, and data bands that display that information to you as a Civil 3D user. These two are intertwined, but you can show the same profile in multiple profile views with widely different settings for styles and labels to create a completely different representation of the same data. You'll look at the profile view in more detail later, but in this section, you'll learn about the two main types of profiles: surface profiles and layout profiles.

Surface Profiles

Surface profiles are the starting point for almost all profile creation, and creating a surface profile in Civil 3D is a straightforward process. Surface profiles are dynamically linked to both the surface and the parent alignment in Civil 3D, meaning that a change in either source data will force a change to the profile data. In this exercise, you'll sample the existing ground surface from the subdivision layout you've been working with, and then create a simple profile view to display this information in a typical manner.

1. Open the Surface Profiles.dwg file. (Remember, all data files can be downloaded from www.sybex.com/go/introducingcivil3d2009.)

2. From the main menus, select Profiles → Create Profile from Surface to display the Create Profile from Surface dialog shown in Figure 9.1.

3. Change the Alignment drop-down list to Parker Place. Notice how the Station Range area displays information about the selected alignment. You can also use the station boxes here to sample a limited range of stations along an alignment if you'd like.

Figure 9.1

Sampling the Parker Place profile

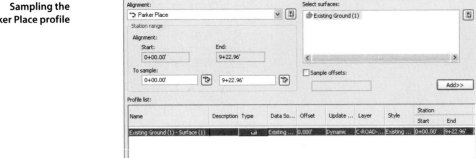

4. Click the Add button at mid-right, and the Existing Ground (1) – Surface (1) profile will be added to the Profile List area as shown in Figure 9.1.

   Congratulations, you've just completed sampling your first profile. Remember, profile data and profile views are not the same thing. To actually display this data in a form that makes sense, you need to draw in a profile view. You'll do that next.

5. Click the Draw in Profile View button at the bottom of the dialog to close it and open the Create Profile View wizard shown in Figure 9.2.

Figure 9.2

**The Create Profile
View wizard**

   This is considered a wizard because it steps you through a number of different options in a linear fashion. Although you can jump from step to step using the links on the left of the dialog, you should follow the steps until you're more familiar with all of the options available. You'll generally accept the defaults, but walking through the wizard gives you a chance to see the location of many settings you might want to explore later.

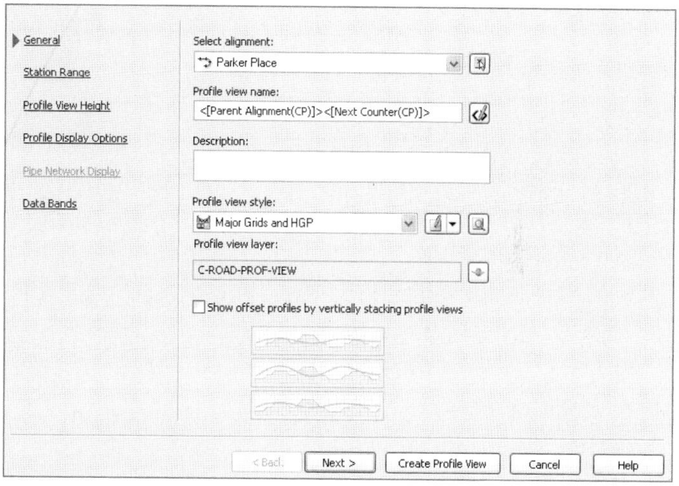

6. In the General step, accept the default values and click Next. (You'll explore profile view styles in a later exercise.)

7. The Station Range step allows you to show a limited portion of the profiles if desired. Make sure the Automatic radio button is selected and click Next.

8. The Profile View Height option allows you to specify a specific height for your view, or to split views that have large vertical displacements so that they fit better into your sheet. Verify that the Automatic option is selected and click Next.

9. The Profile Display Options step allows you to select label sets for profiles, select whether or not to draw a profile on a given profile view, select a profile to use for grid clipping, and a number of other options that make it easy to get just the view you'd like. You're drawing a simple surface profile, so click Next to move to the Data Bands tab.

10. Data Bands are strips of data oriented along the top or bottom of a profile (or section) view that display relevant information based on the profile data at that station. They can be used to display two different surface elevations every 50′, or to display the depth of a design profile, or perhaps to display the general shape of the horizontal geometry at that location. You'll adjust this later, but for now, click the Create Profile View button to dismiss the wizard.

11. Pick a point in your drawing window somewhere to the east of the site. The profile view will be drawn as in Figure 9.3.

Figure 9.3

Completed Parker Place profile view

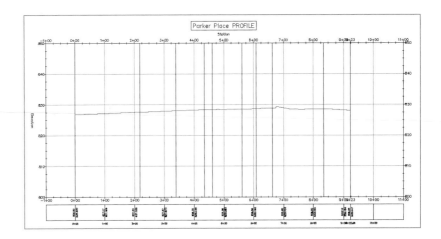

You'll notice that in the entire wizard, you didn't make any changes. Once you have Civil 3D configured and tweaked just how you like it, you'll be able to simply click the Draw in Profile View button right off the bat in the wizard, and skip all the settings tabs. By having all of those options preloaded, you can make it almost instantaneous to create a number of views just the way you need them.

One common development requirement is to show the ground surface at various parallel locations. In highway or subdivision work, this is commonly the right-of-way, and is a simple matter of adding offsets to the profile information, as you'll do in this exercise.

1. Open the Offset Profiles.dwg file (or continue working with the Surface Profiles drawing file if you completed the last exercise).

2. From the main menu, select Profiles → Create Profile from Surface to display the Create Profiles from Surface dialog.

3. Select Parker Place in the Alignments drop-down list at the top-left. The Profile List area reflects the already existing profile.

4. Select the Sample Offsets checkbox to activate the offsets text entry area.

5. Enter **-25,25** into the Sample Offsets box as shown in Figure 9.4, and then click the Add button to add the new profiles to the Profile List area.

Figure 9.4

Completed sampling of left and right offset profiles

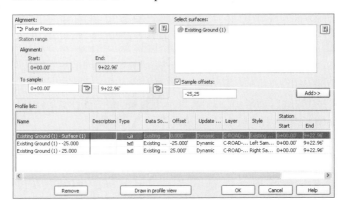

6. In the second row of the Profile List, click the Style cell to display the Pick Profile Style dialog shown in Figure 9.5.

Figure 9.5

Selecting a style for an offset profile

7. Select the Left Sample Profile style as shown, and click OK to dismiss the dialog.

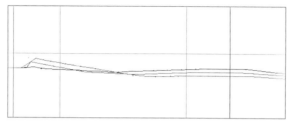

8. In the third row of the Profile list, select the Style cell again, and pick the Right Sample Profile style this time. By using different styles for left and right sample profiles, each will be visually distinctive.

9. Click OK to close the Create Profile from Surface dialog and dismiss Panorama. You don't have to create a profile view this time because you already have one. Zoom in on the profile view to see the distinct profiles. Your screen should look similar to Figure 9.6.

If you zoom in close enough, you'll notice that the left and right profiles have small triangle-shaped markers at every point. That's a part of the style, and you'll look at modifying these markers (or making them disappear) in a later portion of this chapter.

Figure 9.6

The Parker Place profile view with left and right profiles

As mentioned previously, the profile information is dynamically related to both the surface and alignment. If an alignment is lengthened, shortened, or simply relocated, the profile information is updated. In addition, any profiles that were created based on offsets are updates as well. In this exercise, you'll move the road centerline and see this relationship in action.

1. Open the `Dynamic Profile.dwg` file (or keep working with the same file if you've completed the prior exercises). Make sure you can see both the Parker Place alignment and the profile view.

2. Select the alignment to activate its grips. Be sure to pick the alignment—picking a label will simply make it possible to drag the label away from the alignment!

3. Select the starting-point grip and drag it to the southeast. Pick a point near the location shown in Figure 9.7 to set a new starting location for the alignment. Notice that the profile view has lengthened and all of the profiles reflect this new alignment location as shown in Figure 9.7.

This is obviously a temporary location, but the power shouldn't be underestimated. The ability to grab an alignment, manipulate it on screen, and instantly see feedback in the profile view is a powerful design iteration tool. Exploring and searching for vertically optimized design solutions is pick-and-click simple with this tool.

Figure 9.7

**The new alignment
location reflected in
profiles**

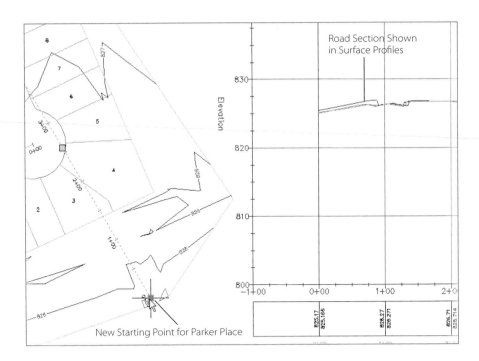

Figure 9.7

**The new alignment
location reflected in
profiles**

The same power can be applied to almost any object in Civil 3D. If you select a polyline
in a Civil 3D drawing and right-click, one of the shortcut menu options is Quick Profile.
Quick profiles give you the ability to get a look at your surfaces in a profile view without
creating an alignment, sampling the surface, and creating a view. They're quick and easy,
and you'll make one in the following exercise.

1. Continuing in the Dynamic Profiles drawing file, draw a line from the center of one
   cul-de-sac to another. (It doesn't really matter which two cul-de-sacs you use.)

2. Select this new line and right-click to display the shortcut menu. Select Quick Profile
   to display the Create Quick Profiles dialog shown in Figure 9.8. Here you can toggle
   on and off the surfaces to be displayed and the style they use, as well as what profile
   view style should be used.

Figure 9.8

**The Create Quick
Profiles dialog**

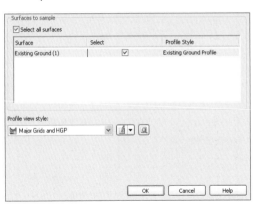

3. Click OK to dismiss the dialog.

4. Pick a point on the screen, and Civil 3D will draw a profile view similar to your typical profile view. Note that the title bar reflects a magic Alignment – (1) or something similar. Behind the scenes, Civil 3D is creating a temporary alignment and cutting a profile for you.

5. Select the line you just drew to activate its grips.

6. Move one end of the selected line to another cul-de-sac center point and watch the profile view update.

In this example, you used a line, but almost any object can be used to generate a quick profile. If you're not sure if a given object will work, select the object, right-click, and if the option is on the shortcut menu, you're in luck. Remember, while the quick profile is essentially the same as a typical alignment-based profile view of the given object cutting through surfaces, the profile view itself is a temporary object. This means that it will disappear the next time you save. That's great for designers, but don't build your construction documents with a quick profile, or you'll be left with nothing.

Once a profile of the existing ground has been created, it's time to begin designing the road or channel by using a layout profile. Layout profiles are the design elements you'll use to design your roads, channels, and other vertical elements throughout Civil 3D.

Layout Profiles

Layout profiles are very similar to alignments in that they can be created simply by connecting points and adding in curves, or they can be created by laying in individual segments based on the idea of fixed, floating, and free elements. Because most users focus on profile design using a collection of PVIs (points of vertical intersection) and parabolic curves between tangents, you'll look at that design method in this exercise.

1. Open the PVI Profiles.dwg file. This drawing has sampled existing ground profiles for all of the site alignments already drawn into the model, and a collection of circles where you're going to place your PVI points.

2. From the main menu, select Profiles → Create Profile by Layout. Click the Parker Place profile view to display the Create Profile dialog shown in Figure 9.9.

3. Change the label set to Complete Label Set as shown, and then click OK to dismiss the dialog. The Profile Layout Tools toolbar shown in Figure 9.10 will appear.

Figure 9.9

The Create Profile dialog

Figure 9.10

The Profile Layout Tools toolbar

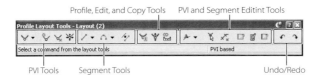

Similar to the Alignment Layouts Tools toolbar, the left portion of the Profile Layout Tools toolbar is for the creation of profiles, the middle segment is for adjusting and copying profiles, the next portion is for editing, and the last buttons perform the Undo and Redo functions.

4. Click the drop-down button on the left and select Curve Settings to display the Vertical Curve Settings dialog. Here you can adjust the type of curve used by Civil 3D in profile designs (parabolic, circular, or asymmetric) and decide what parameters will drive those curves.

5. Change the length to **200′** for both Crest and Sag curves, and then click OK to dismiss the dialog.

6. Click the drop-down button on the far-left of the Profile Layout Tools toolbar again, and select the Draw Tangents with Curves option.

7. Turn on a center snap, and select the center point of the circles drawn in the Parker Place profile view grid. Right-click after the last circle to exit the command. Your screen should look like Figure 9.11.

Figure 9.11

Completed layout profile for Parker Place

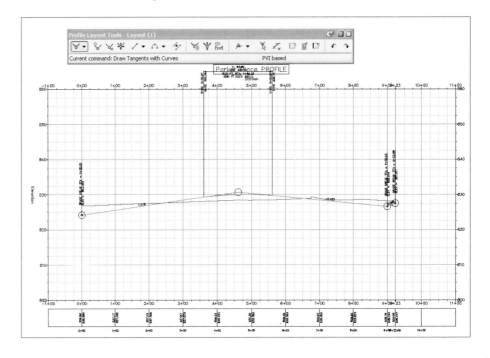

Your first layout profile is complete. The circles were there to guide you, but you can place PVIs anywhere you see fit, just as when drawing an alignment in a plan. As you place PVIs, Civil 3D attempts to fit a parabolic curve based on the predefined settings; but if it cannot fit a curve of the length requested, it will simply skip the curve. To see this in action, zoom in near the right end of your profile and note that the last two segments are simply joined together with no curve between them.

The act of creating an alignment with the most basic tools like this makes it quick and simple to create a number of alternatives, and to edit them as needed. Civil 3D allows the creation of multiple profiles defined as layouts, without requiring any of them to be designated as the primary profile. When you examine profile views in more detail in a later section of this chapter, you'll learn how to control which profile is displayed within a given profile view.

In the first exercise, you ignored the concept of design criteria. Civil 3D includes the ability to use design criteria as a control factor in laying out your design. AASHTO 2001 is built into the box, but you can create and manage your own criteria. Performing highway design (requiring the AASHTO guidance) is beyond the scope of this introductory level text, so now you'll move on to another creation methodology.

Creating a quick layout profile by picking random points as in the previous exercise is great for preliminary design, but when you are trying to tighten up a design, or trying to input a design based on handwritten notes or plans, it's necessary to control the PVI location, profile slopes, and curve information at a more granular level. To that end, Civil 3D includes a series of transparent commands that allow the direct input of station and elevation data, length and slope data, or station and slope data. In the next example, you're going to input a design file based on the following criteria:

Start at 0+00 with an elevation of 826.5. Draw to station 5+00 at 0.5%. Draw 250′ at −1%. Tie back into the existing ground profile at the end of the alignment.

Here are the steps you need to follow:

1. Open the `Designed Profiles.dwg` drawing file.

2. From the main menu, select Profiles → Create Profile by Layout and click the Parker Place profile view to display the Create Profile dialog.

3. Verify that the Profile Label Set is on Complete Label Set and click OK. The Profile Layout Tools toolbar will appear as before.

   At this point, you need to make sure another toolbar is available, the Civil 3D Transparent Commands toolbar. If you have not modified your Civil 3D configuration, this toolbar is typically on the second row of buttons, and it looks like Figure 9.12. If you don't have this toolbar on your screen, you can access it by right-clicking in the grey dock area (but not on a button or toolbar) and selecting Civil → Transparent Commands.

Grade-Station

Station-Elevation   Grade-Length

Once you have the transparent command toolbar, you can proceed.

4. Click the drop-down button on the left of the Profile Layout Tools, and select the Draw Tangents with Curves option. Civil 3D will prompt you to pick a start point. Instead of picking directly, you'll use the Transparent Commands toolbar.

5. Click the Station-Grade button shown in Figure 9.12. Civil 3D will prompt you to select a profile view. Select the Parker Place profile view by clicking a grid line. A sliding jig will appear along the bottom of the profile view, indicating that a station selection is in progress.

6. Type **0** at the command line and press Enter. A jig will now appear along the vertical axis indicating an elevation selection is in place.

7. Type **826.5** at the command line and press Enter. Nothing will appear on the screen, and Civil 3D will prompt you to Specify Station.

8. Press Esc one time, and the prompt will change to Specify End Point.

9. Click the Grade-Station button on the Transparent Commands toolbar, and the prompt will change to Specify Grade.

10. Type **0.5%** and press Enter. Civil 3D will display a jig sliding along from the starting point and heading up at 0.5%, and then it will prompt you for another station input.

11. Type **500** at the command prompt and press Enter. Civil 3D will return to the Specify Grade prompt.

12. Press Esc one time, and the prompt will change to Specify End Point.

13. Click the Grade-Length button on the Transparent Commands toolbar, and the prompt will ask you to specify a grade.

14. Type **-1%** at the command line and press Enter.

15. Press Esc one time to return to the Specify End Point prompt.

16. Use an end snap and select the end of the existing ground profile that's already in the profile view. Your screen should look like Figure 9.13.

By using the transparent commands, you can replicate existing data quickly and easily. Although it may seem like a lot of steps to produce this profile, familiarity breeds speed with the tools, and these transparent commands will become second nature very quickly as you work with profiles.

Once you've made a few profiles, the next step is to edit them. You'll look at that in the next section.

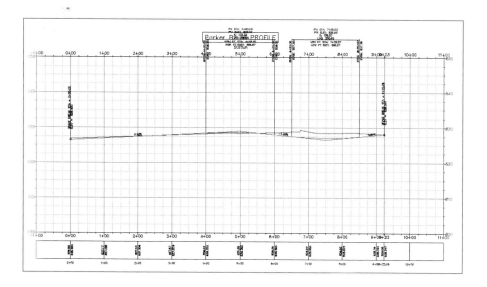

Figure 9.13

Completed profile entered from design data

Editing Profiles

Editing profiles is similar to editing alignments as discussed in Chapter 8, "Alignments." Grip edits are the quick-and-dirty edits, but you also want to be able to manipulate PVI data more precisely, to adjust slopes, and to lengthen or modify curves. Just like other Civil 3D objects, edits made to the profile object are reflected almost immediately on the screen, along with all corresponding labeling. This means that searching for the perfect solution doesn't wipe out all the work you've done labeling, and makes it possible to explore alternative ideas in a time-efficient manner.

Grip editing is usually good for making initial design more palatable. Later on, as you look at corridors in Chapter 10, "Assemblies and Corridors," you will explore the interaction of profiles, corridors, and volumes. Being able to quickly manipulate a profile with grips and then rerun a volume calculation is invaluable in searching for the best engineering solution. In this exercise, you'll simply edit a profile using grips and the transparent commands again to refine a layout profile.

1. Open the `Grip Editing Profiles.dwg` file.

2. Zoom in to the vertical curve near the 7+00 station and select the blue layout profile to activate the grips as shown in Figure 9.14.

3. Select the PVI grip (the red triangle) and, using a center snap, place it in the center of the small circle just to the northwest. The PVI will update, forcing a change in the curves, extension lines, labels, and data.

4. Pan to the left so that the grips for the curve near 2+00 are on your screen.

5. Select the PVI grip for this curve, but instead of picking a point directly, click the Station-Elevation transparent command.

Figure 9.14

Vertical curve grips in a layout profile

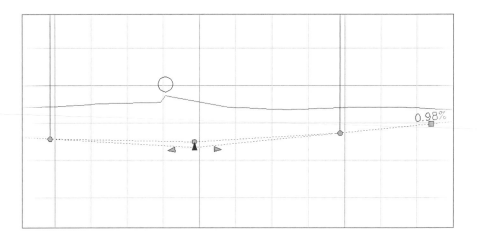

6. Click the Parker Place profile view to select it.

7. Enter a station of **225** at the command line.

8. Enter an elevation of **825.5** at the command line.

9. Press Esc to deselect the profile and zoom out. Your screen should look similar to Figure 9.15.

Figure 9.15

The edited Parker Place layout profile

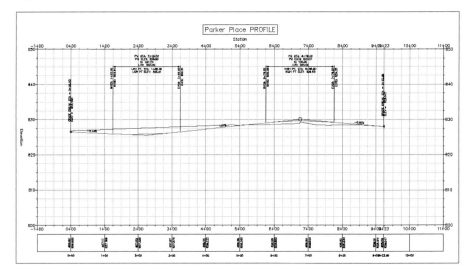

Moving beyond the quick grip edits, it's important to be able to precisely control the layout profile. Common review standards include using even station values for PVI points, and setting slopes to easy values. Although these requirements were more important when profile staking was a manually calculated process, it's still good design to follow these common rules. In this exercise, you'll fix a profile so that the PVI and slope data are more acceptable values.

1. Open the `Tabular Editing Profiles.dwg` file.

2. Select the blue layout profile to activate its grips. Be sure to pick the profile, not one of the labels.

3. Right-click and select Edit Profile Geometry from the menu. The Profile Layout Tools toolbar will appear. (The same toolbar used to originally lay out the profile is used to edit the profile.)

4. Click the Profile Grid View button near the right-hand side to display the Profile Entities tab in Panorama, as shown in Figure 9.16. This view allows you to see all of the data for the profile in one concise manner.

5. Click the PVI Station column for row 2 and change the value to **235**.

6. Click the PVI Station column for row 3 and change the value to **675**.

7. Click the Grade Out column for row 2 and change the value to **1.11%**.

8. Click the Grade In column for row 4 and change the value to **-0.84%**.

9. Scroll to the right and click the Profile Curve Length column for row 2. Change the value to **100**.

10. Click the X on the Panorama title bar to close the palette, and close the Profile Layout Tools by clicking the red X.

Figure 9.16

Profile Entities in Panorama

No.	I Station	PVI Elevation	Grade In	Grade Out	A (Grade Ch...	Profile Curv...	Profile Curve Length	K Va
1	0+00.00'	826.500'		-0.52%				
2	2+35.00'	825.267'	-0.52%	1.11%	1.63%	Sag	100.000'	6
3	6+75.00'	830.130'	1.11%	-0.84%	1.95%	Crest	200.000'	10
4	9+22.96'	828.047'	-0.84%					

The direct input method allows you to drive certain PVI elevations based on whether you used the Grade In or Grade Out column. You may have to play a bit to get used to the way Civil 3D decides which parameters to hold while modifying others. At the end of the day, you can precisely design your profile to match whatever criteria you may need.

Moving points and adjusting grades is relatively simple, but adding to the profile, or adjusting the curves and tangent segments, is almost as simple. In many applications, making a change in the underlying geometry of the profile would mean scrapping the design and starting over. In Civil 3D, you use profile tools to simply add or remove PVIs and curves, as in this exercise.

1. Open the `Adding Profile Components.dwg` file.

2. Select the Parker Place layout profile, right-click, and select Edit Profile Geometry to display the Profile Layout Tools toolbar. (Remember, you can mouse over the tools to get their names as a tooltip!)

3. Select the Delete PVI button. Civil 3D will prompt you at the command line to pick a point near that PVI to delete.

4. Click near the 4+75 station, and the PVI there will disappear, along with the curve.

5. Right-click to exit the command, and the labeling will update.

   As you've seen, deleting and adding PVI information to an existing profile is as simple as two clicks. Adding a curve is almost as simple.

6. Select the drop-down button next to the Fixed Vertical Curve button, and select the Free Vertical Parabola (PVI Based) option as shown in Figure 9.17.

7. Click near the PVI at station 6+75.

8. Enter **150** at the command line or press Enter to accept this default value. The curve will be added, but the labeling won't update.

9. Right-click to exit the command and update the labeling.

There are a number of different ways to build and edit profiles. Using these basic elements will handle a large portion of the profiles seen in land development work, and give you the ability to explore and play with profiles to understand your site design better. Now that you know how to create and manipulate profiles, you'll explore ways to display and label them in the next section.

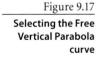

Figure 9.17

Selecting the Free Vertical Parabola curve

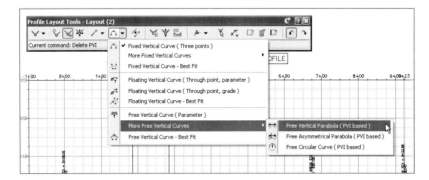

Displaying and Labeling Profiles and Profile Views

To this point, you've been using a basic set of labels along the profile and then around the profile view. Beyond the basics, there are styles in play for both the profile and profile view: labels and label sets for profiles, and data bands along the profile view. Because the profile and the profile view have distinctly different settings, you'll look at each in its own section.

Working with Profile Styles and Labels

Like most other Civil 3D objects, the profile object itself carries a style property reflecting how it will be displayed. Earlier in this chapter, you looked briefly at this option when displaying the left and right offset profiles, but it's important to review these styles and look at some options for their use. In this exercise, you'll modify the styles used in a profile view to reflect the change from a design mode to a plan production mode where extra information is added to meet review requirements.

1. Open the Profile Styles.dwg file.

2. Select the red-and-black layout profile in the Parker Place profile view, and then right-click and select Profile Properties to display the Profile Properties dialog shown in Figure 9.18.

3. Switch to the Information tab if necessary and click the Object Style drop-down button to display the available profile styles.

4. Select the Design Profile style from the list and click OK to dismiss the dialog.

5. Press Esc to unselect the profile. Note the change in the profile display.

As seen in Figure 9.18, there's not much to a profile in terms of properties that would be modified. The style change in this case turned on the parabolic extension lines and changed the colors for the entire profile to be uniform as opposed to color-coded by element type. The use of a color-coded profile style is great during the design phase, and the ease of changing styles later makes it convenient to have styles for all kinds of uses and permutations.

The style of a given profile is often established during the creation of that profile, but labeling often comes as a later process. The labels a designer needs during the analysis and design stage often bear little resemblance to the reviewing agency requirements.

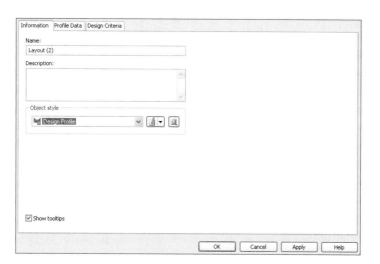

Figure 9.18

The Profile Properties dialog

Thankfully, Civil 3D includes the concept of label sets for profiles just as in alignments, so making a change to the label set across a wide group of designed profiles is a relatively quick and painless task. In this exercise, you'll label one profile one component at a time, establish a label set from those choices, and then apply that label set to another layout profile in the drawing.

1. Open the `Profile Labels.dwg` drawing file.

2. Zoom in on the Parker Place profile view and select the blue layout profile.

3. Right-click and select Edit Labels from the shortcut menu to display the Profile Labels dialog shown in Figure 9.19.

4. Change the Type drop-down list to Grade Breaks, and then change the Profile Grade Break Label Style drop-down list to Station over Elevation if necessary.

5. Click the Add button to add this label to the profile. Note that the labels will not update in the model unless you click OK to close the dialog or Apply to push the changes out to the model.

6. Change the Type drop-down to Lines, and then change the Profile Tangent Label Style drop-down list to Percentage Slope.

7. Click the Add button to add this label to the profile.

8. Change the Type drop-down list to Crest Curves, and then change the Profile Crest Curve Label Style to Crest Only.

9. Click the Add button to add this label to the profile.

10. Within the Labels table, select the Dim Anchor Val in the Crest Curves row, and change the value to **2**.

11. Change the Type drop-down list to Sag Curves, and then change the Profile Sag Curve Label Style to Sag.

12. Click the Add button to add this label to the profile.

Figure 9.19

The empty Profile Labels dialog

13. Within the Labels table, select the Dim Anchor Val in the Sag Curves row and change the value to **2**. Your dialog should now look like Figure 9.20.

14. Click Apply to update your model. Your screen should look something like Figure 9.21. Note that the Profile Labels dialog is still open. Apply lets you see your changes in the model without leaving the dialog.

Figure 9.20

The completed Parker Place labels

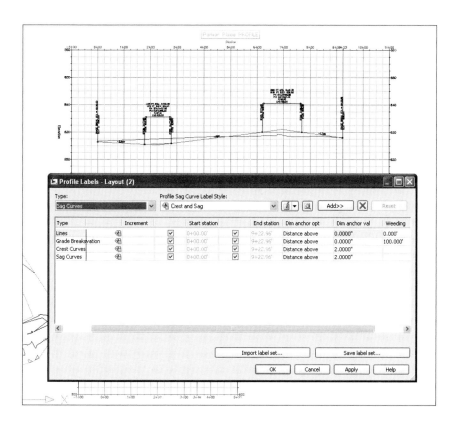

Figure 9.21

Parker Place profile view with labels applied

15. Click the Save Label Set button in the lower right of the Profile Labels dialog to display the Profile Label Set dialog.

16. Switch to the Information tab and change the name to **Intro Roads**.

17. Click OK to return to the Profile Labels dialog, and then click OK again to return to your drawing.

At this point, Parker Place is labeled as needed, but it sure took a lot of picks and clicks to get there! Thankfully, the label set you created in the last few steps of the exercise allows you to reapply those same selections quickly and easily to other profiles. In this exercise, you'll apply that label set, and then make a minor change to the destination profile labels to display all the points required.

1. Continuing within the Profile Labels drawing file, pan down to the Carson Circle profile view.

2. Select the blue layout profile and right-click to display the shortcut menu.

3. Select Edit Labels from the shortcut menu to display the Profile Labels dialog.

4. Click the Import Label Set button near the lower right to display the Select Style Set dialog.

5. Select Intro Roads from the drop-down list, and then click OK to close the Select Set dialog.

6. Click OK to dismiss the Profile Labels dialog. The Carson Circle profile view will look similar to Figure 9.22. Note that the PVI near station 0+12 is missing its label.

7. Select a label and right-click to display the shortcut menu.

8. Select Edit Labels to display the Profile Labels dialog again.

9. In the list of labels, click the Weeding column of the Grade Breaks row and change the value to **5**. Weeding distances tell Civil 3D to ignore label points when they're too close together to make good-looking labels. In this case though, it's missing an important data point.

Figure 9.22

Carson Circle labeled with the Intro Roads label set

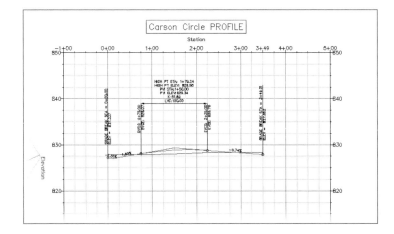

10. Click OK to dismiss the dialog, and the low point should now have a label.

11. Control-click on the new label to highlight the individual label instead of the label set.

12. Right-click and select Flip Label from the shortcut menu. Your screen should now look like Figure 9.23.

As you saw in previous exercises, the profile labels are dynamically tied to the profile geometry. Although the labels were applied in those exercises, there are also options for labeling Horizontal Geometry points or Major and Minor station points. Most people label these Major and Minor station elevations as part of the profile view, as you'll examine next.

Figure 9.23

Completed Carson Circle labels after the Weeding edit

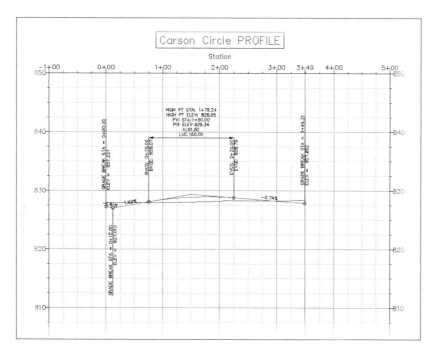

Working with Profile Views and Bands

Labeling profiles is important to review and design, but getting the display right is at least as important. Civil 3D makes it simple to have different grid displays for various uses and to show different pieces of information above and below the profile view as bands of data. Profile view styles control the grid lines and tick marks along the edges, the labeling on all four axis, and the title of the profile view and of each axis. Band styles control the display of information along the top or bottom edge of the profile view, and can include information from simple elevations to complete data about superelevation. In this exercise, you'll manipulate multiple profile views and apply different styles and properties to control each view. Additionally, you'll see how to select which profiles are on and off within a particular profile view.

1. Open the `Profile Views.dwg` file. There are three Parker Place profile views in this drawing, and there is an alternate layout profile called Design 2 displayed in each of them.

2. Select the top profile view grid and then right-click to display the shortcut menu.

3. Select Profile View Properties to display the Profile View Properties dialog shown in Figure 9.24. Change to the Information tab if necessary.

Figure 9.24

**The Information
tab in a Profile
Properties dialog**

4. Change the Object Style drop-down list to Full Grid. The Information tab allows you to change the name of a profile view and change or edit the style in use.

5. Change the name of the profile view to **Parker Place Design 1**.

6. Switch to the Stations tab. The Stations tab allows you to specify a start and end station if you do not want to show the full alignment length in one profile view. This makes showing the profile view for a single sheet's worth of data very simple.

7. Switch to the Elevations tab. This tab allows you to modify the datum elevation, making it an even value, or to limit the height so that your profile views all have the same height.

8. Click the User Specified Height radio button to activate the Minimum and Maximum data boxes.

9. Enter **820** for a Minimum value and **850** for a Maximum value as shown in Figure 9.25.

10. Switch to the Profiles tab and uncheck the Design 2 row under the Draw column as shown in Figure 9.26.

11. Click OK to close the dialog. (You'll look at the Bands tab in the next exercise.)

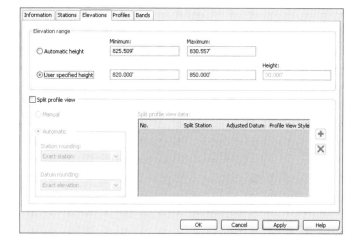

Figure 9.25

User Specified Height values in the Profile Properties dialog

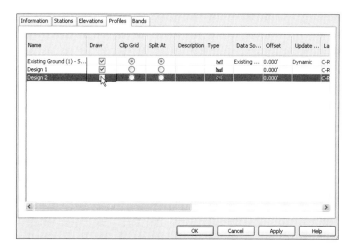

Figure 9.26

Controlling displays on the Profiles tab

With this level of control, you can create multiple displays, using different grids and scales as needed. For practice, repeat the same steps on the middle profile view, changing the name to **Parker Place Design 2** and toggling off the Design 1 profile. With that complete, your drawing will look similar to Figure 9.27. Remember, you still have the original view showing both design profiles at the bottom, and that a change to the profile objects in any view changes them all.

Figure 9.27

Two profile views to display alternative designs

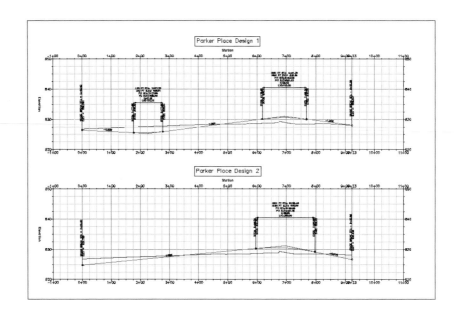

With the profiles in place, you may still need to show a bit more information. In this exercise, you'll add a pair of bands to a profile view, showing horizontal geometry at the top of your profile view grid, and elevation data along the bottom.

1. Open the `Profile Bands.dwg` file.

2. Select the Parker Place profile view and right-click to open the shortcut menu.

3. Select Profile View Properties to access the Profile View Properties dialog and switch to the Bands tab shown in Figure 9.28.

Figure 9.28

Initial Bands tab display

4. Change the Band Type drop-down list to Elevations and Stations, and then click the Add button to display the Geometry Points to Label in Band dialog shown in Figure 9.29. In this case, the dialog selection is somewhat irrelevant because the band is set up to label at major stations only.

5. Click OK to close this dialog and return to the Profile View Properties dialog.

6. Click the Gap column and change the value to **0**.

7. Click the Profile 2 column in the first row, and change the drop-down list to Design 1. The Profile 1 and Profile 2 columns assign various profiles to various label components within the band. Your dialog should look like Figure 9.30 now.

Figure 9.29

Selecting profile points to label

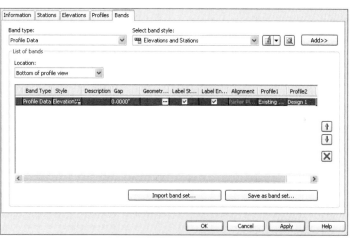

Figure 9.30

Bands tab in Profile View Properties after a band is added to the bottom of the profile view

8. Change the Location drop-down list to Top of Profile View. As mentioned, bands can be applied to both the top and bottom of the view.

9. Change the Band Type drop-down list to Horizontal Geometry.

10. Change the Select Band Style drop-down list to Geometry and click the Add button again.

11. Change the Gap value in the first row to **2″**. This will push the band information up above the title block for the profile view. Your dialog should now look like Figure 9.31.

12. Click OK to close the dialog. Your profile view should look something like Figure 9.32.

Figure 9.31

Bands tab in Profile View Properties after a band is added to the top of the profile view

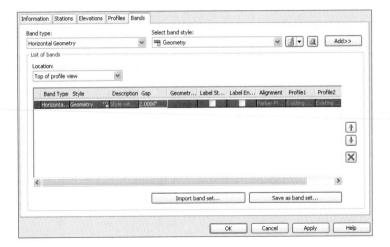

Figure 9.32

Completed profile view with bands

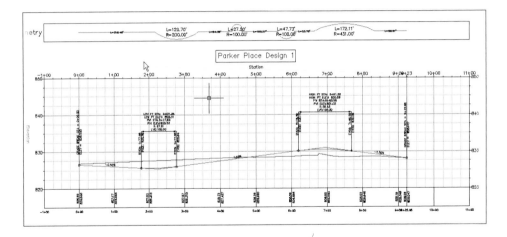

If you zoom in to the data band at the bottom of the profile view, you'll note that the elevations are different, reflecting the existing ground and layout profiles. This assignment was completed in step 7 of the preceding exercise. It's also important to note that the gap values entered are essentially offsets, pushing the band vertically away from a given axis. (You can use negative values here if you need to show something running inside your profile view grid.)

Superimposing Profiles

Although most of the time you'll be working with a single profile, it can be beneficial to understand the relationship between profiles in nonparallel situations. To assist in this understanding, Civil 3D includes a utility to superimpose profiles from one profile view to another. In the following exercise, you'll use this utility to compare the design profiles of two streets that run on adjacent blocks. This can be helpful when you grade the lots between them and need to know how much elevation difference you are covering. That's the use case you'll examine in this exercise.

1. Open the `Superimpose Profiles.dwg` file. Carson Circle and Claire Point both have layout profiles drawn in the respective profile views.

2. From the main menu, select Profiles → Create Superimposed Profiles. Civil 3D will prompt you at the command line to pick the source profile.

3. Select the blue layout profile in the Carson Circle profile view. Civil 3D will prompt you to pick a destination profile view.

4. Select the Claire Point profile view to display the Superimpose Profile Options dialog. The options here are handy if you'd like to show a portion of a longer alignment on the profile view of a shorter one, or just need to show a small range of stations for some reason.

5. Click OK to dismiss the dialog. The Claire Point profile view should look like Figure 9.33. Remember, the projection is a linear point projection, so distances and curves may look exaggerated in some way.

Remember, this is a dynamic link like so much else in Civil 3D. Modifying the design profile in the Carson Circle profile view will reflect in the Marie Court profile view. This gives you the real ability to quickly see how a profile is related to its peers.

Figure 9.33

Superimposed profiles

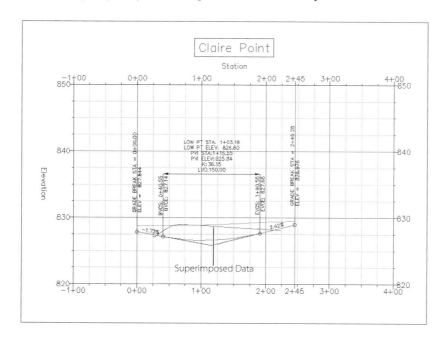

Summary

Profiles and profile views in Civil 3D act together to give you a full measure of ways to display vertical information in your design. Sampled profiles that react to design changes allow you to design based on existing conditions and review alternate alignment placements in an instant. Layout profiles with smart elements that understand the relationship between the tangents and curves of the design and the labeling that comes along make design revision quick and even fun to do. Finally, profile views and bands give you full control of data represented in your construction documents, reducing the drudgery of plan production to almost nil.

CHAPTER 10

Assemblies and Corridors

In land development project design, roads follow one or more typical sections. These typical lane, curb, and sidewalk configurations are usually based on standards put forth by the governing body, such as a state department of transportation or local municipality. Civil 3D provides tools to model these typical sections as assemblies. Once the assembly is created, it is combined with alignments and profiles to create a corridor model.

This chapter includes the following topics:

- Importing a standard assembly

- Customizing lane width in a standard assembly

- Building a road corridor from an alignment, a profile, and an assembly

- Viewing corridor sections

- Building a finished ground surface from a corridor

- Observing the dynamic reaction of the corridor model

Importing a Standard Assembly

Civil 3D includes a robust catalog of road components for building any imaginable typical section as an assembly. In addition to simple lanes, curbs, and sidewalks, the

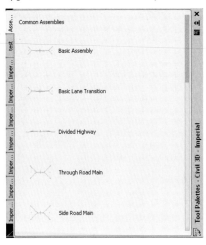

catalog also includes parts for rehabilitation projects, superelevation, and channels, among other options. These parts come preloaded onto several Tool palettes so that they are at your fingertips when you begin building your model. In addition to the smaller components, called *subassemblies,* there are several prebuilt standard assemblies for basic roads, divided highways, intersections, and roundabouts (see Figure 10.1).

In the following exercise, you'll bring in one of these assemblies, which you'll later customize.

1. Open the drawing file Corridors1.dwg, which you can download from www.sybex.com/go/introducingcivil3d2009.

2. Choose Corridors → Subassembly Tool Palettes. The Tool palettes will appear.

3. On the Tool palettes, switch to the Assemblies - Imperial Tool Palette, as shown in Figure 10.1.

4. Click the Through Road Main assembly. The AutoCAD Properties palette will appear.

5. At the Specify Location for Assembly: prompt, pan over to the right of the site, below the profile, and select any location where there is room to work. An assembly will appear in the drawing. Press Esc to exit the command. The assembly will look like Figure 10.2.

6. Save the drawing—you will need it for the next exercise.

Figure 10.2

The Through Road Main assembly

Customizing Lane Width in a Standard Assembly

The prebuilt assemblies are excellent for getting started, but they are rarely a perfect fit to the required design. Sometimes, only small changes are necessary, such as lane width or curb height, while other times you may have to build an assembly from scratch using the catalog subassemblies. For this example, you will change the lane width parameter and lane slope parameter to customize the assembly.

1. Select the assembly by clicking the vertical red line. Right-click and choose Assembly Properties. The Assembly Properties dialog will appear.

2. Switch to the Construction tab of the Assembly Properties dialog.

3. Select the Lane entry under Through Road Main - Right. Information about this lane will appear on the right side of the dialog under Input Values.

4. Change the Width entry from 13.5′ to **10′**, as shown in Figure 10.3.

5. Change the Default Slope entry from -2.00% to **-3.00%**.

6. Repeat steps 1 through 5 for Through Road Main - Left.

7. Click OK to exit the dialog. The slope and width of each lane has been changed.

8. Save the drawing—you will need it for the next exercise.

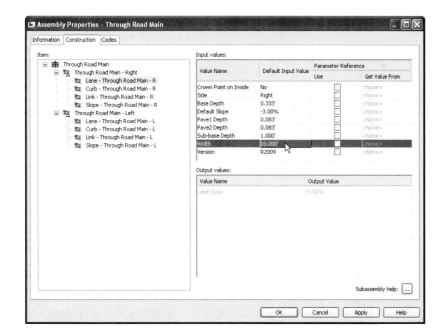

Figure 10.3

The construction tab of the Assembly Properties dialog showing the lane width parameter

Building a Road Corridor from an Alignment, a Profile, and an Assembly

Once the typical section has been built as an assembly, it can be combined with an alignment and profile to build a corridor model. A corridor takes the horizontal design of the alignment combined with the vertical design of the profile and the cross-sectional aspect of the assembly and combines them into one three-dimensional model.

Figure 10.4 shows the corridor from this chapter in an isometric view. Note how each assembly is applied along the proposed alignment, and vertical rise can be observed, which comes from the design profile.

Figure 10.4

A corridor model in isometric view

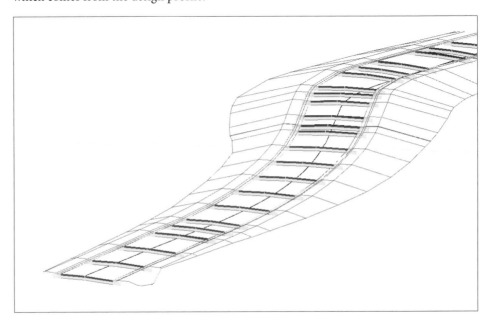

The following exercise will give you hands-on experience building a corridor model from an alignment, a profile, and an assembly.

1. Continue working in `Corridors1.dwg`.

2. Choose Corridors → Create Simple Corridor. The Create Simple Corridor dialog will appear.

   If you knew the name of the design alignment, you could type it by hand, but it would be better to have Civil 3D read the name of the alignment and automatically build it into the corridor name with a name template. Once a name template is created, all new corridors will be automatically named to your specifications.

3. Click the Edit Name Template button. The Name Template dialog will appear.

4. Delete the information in the Name field.

5. Use the Property Fields pull-down list to select Corridor First Baseline. Click the Insert button. The Name field will now be populated with <[Corridor First Baseline]>, which is a special formula that will read the name of the alignment you choose as your first baseline.

6. In the Name field, type a space followed by the word **Corridor** to the right of the <[Corridor First Baseline]> formula, as shown in Figure 10.5.

7. Click OK to dismiss the Name Template dialog. The Create Simple Corridor dialog will return. Click OK.

   This named your corridor using a name template. The resulting corridor will appear in Prospector with the name Parker Place Corridor.

Figure 10.5

The Name Template dialog

8. At the `Select a baseline alignment <or press enter key to select from list>:` prompt, press ↵. The Select an Alignment dialog will appear. Select Parker Place, and then click OK.

9. At the `Select a profile <or press enter key to select from list>:` prompt, press ↵. The Select a Profile dialog will appear. Use the Select a Profile drop-down list to select Parker Place FG. Click OK.

10. At the `Select an assembly <or press enter key to select from list>:` prompt, press ↵. The Select an Assembly dialog will appear. Use the drop-down list to select Through Road Main. Click OK.

    The Through Road Main assembly includes a daylight subassembly called BasicSideSlopeCutDitch, as shown in Figure 10.6.

    A daylight subassembly gives the corridor information about how the designer wants to tie into existing ground, as shown in Figure 10.7. The BasicSideSlopeCutDitch has parameters for both cut and fill, including adding a ditch when a section is in an area of cut.

    Before the daylight subassembly can do its work, you must select which surface will act as the existing ground, or target surface. After completing step 10, the Target Mapping dialog will appear to prompt you to choose a surface.

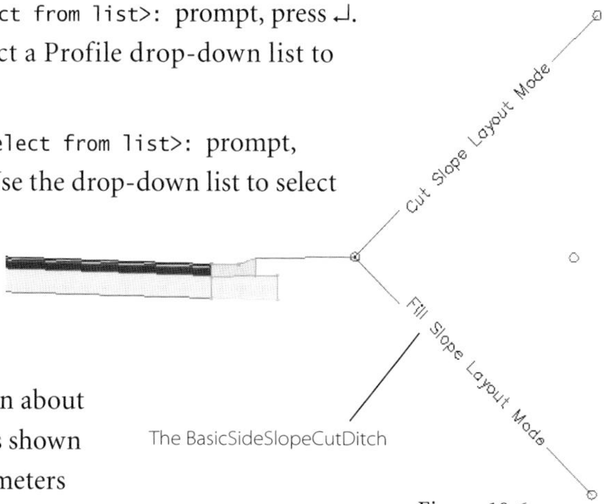

Cut Slope Layout Mode

Fill Slope Layout Mode

The BasicSideSlopeCutDitch

Figure 10.6

The BasicSide-SlopeCutDitch assembly provides information to the corridor about how to connect with existing ground, including adding a ditch in the cut condition.

Figure 10.7

Daylight links in a corridor section. Daylighting determines how the assembly will tie to existing ground.

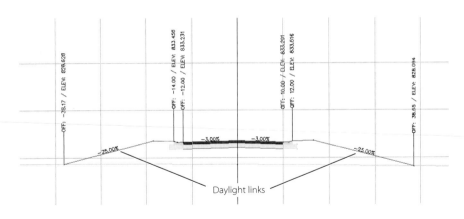

11. The Target Mapping dialog will appear. Click inside the Surfaces field that says <Click here to set all>. The Pick a Surface dialog will appear. Choose Existing Ground, and then click OK. A surface is now assigned to both sides of the road for daylight calculations, as shown in Figure 10.8.

12. Click OK to exit the Target Mapping dialog. The corridor will build, and the message `Corridor → Parker Place Corridor created` will appear in the command line. The corridor will appear in the drawing, as shown in Figure 10.9.

Figure 10.8

The Target Mapping dialog with a target surface assigned

Figure 10.9

The Parker Place corridor

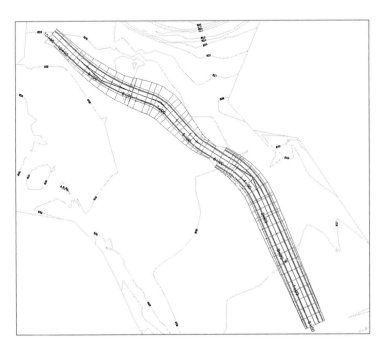

Viewing Corridor Sections

Once a corridor model has been created, you will often want to explore each section quickly to get a feel for what has been built and make notes of what needs to be changed with the design, adjusted, or modeled differently. An easy way to view each section is by using the View/Edit Corridor Surfaces tool. The following exercise will lead you through exploring your corridor model with this tool.

1. Continue working in Corridors1.dwg.

2. Choose Corridors → View/Edit Corridor Section.

3. At the Select a corridor <or press enter key to select from list>: prompt, pick the Parker Place Corridor object in the drawing. The View/Edit Corridor Section Tools dialog will appear, as shown in Figure 10.10.

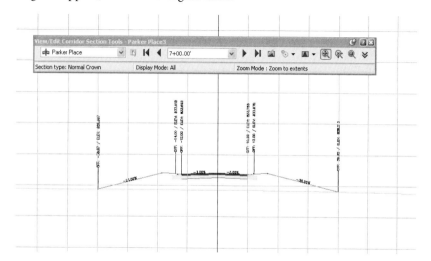

Figure 10.10

The View/Edit Corridor Section dialog and interface

4. Use the Next Station button to advance through each corridor station to get an idea of what is happening in the corridor.

5. Use the Select Station pull-down list to advance to station 2+00.00. Note that the BasicSideSlopeCutDitch subassembly has made a ditch for this section because the profile drives this section into cut.

6. Use the Select Station pull-down list to advance to station 7+00. Note that the Basic-SideSlopeCutDitch subassembly has used the 50 percent slope to connect to existing ground because the profile drives this section into fill.

7. Use the Override Station Range pull-down menu (shown in Figure 10.11) to select Edit/View Options. The View/Edit Corridor Section Options dialog will appear.

Figure 10.11

Use the Edit/View Options choice to bring up the View/Edit Corridor Options dialog.

8. Click in the Code Set Style field until you see an ellipsis button. Click the ellipsis button. The Code Set Style dialog will appear.

9. Use the pull-down to change the Code Set Style from View-Edit with Shading to View-Edit. Press OK to exit the dialog.

10. Click OK to exit the View/Edit Corridor Section Options dialog. Note that the assembly shading disappears.

11. Click the Zoom to a Subassembly button. The Pick Subassembly dialog will appear. Use the pull-down list on the Pick Subassembly dialog to select Curb - Through Road Main – L and click OK. The view will zoom in on the curb subassembly.

12. Explore some of the other tools on the View/Edit Corridor Section Tools dialog. Observe what happens when using the wheel mouse pan and zoom features.

13. Press Esc to exit the command. Explore the corridor by toggling through additional stations. When you're done exploring, click the red X to exit the View/Edit Corridor Section Tools dialog.

14. Save the drawing—you will need it in the next exercise.

Building a Finished Ground Surface from a Corridor

A corridor is a complete road model that can be used to build one of many surfaces. Surfaces are commonly built to represent the final finished grade (top surface) or to represent subgrade (datum surface). The following exercise will give you experience building a surface from the pieces of the corridor that represent a final finished grade.

1. Continue working in `Corridors1.dwg`.

2. Select the corridor in the drawing and right-click. Choose Corridor Properties from the menu. The Corridor Properties dialog will appear.

3. Switch to the Surfaces tab of the Corridor Properties dialog.

4. Click the Create a Corridor Surface button. A surface entry will appear.

5. Confirm that the Data Type is set to Links and Specify Code is set to Top.

6. Click the plus button. A data type entry will appear.

7. Click OK.

8. Zoom in on your corridor to see the contours from the corridor surface, as shown in Figure 10.12.

   Every good surface should have a boundary. Boundaries clean up bad triangulation around the edges of a surface and are critical for corridor surfaces because bends in the road can encourage improper triangulation. For single-baseline corridors—that is, corridors that are built using one alignment—there is an automatic boundary feature.

9. Select the corridor in the drawing and right-click. Choose Corridor Properties from the menu. The Corridor Properties dialog will appear.

10. Switch to the Boundaries tab of the Corridor Properties dialog.

11. Right-click the surface entry on the Boundaries tab (capture) and use the Add Automatically fly-out menu to select Daylight as shown in Figure 10.13.

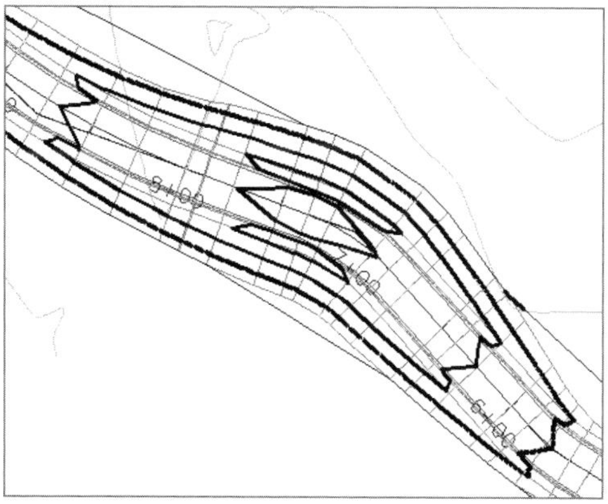

12. Click OK.

13. Zoom and pan around the corridor. Notice that the surface has been constrained to the outermost corridor feature line, which is the piece of the corridor that represents the daylight connection with existing ground.

14. Save your drawing—you will use it in the next exercise.

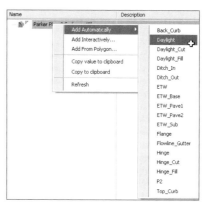

Figure 10.12

A corridor surface created using top link information

Figure 10.13

The Add Automatically fly-out menu

Observing the Dynamic Reaction of the Corridor Model

Now that you understand how a corridor is constructed, it is important to see how this model will react as your design evolves. It is not necessary to have your alignment, profile, or assembly design perfected before you model the road, because the corridor will update as you design and help you understand how your design is evolving.

The following exercise will lead you through making design changes to the profile and a lane width so that you can see how a corridor reacts dynamically.

1. Continue working in `Corridors1.dwg`.

2. Locate the Prospector tab of the Toolspace. Expand the Corridors entry. Right-click Parker Place Corridor and choose Rebuild Automatic.

3. Still on the Prospector tab, expand the Surfaces entry. Right-click Parker Place Corridor Surface and select Rebuild Automatic (if it is not already selected).

4. Choose View → Viewports → 2 Viewports.

5. At the `Enter a configuration option [Horizontal/Vertical] <Vertical>:` prompt, type **H** and press ↵. The view will be split into two pieces, as shown in Figure 10.14.

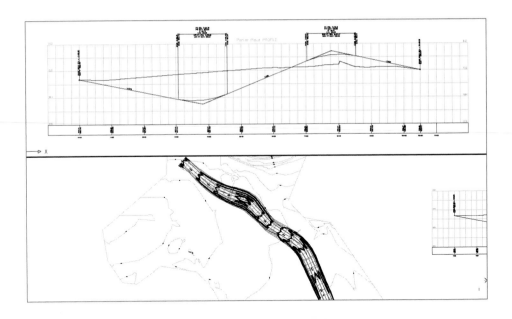

6. Click inside the top viewport to activate it. Zoom in on the profile view.

7. Click inside the bottom viewport to activate it. Zoom in on the road.

8. Click inside the top viewport to activate it. Select the finished ground profile. Use a PVI grip to change the second PVI from a fill condition to a cut condition, as shown in Figure 10.15.

9. The corridor will rebuild. Use the bottom viewport to note the change in contours. Experiment with other profile edits.

10. Click inside the top viewport to activate it. Zoom in on the assembly.

11. Select the assembly by clicking the vertical red line. Right-click and choose Assembly Properties. The Assembly Properties dialog will appear.

12. Switch to the Construction tab of the Assembly Properties dialog.

13. Select the Lane entry under Through Road Main - Right. Information about this lane will appear on the right side of the dialog under Input Values.

Figure 10.15

Use the PVI grip to move the second PVI from fill into cut.

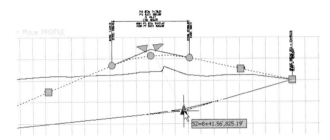

14. Change the Width entry from 10′ to **15′**.

15. Click OK.

16. The corridor will rebuild. Use the bottom viewport to note the visible change in the corridor for the right lane and the change in surface contours.

17. Save your drawing.

Summary

In this chapter you were introduced to the power of the Civil 3D corridor model. The foundations of a corridor model are an alignment, a profile, and an assembly. These three elements are strung together to form a dynamic 3D model called a corridor. Once an alignment and profile are in place, one of several standard assemblies can be used to build the corridor, or a custom assembly can be constructed from the subassembly catalog. A corridor can be viewed through the View/Edit corridor interface, and surfaces can be built using some of the built-in intelligence of the model. Understanding these key skills will lead the way to create more advanced models and enable you to go through may design iterations to optimize your road design with fewer drafting delays.

CHAPTER 11

Sections

Many projects require the designer to create sections along an alignment. These sections may show existing ground along a river, a combination of existing ground and proposed ground along an embankment, or detailed design elements of a road or pipes under a highway. Civil 3D provides tools to sample, view, and analyze this necessary information.

This chapter includes the following topics:

- **Sampling section data along an alignment**

- **Creating a section view**

- **Labeling pipe crossings in a section view**

- **Creating multiple section views**

- **Analyzing construction materials by section**

Sampling Section Data Along an Alignment

Just as a profile is sampled along an alignment, a section is sampled along a sample line. Before you can draw sections or create section views, you must create sample lines along an alignment. In their simplest form, sample lines are placed perpendicular to an alignment and a certain interval (see Figure 11.1).

Sample lines can also be created from polylines, set at specific stations, or customized in several other ways. You are not limited to using perpendicular sample lines (see Figure 11.2). For example, most river sections would be cut perpendicular to the existing ground contours as opposed to perpendicular to the centerline alignment. This could be accomplished by converting a polyline to a sample line.

Figure 11.1

Sample lines are created based on an alignment. By default, sample lines are created perpendicular to their parent alignment.

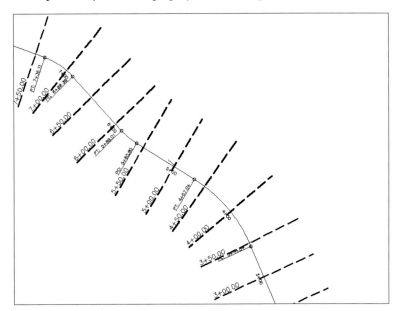

Figure 11.2

Sample lines can be created from polylines to cross their parent alignment at odd angles.

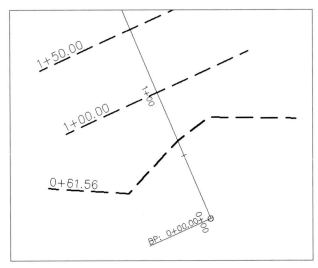

When sample lines are created, there are several types of information that they can process. Think of the sample line as a knife cutting through a casserole; and surfaces, corridors, and pipe networks as ingredients in that casserole (see Figure 11.3). When the knife slices through, it registers what elements are contained in that slice. Once the sample line is created, it remembers which elements it is keeping track of, and those elements can be drawn on section views and will be dynamically updated.

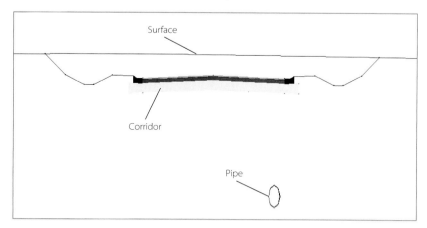

Figure 11.3

Surfaces, corridors, and pipe network objects can be sampled with sample lines, and later drawn in section views.

The following exercise leads you through creating a sample line group that will process data for two surfaces, a corridor, and two pipe networks.

1. Open the drawing file Sections1.dwg, which you can download from www.sybex.com/go/introducingcivil3d2009.

2. Choose Sections → Create Sample Lines. At the Select an alignment <or press enter key to select from list>: prompt, press ↵. The Select Alignment dialog will appear.

3. In the Select Alignment dialog, choose Parker Place. Click OK. The Create Sample Line Group dialog will appear, as shown in Figure 11.4.

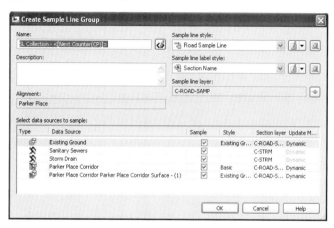

Figure 11.4

The Create Sample Line Group dialog

4. In the Create Sample Line Group dialog, note that all of the Data Source types are checked. This means that the existing ground surface, the sanitary sewers, the storm drainage system, the corridor, and the corridor surface will all be sampled and available to draw on cross section views. Click OK. The Sample Line Tools dialog will appear.

5. Use the Sample Line Creation Methods pull-down menu to choose the By Range of Stations option (shown in Figure 11.5). The Create Sample Lines - By Station Range dialog will appear.

6. In the Create Sample Lines - By Station Range dialog, change the left and right swath width from 50.000′ to **75.000′**.

7. Staying in the Create Sample Lines - By Station Range dialog, change the sampling interval to **25.000′** along Tangents and **25.000′** along curves.

8. Staying in the Create Sample Lines - By Station Range dialog, change the At Range Start, At Range End, and At Horizontal Geometry Points settings from false to **true** (see Figure 11.6). Click OK.

9. The Sample Line Tools dialog will remain on the screen, and blue sample lines will appear in the drawing.

10. Press ⏎ to exit the command. Labels will appear on each sample line, as shown in Figure 11.7.

Figure 11.5

Choose the By Range of Stations menu option.

Figure 11.6

The Create Sample Lines - By Station Range dialog

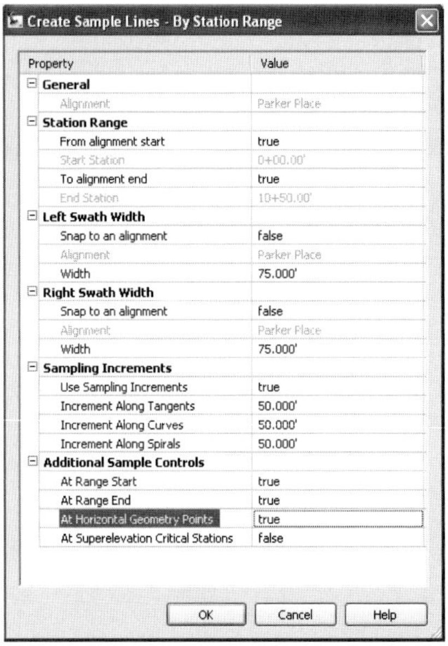

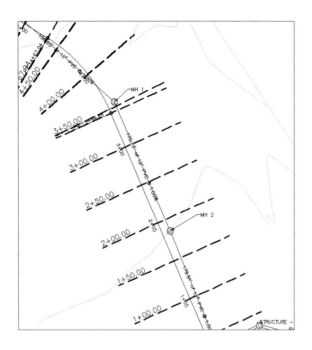

Figure 11.7

Labeled sample lines will appear in the drawing.

Creating a Section View

When sample lines are created, they perform two tasks. They mark the location where section views can be drawn, and they process the data elements that can be shown, such as surfaces, corridors, and pipe network objects. A section view provides a way to show this information.

Much like a profile view, the section view is a medium for drawing existing and proposed data along an alignment. While the profile view presents this data parallel to the parent alignment, a section view shows this information with respect to the sample line, which is often perpendicular to the alignment (see Figure 11.8).

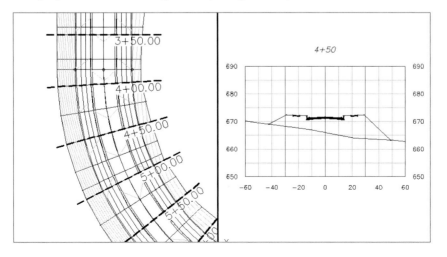

Figure 11.8

The section view (right) shows the information "sliced" by the sample line for station 4+50.00.

In the following exercise, you create a single section view:

1. Continue working in the drawing from the previous exercise, or open the drawing file Sections2.dwg (which you can download from www.sybex.com/go/introducingcivil3d2009).

2. Choose Sections → Create Section View. The Create Section View - General dialog will appear.

3. Use the Station: pull-down menu to choose station 5+00.00′ as shown in Figure 11.9.

4. Click Next twice to advance through the Create Section View - Offset Range and Elevation Range dialog. Note that the Automatic radio button is toggled on for both elements (see Figure 11.10). This means that the program will make a decision about how wide and how tall to make the section view.

5. Click Next to advance to the Create Section View - Section Display Options dialog. This dialog lists all of the different Civil 3D objects that could be displayed in this Section View. Note that the Draw box for each object is checked, which means all of these objects will be shown (see Figure 11.11).

Figure 11.9

Choose Station 5+00.00′.

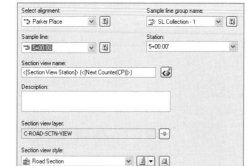

Figure 11.10

The Automatic radio button is toggled on, which means that the section view will be drawn to the limits of the sample line. If you wanted the view to be expanded, you could make a manual adjustment.

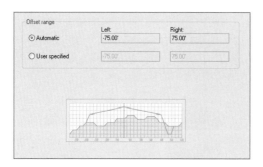

Figure 11.11

Each sampled element is checked, which means they will all be drawn on the section view.

6. Use the scroll bar to slide over to the Change Labels column of the dialog. Click inside the Change Labels field, as shown in Figure 11.12, for the Existing Ground surface. The Select Style Set dialog will appear.

Figure 11.12

Move your mouse over the Change Labels field, and then click.

7. Use the Select Style Set pull-down list to choose the _No Labels style set, as shown in Figure 11.13. Click OK to dismiss the dialog and return to the Create Section View dialog. When the section view is drawn, only the corridor surface will be labeled.

Figure 11.13

The Select Style Set dialog

8. Use the scroll bar to slide over to the Style column of the dialog. Click inside the Style field for the corridor surface. The Pick Section Style Set dialog will appear.

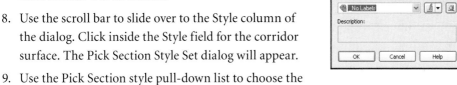

9. Use the Pick Section style pull-down list to choose the Finished Ground style. Click OK to dismiss the dialog and return to the Create Section View dialog (Figure 11.14) When the section view is drawn, the corridor surface will use the Finished Ground style so that you can distinguish it from the existing ground.

10. Click the Create Section View button. At the Identify section view origin: prompt, select a location in the drawing for the section view (somewhere under the profile view would be good).

11. The section view is created, and will look like Figure 11.15.

Figure 11.14

The dialog after step 9

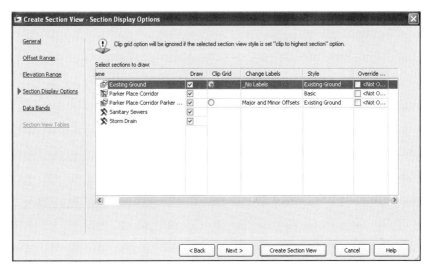

Figure 11.15

The section view for station 5+00.00′

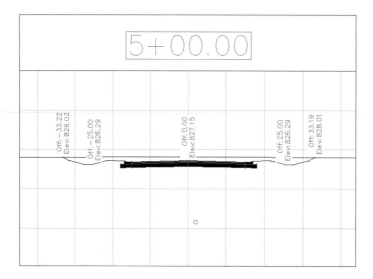

Labeling Pipe Crossings in a Section View

When a sample line crosses a pipe network part, that pipe can be drawn in a section view, as you saw in the last exercise. Many jurisdictions use cross-section views to assist in locating possible pipe conflicts and confirm separation distances between different types of pipe, such as sewer and water. In many cases, these regulations require that the pipe inverts be labeled. Without Civil 3D, this was a tedious manual calculation that required careful bookkeeping, especially if the design changed after the pipe was labeled.

The next exercise will lead you through creating a dynamic pipe invert label.

1. Continue working in the drawing from the previous exercise, or open the drawing file Sections3.dwg (which you can download from www.sybex.com/go/introducingcivil3d2009).

2. Zoom in on the section view that you created in the last exercise for Station 5+00.00′. Note that this section crosses through a sanitary pipe.

3. Choose Pipes → Add Pipe Network Labels → Add Pipe Network Labels. The Add Labels dialog will appear.

4. Use the Label Type: drop-down list to choose Single Part Section.

5. Use the Pipe Label Style drop-down list to choose Pipe Invert in Section. Your selections will look like Figure 11.16.

6. Click the Add button.

Figure 11.16

Choose Single Part Section as the element to label and Pipe Invert in Section as the label style.

7. At the `Select the part in a network section
   to label:` prompt, select the pipe shown in the
   section view. A label will appear, as shown in
   Figure 11.17. Press ↵ to end the command. Click
   Close to dismiss the Add Labels dialog.

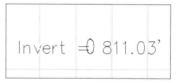

Figure 11.17

**The pipe invert
label when initially
placed**

8. Select the label so that a grip
   appears. Use the grip to drag the
   label off to the side. A leader will
   appear, as shown in Figure 11.18.
   Press Esc to deselect the label.

Figure 11.18

**The pipe invert label
in the dragged state**

9. Choose View ➤ Viewports ➤ 2 Viewports. At the `Enter a configuration option
   [Horizontal/Vertical]<Vertical>:` prompt, type **H** to choose horizontal, and then
   press ↵. The screen will split into two viewports.

10. Click inside the top viewport to activate it. Zoom in on Pipe No. 3. This is the pipe
    shown in the section view. Your screen should look similar to Figure 11.19.

11. Select the pipe so that grips appear. Use the square grip at the center of the pipe to
    move it up approximately 3′, as shown in Figure 11.20. Note that the pipe shown in
    the section view moves to reflect the change in profile.

12. Choose View ➤ Viewports ➤ 1 Viewport. The screen will return to having one active
    viewport.

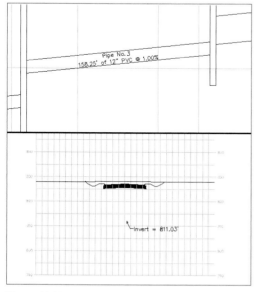

Figure 11.19

**With your viewport split, zoom into Pipe No. 3 in pro-
file and section views.**

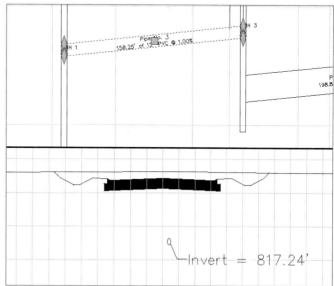

Figure 11.20

**Use the center pipe grip to move Pipe No. 3 up approximately 3′.
Note that the pipe shown in section view dynamically updates.**

Creating Multiple Section Views

Although it might be useful to make one section view at a time when studying special sections, it is more typical to make a section view for each sample line in one batch, such as in Figure 11.21.

An optional, but powerful component of section views is the *section view band*. Section view bands, like profile view bands, can include information about the parent alignment, sample line, surface elevation, and offset information. Figure 11.22 is an example of a band showing horizontal offset information.

Figure 11.21

A collection of section views

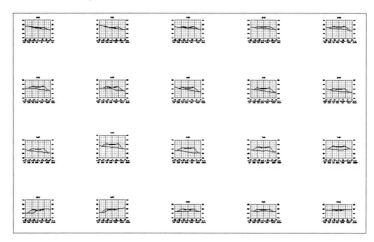

Figure 11.22

A band showing horizontal offsets from a parent alignment

The next exercise gives you hands-on practice creating multiple section views, and applying a band set to the section views that shows the horizontal offset, existing ground elevation, and finished ground elevation.

1. Continue working in the drawing from the previous exercise, or open the drawing file Sections4.dwg (which you can download from www.sybex.com/go/introducingcivil3d2009).

2. Choose Sections → Create Multiple Section Views. The Create Multiple Section Views → General dialog appears, as shown in Figure 11.23. This dialog is very similar to the Create Section Views dialog with a few key differences.

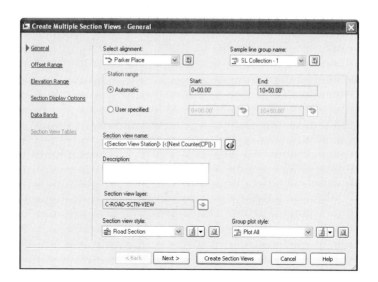

3. Click the Next button three times to get to the Create Multiple Section Views → Section Display Options dialog.

4. Use the scroll bar to slide over to the Style column of the dialog. Click inside the Style field for the Parker Place Corridor Surface. The Pick Section Style Set dialog will appear.

5. Use the Pick Section Style pull-down list to choose the Finished Ground style. Click OK to dismiss the dialog and return to the Create Section View dialog (see Figure 11.24). When the section view is drawn, the corridor surface will use the Finished Ground style so that you can distinguish it from the existing ground.

6. Click Next to advance to the Create Multiple Section Views- Data Bands dialog.

7. Use the Select Band Set pull-down list to choose Major Stations Elevations.

8. In the Set Band Properties portion of the dialog, click inside the Surface 1 column for each style and change the EG Elevations style to Existing Ground, and confirm that the FG Elevations style is the Parker Place Corridor Surface, as shown in Figure 11.25. Each sampled surface will appear on its own band, so you can ignore the Surface2 field.

Existing Ground	☑	⊙	_No Labels	Existing Ground	☐ <Not Overridden>
Parker Place Corridor	☑			Basic	☐ <Not Overridden>
Parker Place Corridor Parker ...	☑	●	_No Labels	Finished Ground	☐ <Not Overridden>
Sanitary Sewers	☑				
Storm Drain	☑				

Figure 11.24

Change the corridor surface style to Finished Ground.

Set band properties:		
Band Type	Style	Surface1
Section Data	EG Elevations	Existing Ground
Section Data	FG Elevations	Parker Place Corridor ...

Figure 11.25

Assign Surface1 for both band styles.

9. Click the Create Section Views button. At the `Identify section view origin:` prompt, pan over to the large open space to the right of the profile view and click on-screen. The section views will appear using that point as a starting point, as shown in Figure 11.26.

10. Zoom in on one of the sections and note the band information (see the example in Figure 11.27).

11. Save your drawing—you will need it for the next exercise.

Figure 11.26

The result of creating multiple section views

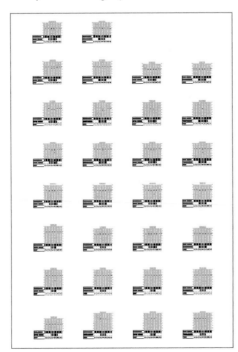

Figure 11.27

The band set shows existing and proposed elevations at major offset locations.

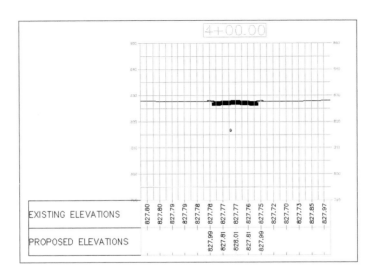

Analyzing Construction Materials by Section

Before Civil 3D, designers had to do tedious manual calculations to determine quantities of road material using the Average End Area method. With a combination of a road corridor and sample lines, it is now easy to create dynamic materials tables that calculate quantities of pavement, subbase material, and base material.

In the following exercise, you assign materials based on subassembly intelligence and generate dynamic materials tables:

1. Continue working in the drawing from the previous exercise, or open the drawing file Sections5.dwg (which you can download from www.sybex.com/go/introducingcivil3d2009).

2. Choose Sections → Compute Materials. The Select a Sample Line Group dialog will appear.

3. The Select a Sample Line Group dialog shows Parker Place as the alignment and SL Collection - # as the sample line group. (Depending on how many times you have worked through the exercise, your # will vary.) Leave these set and press OK. The Compute Materials dialog will appear.

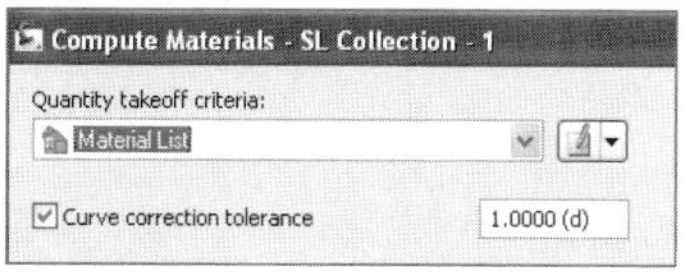

Figure 11.28

Choose Materials List as the Quantity Takeoff Criteria.

4. In the Compute Materials dialog, use the Quantity Takeoff Criteria pull-down list to choose Materials List as shown in Figure 11.28.

5. Click in the Object Name field next to Pavement Material (where it says "<<click here…>"), and choose Parker Place Corridor Pave1 as shown in Figure 11.29.

Figure 11.29

Use the pull-down list to choose Parker Place Corridor Pave1.

6. Click in the Object Name field next to Subbase Material (where it says "<<click here…>"), and choose Parker Place Corridor Subbase from the pull-down list.

7. Click in the Object Name field next to Base Material (where it says "<<click here…>"), and choose Parker Place Corridor Base from the pull-down list. The dialog should now look like Figure 11.30.

Figure 11.30

Each corridor shape is assigned a material.

8. Click OK. The information will be processed, but nothing will appear on-screen yet.

9. Choose Sections → Add Tables → Material Volume. The Create Material Volume Table dialog will appear.

10. Make sure that Pavement is selected under Select Material, as shown in Figure 11.31. Click OK.

Figure 11.31

Assign Pavement for the first table.

Figure 11.32

Parker Place Pavement table

Parker Place Pavement			
Station	Area	Volume	Cumulative Volume
0+00.00	2.49	0.00	0.00
0+50.00	2.49	4.61	4.61
1+00.00	2.49	4.61	9.22
1+50.00	2.49	4.61	13.83
2+00.00	2.49	4.61	18.44
2+50.00	2.49	4.61	23.06
3+00.00	2.49	4.61	27.67
3+44.84	2.49	4.14	31.80
3+50.00	2.49	0.48	32.28
4+00.00	2.49	4.61	36.89
4+50.00	2.49	4.61	41.50
4+67.04	2.49	1.57	43.07
5+00.00	2.49	3.04	46.11
5+50.00	2.49	4.61	50.72
5+60.80	2.49	1.00	51.72
5+88.01	2.49	2.51	54.23
6+00.00	2.49	1.11	55.33
6+50.00	2.49	4.61	59.94
6+88.38	2.49	3.54	63.48
7+00.00	2.49	1.07	64.56

Parker Place Pavement			
Station	Area	Volume	Cumulative Volume
7+36.11	2.49	3.33	67.89
7+50.00	2.49	1.28	69.17
7+89.88	2.49	3.68	72.84
8+00.00	2.49	0.93	73.78
8+50.00	2.49	4.61	78.39
9+00.00	2.49	4.61	83.00
9+50.00	2.49	4.61	87.61
9+61.99	2.49	1.11	88.72
10+00.00	2.49	3.51	92.22
10+50.00	2.49	4.61	96.83

11. At the `Select upper left corner:` prompt, pick a location in the drawing where there is room for a table. The table will appear, as shown in Figure 11.32. Note that your numbers may not match exactly.

12. Choose Sections → Add Tables → Material Volume. The Create Material Volume Table dialog will appear.

13. Use the Select Material pull-down list to select Subbase. Click OK.

14. At the `Select upper left corner:` prompt, pick a location in the drawing where there is room for a table. The table will appear.

15. Repeat steps 12 through 14, choosing the Base material in the Create Material Volume Table dialog.

Before Civil 3D, the designer would have left the material quantity takeoff until the very end of the project — after the design has been completely finalized. Now, these tables can be generated early in the modeling process because they will react with each iteration. The following exercise shows you that dynamic reaction in action:

1. Continue working in the drawing from the previous exercise, or open the drawing file Sections6.dwg (which you can download from www.sybex.com/go/introducingcivil3d2009).

2. Choose View → Viewports → 2 Viewports. At the `Enter a configuration option [Horizontal/Vertical]<Vertical>:` prompt, type **V** to choose vertical. Press ↵, and the screen will split into two viewports.
3. Click in the left viewport to activate it. Zoom in so that the pavement quantities table is fully visible. Note the cumulative pavement quantity in the last row of the table.
4. Click in the right viewport to activate it. Zoom in on the road assembly. Your screen should look similar to Figure 11.33.

Parker Place Pavement			
Station	Area	Volume	Cumulative Volume
7+36.11	2.24	3.00	61.10
7+50.00	2.24	1.15	62.25
7+89.88	2.24	3.31	65.56
8+00.00	2.24	0.84	66.40
8+50.00	2.24	4.15	70.55
9+00.00	2.24	4.15	74.70
9+50.00	2.24	4.15	78.85
9+61.99	2.24	1.00	79.85
10+00.00	2.24	3.15	83.00
10+50.00	2.24	4.15	87.15

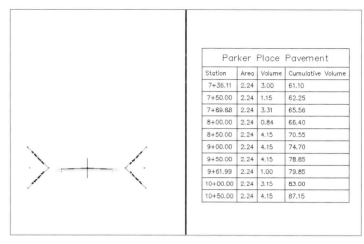

Figure 11.33

Split your viewport so that you can see both the road assembly and the final cumulative volume in your pavement table.

5. Select the red, vertical line that represents the assembly. Right-click and choose Assembly Properties. The Assembly Properties dialog will appear.
6. Switch to the Construction tab of the assembly properties dialog. Select the right Lane entry. Information about the lane will appear on the right side of the dialog, including the lane width. Change the Width from 13.5′ to **15′**, as shown in Figure 11.34.
7. Repeat step 6 for the left lane width.
8. Click OK to exit the dialog.
9. Locate the Parker Place Corridor entry on the Prospector. Right-click the entry and choose Rebuild as shown in Figure 11.35.

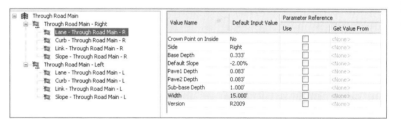

Figure 11.34

Change the road lane width from 13.5′ to 15′.

10. Note that each row of the pavement quantity table has increased to reflect the additional lane width, and the cumulative quantity has also changed to reflect this. The other two tables are similarly adjusted. Also note that the lanes as shown in section view have widened to 15′.

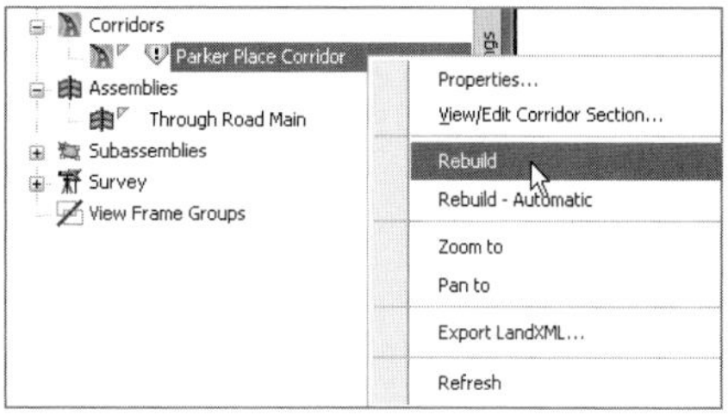

Figure 11.35

Rebuild the corridor to update the quantities.

Summary

In this chapter, you learned how sample lines are related to an alignment and that they can sample surfaces, corridors, and pipe network objects. This sampled information can then be shown, labeled, and analyzed using section views, section view labels, and materials information.

Understanding how to create sample lines and how they dynamically interact with surfaces, corridors, and pipe networks will enable you to go through many design iterations to optimize your design with fewer drafting delays.

CHAPTER 12

Grading

Beyond working with points, alignments, and profiles to create your proposed model, you'll eventually need to get into the grading features of Civil 3D. Civil 3D's grading features are divided into two main components: feature lines and grading groups. These tools can be used to describe a number of different grading ideas, and most users will need both to achieve their desired results efficiently.

Feature lines generally describe linear relationships between points of vertical intersection (PVIs). Generally similar to 3D polylines, but more powerful in that they can be made from true arcs and will also display line types properly, feature lines tend to be the starting point for many users. For some, they are the ending point as well, solving all the problems presented in a given design scenario.

Grading groups generally consist of a feature line object describing some linear feature with its given PVIs and then the gradings themselves. *Gradings* are lines projected perpendicularly from the feature line, and the properties of the grading lines are based on criteria. These criteria can be things such as "Daylight to a surface at a 4:1 slope," or "Project for 10′ at a 5% grade." This combination of feature line and grading creates the grading groups, and grading groups generally are used to describe surface areas for modeling.

This chapter includes the following topics:

- **Creating feature lines from existing objects**
- **Modifying a feature line**
- **Creating a grading group**
- **Creating a surface from a grading group**
- **Adding feature line data to a surface**
- **Creating a composite surface**
- **Editing the surface build order**

Working with Feature Lines

Feature lines are the starting point for most grading work in Civil 3D. They can be used to describe everything from building pads to curb lines; from ditch bottoms to water lines. The feature line functionality in Civil 3D is slightly different from many other features in that most of the commands are built into a typical AutoCAD toolbar. The Feature Line toolbar is shown in Figure 12.1.

Figure 12.1

**The Feature
Line toolbar**

It's interesting to note that while the Feature Line toolbar is part of the stock Civil 3D workspace, all of the commands in this chapter can also be accessed under the Grading menu. Most exercises will refer to the command from the toolbar, but if you prefer menus, you can search through the menu for the same commands.

Before you wade too far into feature lines, remember that the concept of Civil 3D sites comes into play with feature lines and grading groups. What this means to you is that when two feature lines are in the same Civil 3D site, they will react to each other if they cross. This can be used to your advantage (for instance, when you need to keep driveways tied to building pads), but it can also be a headache if you are seeing odd elevation jumps or grade changes due to crossing elements for which you didn't account. . Just keep the site idea in the back of your mind, and it will help decipher any grading puzzles you run across.

Creating Feature Lines

Once you are ready to begin modeling your site in Civil 3D, you'll need to start creating feature lines. Many of the tools you'll use to manipulate feature line objects can also be used on 3D polylines, survey figures, and parcel segments, but we consider it best practice to use feature line objects when trying to describe 3D model elements instead of making something like a lot line do double duty. There are three primary methods of creating feature lines:

- **Creating from scratch:** Entering points and elevations manually
- **Extracting from corridor objects:** Creating all the data automatically
- **Converting from existing objects:** Picking up location information from the object, but entering or deriving the elevations manually or from other objects

The Feature Line toolbar in Figure 12.1 is pretty long and can be confusing, so before you get into the exercises in this chapter, here is a brief look at the most common buttons and commands:

- The Create Feature Line tool allows you to create a feature line from scratch, assigning elevations as you go. These elevations can be based on direct data input at the command line, slope information, or surface elevations.

- The Create from Objects tool converts lines, arcs, polylines, and 3D polylines into feature lines. This process also allows elevations to be assigned from a surface or grading group.

- The Create from Alignments tool allows you to build a new feature line from an alignment, using a profile to assign elevations. This feature line can be dynamically tied to the alignment and the profile, making it easy to generate 3D design features based on horizontal and vertical controls.

The second method tends to be the most popular for users who draw elements in a plan view and then want to use the geometry as the design goes vertical. In the following exercise, you create a feature line based on polyline and surface data:

1. Open the `Creating FL.dwg` file. (Remember, all data files can be downloaded from `www.sybex.com/go/introducingcivil3d2009`.) This file contains the sample site, along with some vertical design data for Parker Place and a polyline around the subdivision that should be the limits of grading.

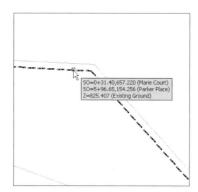

Figure 12.2

Selecting a polyline for feature line conversion

2. Zoom in to the site boundary (the green line running around the site). There is a dashed polyline running just inside the boundary that defines the limits of grading. This is the first feature line you'll create.

3. Select the Create from Objects tool, and then select the dashed polyline as shown in Figure 12.2. Press Enter to finish the selection. Civil 3D will display the Create Feature lines dialog.

Figure 12.3

The Create Feature Lines dialog

4. Toggle on the Style option and the Assign Elevations option as shown in Figure 12.3.

5. Click OK. Because you toggled on the Assign Elevations option, Civil 3D will display the Assign Elevations dialog shown in Figure 12.4.

When assigning elevations during the creation process, you can assign a constant elevation to all points in the feature line, or you can drape the feature line across a surface, assigning elevations based on the surface elevation. With this option, you also have the further option to Insert Intermediate Grade Break Points as shown in Figure 12.4. This option will add vertices to the object being converted every place the feature line crosses a surface TIN line, creating a true draped effect. Toggling this option off will skip those intersections, possibly creating a feature line that skips over and through the surface as the terrain varies between PVIs.

6. Click OK to close the Assign Elevations dialog and complete the creation of the feature line.

Figure 12.4

Draping a feature line on a surface

If you zoom in and select this new feature line, you'll see grips similar to what's shown in Figure 12.5. It's important to understand the difference between these grips and how they can affect your design. The square grips are PVIs, and they can be manipulated in the horizontal and vertical planes. These are the vertices from the original polyline. The circular grips are the elevation points, and they control only the vertical information. If you activate a circular grip, you'll be able to slide it along the segment, but you cannot break it out of the linear portion of the segment. These points came about as a result of the Insert Intermediate Grade Break option selected in the Assign Elevations dialog.

Figure 12.5

Feature line grips

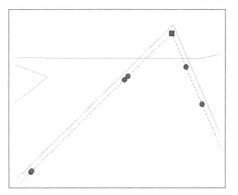

The last method of creating a feature line directly is to base it on an alignment and profile. This allows for the creation of quick grading objects. These in turn can be used to quickly model other pieces of the design. In the following exercise, you create feature line down the center of Parker Place that you'll use later to describe the whole street grading quickly and easily:

1. Open the `Creating Feature Lines from Alignments.dwg` file.

2. Select the Create from Alignment tool on the Feature Line toolbar. Civil 3D will prompt you to select an alignment.

3. Press Enter to display a list of alignments in a dialog.

4. Select Parker Place. Click OK to close the current dialog and display the Create Feature Line from Alignment dialog shown in Figure 12.6.

5. By default, the Profile Design 1 is selected. Click OK to close the Create Feature Line from Alignment dialog and display the Weed Vertices dialog. This dialog allows you to reduce the number of PIs in a feature line by attempting to eliminate redundant data based on the distance between points or the deflection angle.

6. Click OK to close the Weed Vertices dialog. Your new feature line will be created.

This new feature line cannot be edited directly, but must be edited by modifying the alignment or profile associated with it. The next section describes how to do this.

Figure 12.6

The Create Feature Line from Alignment dialog

Modifying Feature Lines

There are several tools to edit feature line objects, but they can be divided into two basic types: horizontal controls and vertical controls.

Horizontal edits can include common things such as Trim or Extend, as well as options like joining, splining, or fitting curves along feature line objects. Because these operations tend to happen a bit independently of each other, you'll look at them in distinct exercises.

Vertical edits include options like setting elevations from surface, setting elevations by a reference from another object, or simply setting the grade between to points on the feature line to force the intermediate points to fall in grade.

Modifying Horizontal Data

The feature line tools for modifying horizontal data operate quite similarly to the standard AutoCAD modify commands such as Trim, Extend, Break, Join, and so on, but because elevations are typically involved, they're written to handle this additional bit of data and account for the changes that this creates in the results. In the following exercise, you'll look at trimming, joining, and filleting a series of feature lines to lay out some preliminary grading on the sample subdivision:

1. Open the `Modifying FLs Horizontal.dwg` file, and pan to the northernmost intersection as shown in Figure 12.7. This sort of layout is the goal for the southern intersection. There are two feature lines describing the edge of the street section, and a feature line describing the centerline.

Figure 12.7

**Intersection design
via feature lines**

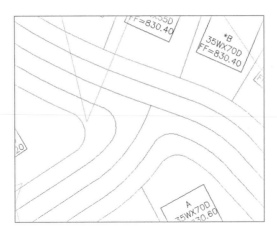

2. Pan to the next intersection south. You'll see the center line of the cul-de-sac running east–west, and the feature line from the Parker Place alignment (and its edge of streets) running north–south.

3. Use the standard AutoCAD offset command to offset the centerline feature line 13′ left and right. Your drawing should look like Figure 12.8.

4. Select the Trim command from the Feature Line toolbar.

5. Select feature line A (it's the same as D) in Figure 12.8 as the cutting edge, and press ↵ to finish the selection.

6. Select feature lines B and C (shown previously in Figure 12.8) at a point to the east of feature line A to trim them back to the edge of the Parker Place paving. Press ↵ to exit the command.

7. Select the Break command from the Feature Line toolbar.

Figure 12.8

Offset feature lines

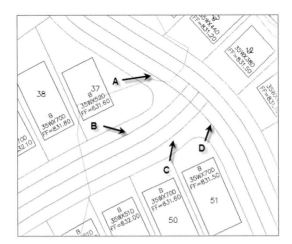

Figure 12.9

Completed feature line Trim and Break commands

8. Select feature line A to begin the Break command.

9. Enter **F** at the command line to tell Civil 3D you want to pick the first point of the break.

10. Use an end snap and pick at the newly trimmed end of feature line B.

11. Use an end snap and pick the end of feature line C. Your drawing should look like Figure 12.9.

12. Select the Join command from the Feature Line toolbar.

13. Select feature line A and then feature line B to join them into one feature line. Repeat this procedure to join feature lines C and D.

14. Select the Fillet command from the Feature Line toolbar.

15. Select feature line AB to begin the command.

16. Hover your mouse over the corner as shown in Figure 12.10, and Civil 3D will present you with a solution based on the given radius and the feature line segments available. Click one time to accept this solution.

17. Repeat steps 15 through 17 on the southern intersection corner to complete the intersection layout. When complete, your drawing should look like Figure 12.11.

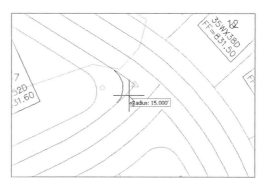

Figure 12.10

Filleting a feature line

Figure 12.11

**Completed intersec-
tion layout**

Figure 12.11

**Completed intersec-
tion layout**

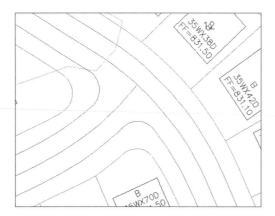

Although it's certainly common to have linework from another source to work with as a street intersection layout, the preceding exercise is a good way of looking at a number of tools that are available for performing basic grading tasks. You'll circle back to the Stepped Offsets command in a little bit as you build up a basic surface design. Because that is the goal, you now need to assign some elevation data to all the feature lines you just created.

Modifying Vertical Data

With a layout in place, the next step in the design is to go up. In many cases, you'll have control or attachment points where your design has to match up with existing elevations or surfaces. The ability to use elevations from one object to drive another in a daisy-chain type of workflow makes building up preliminary grades for feature line objects a pretty straightforward exercise.

The beginning of this section on feature lines discussed the idea of sites and how the feature line objects within a site react to each other at crossing points. To see an example of this, take a look at Figure 12.12. This is the elevation information from the Parker Place centerline feature line. You created this feature line earlier based on the alignment and profile data.

Figure 12.12

**Elevation data in
tabular form**

	Station	Elevation	Length	Grade Ahead	Grade Back
⚠	0+00.00	826.500'	177.665'	-0.52%	0.52%
⊙	1+77.66	825.585'	40.811'	-0.16%	0.16%
⚠	2+18.48	825.520'	59.189'	0.71%	-0.71%
⊙	2+77.66	825.939'	26.635'	-3100.97%	3100.97%
	3+04.30	0.000'	34.879'	2370.14%	-2370.14%
⚠	3+39.18	826.692'	94.588'	1.22%	-1.22%
⚠	4+33.77	827.850'	27.204'	1.22%	-1.22%
⚠	4+60.97	828.183'	100.367'	1.22%	-1.22%
⚠	5+61.34	829.411'	47.730'	1.22%	-1.22%
⚠	6+09.07	829.995'	9.522'	1.22%	-1.22%
⊙	6+18.59	830.112'	17.366'	-4780.03%	4780.03%
	6+35.96	0.000'	26.889'	3088.63%	-3088.63%
⚠	6+62.85	830.489'	52.873'	0.03%	-0.03%
⊙	7+15.72	830.507'	52.873'	-0.86%	0.86%
⊙	7+68.59	830.054'	66.362'	-1.30%	1.30%

The important part to consider here is that the elevation at station 3+04.30 and 6+35.96 is 0. This obviously isn't part of the design profile, but it's coming about because of the two cul-de-sac intersections. The oddly simplistic way Civil 3D handles these interactions is that the last feature line created rules the elevation at the point of intersection. Because the cul-de-sac street centerlines don't have elevation data, they pushed the Parker Place feature line down to zero.

There are a number of ways to fix the problem. The easiest is to simply move the end of the cul-de-sac feature line just off the Parker Place feature line, and then use the elevation from the centerline to set the grade of your other street's beginning. You'll perform this quick edit in the following exercise:

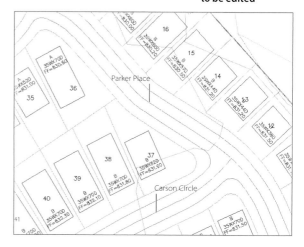

Figure 12.13

The intersection to be edited

1. Open the `Modifying FLs Vertical.dwg` file, and zoom to the intersection of Parker Place and Carson Circle that was laid out in the last section and is shown again in Figure 12.13.

2. Zoom in very close to the intersection and select the centerline feature line for Carson Circle.

3. Select the grip at the intersection, and using a nearest snap, move it just off the intersection point but still inside the marker that's there from the Carson Circle alignment, as shown in Figure 12.14.

4. Select the Set Elevation by Reference tool, and Civil 3D will prompt you to select a reference point.

5. Using an apparent intersection snap, pick the Parker Place feature line first, and then the Carson Circle feature line. Civil 3D should return an elevation of 826.265′ at the command line and ask you for an object to edit.

6. Pick the Carson Circle feature line, and Civil 3D will prompt you for a point to edit.

7. Pick the end point you just moved (a triangle glyph will appear over it when you have the correct selection point).

8. Enter **D** at the command line to tell Civil 3D you are going to specify a difference in elevation between the reference point and the point being modified.

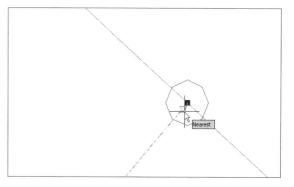

Figure 12.14

Modifying the start point of the Carson Circle feature line

9. Enter **0** as the difference. This will place the Carson Circle feature line end point at the intersection elevation.

10. Press ↵ to exit the command.

11. Select the Carson Circle feature line, right-click, and select Elevation Editor to display the tabular format shown previously in Figure 12.12. Your edited feature line data for Carson Court should look like Figure 12.15.

12. Close Panorama or move it out of the way so you can continue working.

Figure 12.15

Carson Circle feature line elevation data after the beginning point it edited

	Station	Elevation	Length	Grade Ahead	Grade Back
⚠	0+00.00	826.265'	7.757'	-10652.24%	10652.24%
⚠	0+07.76	0.000'	82.916'	0.00%	0.00%
⚠	0+90.67	0.000'	31.666'	0.00%	0.00%
⚠	1+22.34	0.000'	226.850'	0.00%	0.00%
⚠	3+49.19	0.000'			

You could have also simply typed in the elevation of 826.265 in the elevation editor to make this change, but you would have had to either write it down or have a good memory. Both of those methods leave the data open to a mistake in entry or recall, something you avoid by using reference information. Now that you have one point, you'll use other tools in the Feature Line toolbar to set the grade for the street, the grades for the edge of paving feature lines, and the grade around the curb returns.

1. Select the Set Grade/Slope between Points tool from the Feature Line toolbar, and select the Carson's Circle center feature line.

2. Select the point at the intersection as the start point.

3. Press ↵ to confirm the elevation of 826.265.

4. Select the end point in the cul-de-sac area as the end point of the edit. Notice that all the PVIs along the feature line have green glyphs, indicating that they will be modified by this overall edit.

5. Enter **G** at the command line to confirm a grade input format.

6. Enter a grade value of **1.1**. Civil 3D will set the grade between the beginning and end of the feature line as 1.1% and set the end point elevation as 830.106. It will also display this information back at the command line.

7. Press Enter to exit the command.

8. Select the Adjacent Elevations by Reference tool on the Feature Line toolbar. It is on a flyout of buttons under the Set Elevation by Reference tool, so you may need to click and hold to get the button shown here.

9. Select the Carson Circle feature line as the reference.

10. Select the feature line to the north as the object to edit. A series of glyphs will appear, indicating the points to be edited on this feature line as well as the location along the Carson Circle that these points will be set in relation to.

11. Enter **G** at the command line to select a grade reference

12. Enter **-2** at the command line to set the slope between the centerline and the edge-of-paving feature line being edited.

13. Repeat steps 9 through 12, but this time, select the feature line to the south of the centerline as the object to be edited.

At this point, all of the feature line data for the two northern cul-de-sacs is complete for a preliminary grading concept. There are lots of cleanup (and finish-out) items that still need to be completed, but they're more of the same. Using references, slopes, and other editing tools on the feature line, almost any model can be created in plan, pushed vertically, and then edited and analyzed for quick use. Now you'll look at grading groups as another method for dealing with more elaborate or complex areas of grading.

Working with Grading Groups

After a feature line has been established as a baseline for horizontal and vertical control, you can work with grading groups to build more complex 3D shapes. These grading criteria can be defined as slope and height, distance at grade, or simply project to a surface. These gradings are part of a larger group, and groups can be turned into surfaces for use in the overall site-grading scheme. In this section, you'll create a grading group and make a surface from it to analyze the volume of dirt being removed.

It should be noted that many users consider grading groups to be the weakest function in Civil 3D. It can be downright infuriating at times if you are working on a large site and the grading seems to crash the program frequently. The large number of possible permutations in the feature line setup and grading criteria, combined with the very complex mathematics involved in projections seem to give the program fits. To that end, we suggest that you use grading objects where you need them, but do keep in mind that often, the same results can be determined with a combination of feature line objects, corridors, points, or other methods of setting elevation model data.

Creating a Basic Grading Group

When you're working with grading groups, it's important to remember the site interaction, because grading groups created in a site will affect feature line objects or parcel lines within the same site, which can sometimes cause problems.

In the following exercise, you create a basic drainage channel using grading criteria to create the bottom of the channel, and then daylight the channel to the existing ground surface. You'll use a drawing that already has a new site called Channel so that your channel feature line and grading group don't wreak havoc with the lot lines and grading limits feature line that has already been created.

1. Open the `Create Grading Group.dwg` file

Figure 12.16

**Grading
Creation Tools**

2. Select Grading ⇒ Create Grading to display the Grading Creation Tools toolbar shown in Figure 12.16. This toolbar works like most of the Civil 3D toolbars—it is displayed when needed and then goes away after the task is complete. Working left to right is generally a good idea!

3. Select the Set Grading Group button on the far left, and the Site dialog will appear. Verify that Channel is selected in the drop-down list, and then click OK to display the Create Grading Group dialog shown in Figure 12.17.

4. Change the Name field to **Channel** just for clarity and click OK. Note that the name Channel is now displayed in the toolbar next to the Group indicator.

5. Select Grade to Distance from the Select a Grading Criteria drop-down list.

6. Select Create Grading tool, and Civil 3D will prompt you to select a feature.

7. Select the feature line that describes the proposed channel.

8. Click to the right of the channel to set the side to grade.

9. Press ↵ to apply the grading to the entire length.

10. Enter **0.5** as the distance.

11. Enter **S** to set the input type to Slope.

12. Enter **5:1** as the slope of the channel bottom.

13. Repeat steps 7 through 12, but click to the left to set the side to grade.

Figure 12.17

The Create Grading Group dialog

You've created the pilot channel for your overall channel, a 1′ v-section with a depth of 0.1′. It's designed to merely keep a trickle of water in the middle of the channel instead of causing any erosion issues at the sideslope edges. This sort of basic creation can be used to describe channels, or a mountable curb, alley paving, or berm top. The uses are infinite. In the following exercise, you'll daylight this v-channel to create a tie-in to the existing ground surface:

1. Select the Grade to Surface option from the pull-down list on the Grading Creation Tools toolbar.

2. Select the Create Grading tool.

3. Select the outer edge of the v-section as shown in Figure 12.18, and then press ↵ to accept grading the entire length.

4. Enter **S** to verify Slope as the input method for the Cut format, and enter **3:1** as the cut slope.

5. Enter **S** to verify Slope as the input method for the Fill format, and enter **3:1** as the fill slope.

6. Repeat steps 2 though 5 on the left side of the v-channel, and your drawing should look something like Figure 12.19.

These gradings are dynamically related to the feature line that was used in the previous exercise to start the grading group. A modification to this feature line would ripple through the design, causing changes at each individual grading and in the overall appearance of the group. It's worth noting that the anomaly on the north end of your proposed channel is indicative of a wall (or sharp drop-off) being part of the existing ground surface in that location. Now that you've made a group, it's time to make a surface from it and prepare some preliminary analysis.

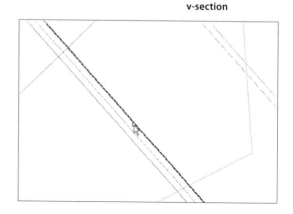

Figure 12.18

Selecting the right-hand edge of the v-section

Creating a Grading Group Surface

Programatically, a grading group is simply a series of feature lines with perpendicular lines running up and down to connect them based on a given slope. Because feature lines and sloped lines are some of the backbone elements of surface modeling in Civil 3D, it's easy to see how close a grading group is to being an actual surface. And once you have a surface, you can compare it to another surface to come up with some sort of volume analysis. In the following exercise, you'll walk through making a surface and getting a quick earthwork volume for your grading group:

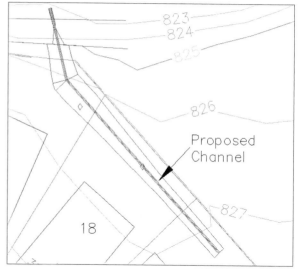

Figure 12.19

Completed channel grading

1. Open the `Creating a Grading Group Surface.dwg` file. The channel prepared in the previous section has been tweaked after some review.

2. Select one of the diamonds that function as anchors for the gradings, right-click, and select Grading Group properties from the menu as shown in Figure 12.20.

Figure 12.20

**Accessing the
grading group
properties**

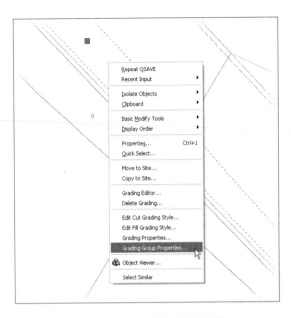

3. Change to the Information tab if necessary, and toggle on the Automatic Surface Creation option to display the Create Surface dialog.

4. Click OK to accept the defaults and return to the Grading Group Properties dialog. The tessellation spacing and tessellation angle values help convert any curves in the feature line into straight segments as required in TIN surface modeling.

5. Toggle the Volume Base Surface option on. Your dialog should look like Figure 12.21.

6. Click OK to close the dialog, and the channel will now have contours displayed along its length. You can also pause over the channel area, and your tooltip should reflect elevations for both the existing ground surface and the channel surface. (See Figure 12.22.)

Figure 12.21

**Completed surface
creation and
volume setup**

Information	Properties

Name:

Channel

Description:

─ Automatic Surface Creation ─

☑ Channel

Tessellation spacing:

10.000'

Tessellation angle:

3.0000 (d)

─ Volume Base Surface ─

☑ Existing Ground

7. Reenter the grading group properties and switch to the Properties tab. The left portion of the dialog will display the cut and fill volumes for the grading group along with a net.

8. Click OK to close the dialog.

Figure 12.22

Tooltip showing two surface elevations after creating a grading group surface

By using grading groups to describe land-development site objects (such as berms, spoils piles, ponds, or swales), you can accurately and quickly get a feel for the volume being created in these objects. This type of quick analysis is part of the power of Civil 3D. Now that you've created both feature lines and grading groups, it's time to look at pulling all these concepts together and creating a composite surface that describes the overall site.

Working with Composite Surfaces

Each of the pieces created so far in this chapter is essentially useless without the final step of building up a proposed model surface. Much of land development is based on proposed gradings that are then labeled to produce construction documents, so it's important to understand how to pull these pieces into a cohesive whole. It is generally a good idea to start with some tie-in points to make sure the site isn't floating in space.

The process then forks for many users. Subdivision designers will set pads or grades to get rough grading, working them in conjunction with stormwater detention areas or other drainage issues to create a comprehensive plan for the site model. Commercial users will often set a building pad based on architectural requirements, and then use the parking and travelway areas to transition between the building and the site boundary tie-ins. In every case, being able to use the feature lines and grading groups as pieces to make a larger whole is crucial. In the following exercise, you create a new composite surface that will act as a container for the other grading elements and then add in the street elements:

1. Open the `Creating a Composite Surface.dwg` file.

2. In Prospector, right-click Surfaces and select Create Surface to display the Create Surface dialog.

3. Change the Name field to **Proposed** and the Style to **Contours 1′ and 5′ (Design)**, as shown in Figure 12.23.

4. Click OK to close the dialog.

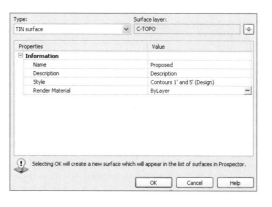

Figure 12.23

Setting up the Proposed surface

5. Select one of the street-centerline feature line objects.

6. Right-click and choose Select Similar. The street should be highlighted as in Figure 12.24.

   Select Similar is a very powerful tool when selecting elements in Civil 3D. It allows you to quickly and easily select all of the objects that are the same type, taking into account their styles, layers, and types. In this case, it ignores the feature lines that describe the pads, curbs, and other elements of your site.

7. Right-click and select Add to Surface as Breakline to display the Select Surface dialog.

8. Pick Proposed from the drop-down list, and then click OK to dismiss the Select Surface dialog. The Add Breaklines dialog shown in Figure 12.25 will appear.

Figure 12.24

Selecting the road centerline feature lines

Figure 12.25

The completed Add Breaklines dialog

9. Change the Description field to **CenterLines**.

10. Toggle on the Supplementing Factors and set the Distance to **50′**. This ensures that Civil 3D will add a surface point as least every 50 feet along the road centerlines.

11. Click OK to close the dialog. You now have a surface covering a portion of the site, but not nearly to the edges. Panorama may also appear, complaining of a crossing breakline. It's safe to dismiss it at this point.

12. Select one of the feature lines that describes the edge of paving or curb lines.

13. Right-click to use the Select Similar tool again.

14. Repeat steps 8 through 11, only this time, use **Curbs** for the Description and using a 25′ supplementing distance. When you complete these steps, the drawing should look like Figure 12.26.

Figure 12.26

The Proposed surface, after adding the street feature lines

Because the feature lines for the edge of paving and curb were built based on the simple relationship typical in a street section, they contour like you would expect. The crown of each road is shown with a 2 percent slope to the edge. In the following exercise, you will add one final set of feature lines that describe the pads before bringing in the channel surface you created earlier:

1. Select one of the building pads within a lot, right-click, and choose Select Similar. Note that the pads have all been converted to feature lines, with elevations based on the text labels.

2. Right-click and select Add to Surface as Breaklines. Use a description of **Pads** and step through the dialogs just as before.

3. Pan to the area near lots 20 through 24. Your screen should look something like Figure 12.27. These solid fill areas are actually contour lines dropping to 0, because those pads were missed during the setup of the feature line data.

4. Select the blue feature line that is the lot 23 pad.

5. Right-click and select Raise/Lower from the menu.

6. Enter **E** at the command line to change to the Elevation input option, and then enter **830.9** as the correct elevation for that pad.

7. Select the pads on lots 21 and 22, and repeat the Raise/Lower process to set the pad at **830.8**. Notice that Prospector has also added chevron icons to your Proposed surface, indicating that the data it is based on has changed. (See Figure 12.28.)

8. Right-click the Proposed surface in Prospector and rebuild. The contours should update, reflecting the expected grading scheme.

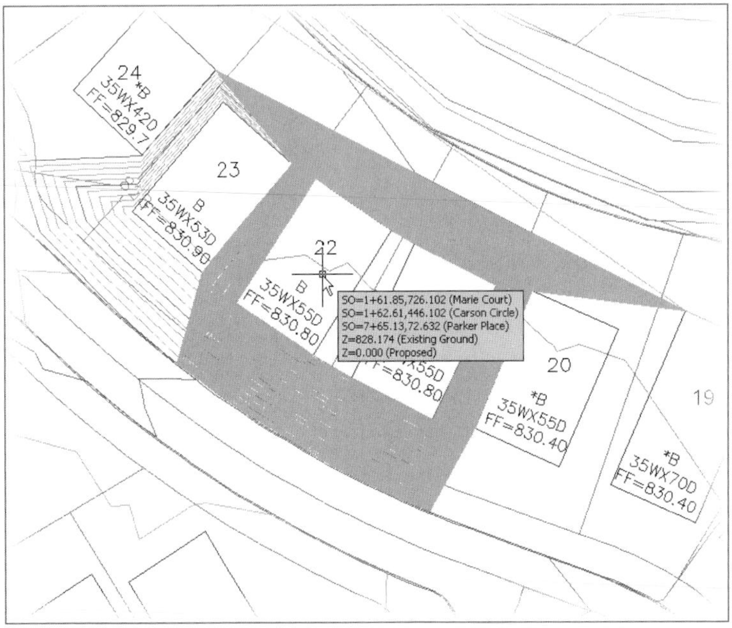

Figure 12.27

Busts in the proposed surface contouring

Figure 12.28

Out-of-date Proposed surface in Prospector

The benefit to remember here is the simple ability to tweak various elements of your grading scheme. Any of the changes you made earlier in terms of editing slopes or modifying the relationships between grading elements using the Feature Line toolbar can be directly reviewed by simply rebuilding your surface and looking at the changes. Now that much of the street and road grading has been added, you'll bring in your channel in the following exercise:

1. Open the Tying Surfaces Together.dwg file. Remember, early in the chapter you used the Assign Elevations option to drape a feature line around your site on the existing ground surface. You'll now use that to tie the surfaces together.

2. Zoom in to the channel location behind lots 18 and 19 if necessary.

3. Within Prospector, expand the Surfaces → Proposed → Definition branch.

4. Right-click the Edits option and select Paste Surface to display the Select Surface to Paste dialog shown in Figure 12.29.

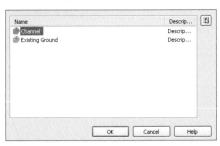

Figure 12.29

Selecting the Channel Surface for pasting

5. Select Channel as shown in Figure 12.29, and then click OK. The surface will update, but not much else will happen. Civil 3D doesn't know how to tie all of this together.

6. Back in Prospector, right-click the Breaklines option and select the Add option to display the Add Breaklines dialog. (This is just another way to get to the same dialog you used previously.)

7. Change the Description field to **Daylight** and click OK to close the dialog. Civil 3D will prompt you to select an object.

8. Select the dashed feature line just inside the property line, and right-click to exit the selection. Your surface should look something like Figure 12.30.

   There still isn't good surface data between the pads on lots 17 through 19 and the channel area. Sometimes Civil 3D will triangulate poorly, but a quick change in the order of calculations will solve the problem.

9. Select the surface, right-click to display the shortcut menu, and select Surface Properties to display the Surface Properties dialog.

10. Switch to the Definition tab as shown in Figure 12.31. The operations that make up a surface are shown in the lower list box.

11. Select the Paste operation in the list box.

12. Click the Move Down button indicated to the left, and notice that the Paste operation and the Add Breakline operation have now switched places and both display chevrons indicating the operations are out of date.

Figure 12.30

Surfaces tied together

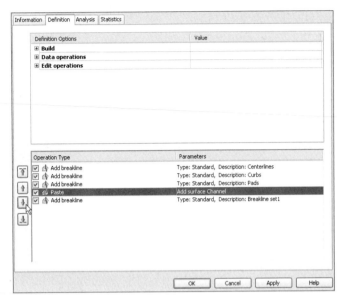

Figure 12.31

The Definition tab of the Surface Properties dialog

Figure 12.32

Completed surface after reordering operations

13. Click OK, and Civil 3D will display the Surface Properties-Rebuild Surface dialog. Because you changed the definition via the Surface Properties dialog, Civil 3D asks you to confirm that you want to rebuild the surface.

14. Select the Rebuild the Surface option. When complete, your surface should look like Figure 12.32.

This drawing is by no means complete—there are additional areas that need refinement—but it serves as a good example of how to manipulate the build order to make changes. By using a feature line that draped on the ground, features lines that describe the site features, and a channel surface defined from the grading group, and then using the surface properties to reorder some operations, you've now completed building up a proposed surface that can be used for further analysis, labeled, profiles, or any number of construction and engineering functions.

Summary

The grading functionality in Civil 3D is designed to let you model almost any scenario you can dream up. In some cases, the feature line object will handle everything you need, and in other cases, a grading group with its projected linework will be up to the task. A proposed grade surface at both a preliminary and final level of detail is a critical part of the Civil 3D workflow, and using the built-in tools to model all of the site design pieces quickly and see changes reflected almost instantly makes it easy to perform this task.

CHAPTER 13

Pipes

Pipe networks are fundamental parts of many civil engineering projects. New development, municipal design, and rehabilitation projects frequently include gravity systems, such as sanitary sewers and storm drainage. Civil 3D provides tools for pipe network design, and editing that is dynamically tied in with labels, profile views, and tables.

This chapter includes the following topics:

- Creating a sanitary sewer pipe network
- Drawing a sanitary sewer network in profile view
- Creating an alignment from storm drainage network parts
- Labeling a pipe network in profile view
- Showing pipe crossings in profile view
- Creating a dynamic pipe table
- Editing a pipe network

Creating a Sanitary Sewer Pipe Network

The municipality for this sample project requires that the site be serviced with a gravity sewer system. Before Civil 3D, the designer might have taken a paper copy of the plan, sketched a few different horizontal alignments with a red pen, and made estimates for rim elevations before creating a spreadsheet for iterating the vertical design. Then, once the network was almost entirely ironed out, the sketch and spreadsheet would be handed off to a technician for drafting.

With Civil 3D, that sketch can be done right in the drawing. As the model is created, the program gives instant feedback regarding rim elevation, slopes, and inverts. Pipe and structure rules can be established to assist the designer in maintaining minimum slopes and cover. Pipe and structure styles can be created to make sure the plan has the correct cosmetic appearance.

The following exercise will lead you through building a sanitary sewer pipe network, including several branches and associated labeling:

1. Open the drawing file Pipes1.dwg, which you can download from www.sybex.com/go/introducingcivil3d2009.

2. Choose Pipes → Create Pipe Network by Layout. The Create Pipe Network dialog will appear.

3. In the Create Pipe Network dialog, change the Network name to **Sanitary Sewer Network**. Verify that the Sanitary Sewer parts list, the existing ground surface, and Parker Place for the alignment are selected. Change the Structure Label Style to Data with Connected Pipes (Sanitary), and change the Pipe Label Style to Length Material and Slope. The dialog should now look like Figure 13.1.

Figure 13.1

The Create Pipe Network dialog after step 3

4. Click OK. The Network Layout Tools dialog will appear. Verify that the Network Layout Tools dialog is set so that the Concentric Structure is selected and the 8 Inch PVC is selected, as shown in Figure 13.2.

Figure 13.2

The Network Layout Tools dialog

5. The drawing contains a series of markers that have been placed as guides for placing sanitary manholes (see Figure 13.3). Click the Draw Pipes and Structures button. At

the `Specify the structure insertion point:` prompt, zoom in to the Parker Place cul-de-sac in the drawing and use your center osnap to place a structure at the first marker.

Figure 13.3
Markers have been placed in the drawing to serve as guides for a sanitary sewer layout.

6. The command line will now read `Specify next structure insertion point or [Curve]:`. Use your center osnap to continue placing structures for the remaining six markers along Parker Place, as shown in Figure 13.4. (Your labels will be moved out of the way later in the exercise.)

7. Note that labeled pipes have appeared between each structure as shown in Figure 13.5. Press ↵ to exit the command. The Network Layout Tools dialog will remain on the screen.

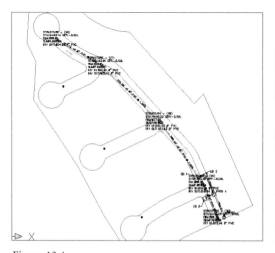

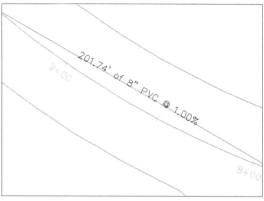

Figure 13.4

Place the pipes and structures for all six markers along Parker Place.

Figure 13.5

Pipes have been drawn between each structure with slopes automatically assigned based on pipe rules from the parts list.

8. On the Prospector tab of the Toolspace, locate the Sanitary Sewer Network under the Pipe Networks tree, as shown in Figure 13.6.

Figure 13.6

A Sanitary Sewer entry appears under the Pipe Networks tree in Prospector.

9. Expand the Sanitary Sewer Network branch, and highlight the Structures entry. A list of structures will appear in the item view at the bottom of the Prospector.

10. Use the Name column to rename each Manhole according to the Figure 13.7. Note that once you change each name in Prospector, the plan labels immediately change to match.

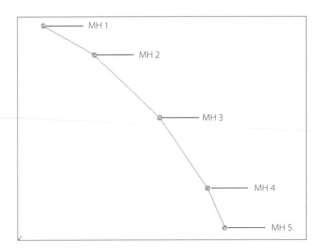

Figure 13.7

Change the structure names according to this figure.

11. Back in the drawing, locate the Network Layout Tools dialog. (If this dialog has disappeared, select any pipe in the network, right-click, and choose Edit Network.) Use the structure pull-down list to switch from Concentric Structure to Eccentric Structure (Figure 13.8).

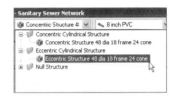

Figure 13.8

Change the structure from concentric to eccentric.

12. Click the Draw Pipes and Structures button. At the `Specify the structure insertion point:` prompt, place a structure at marker A for the northeastern cul-de-sac, and then move your mouse over to MH 2 on Parker Place. A circular glyph will appear alerting you that you are about to tie into a structure. When the glyph is present, click to connect the pipe to MH 2.

13. Use the same process from step 12 to create a pipe run from marker B in the southeastern cul-de-sac to MH 3, and then marker C in the southernmost cul-de-sac to MH 4.

14. Use Prospector to change the names of the two new manholes to the names shown in Figure 13.9.

15. Select the label for MH 1. A grip will appear. Grab this grip and use it to drag the label somewhere off to the side so that the plan is more readable, as in Figure 13.10. Press Esc to exit the Label Drag mode. Repeat this process for each structure label.

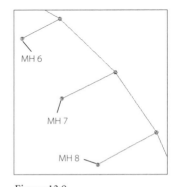

Figure 13.9

Change the structure names according to the figure.

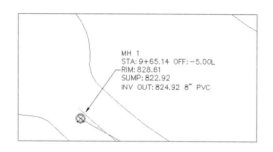

Figure 13.10

Stretch each label out of the way using its grip.

A WORD ABOUT PIPE AND STRUCTURE RULES

When you drew the sanitary sewer network, you probably noticed that the pipes seemed to know how deep to be and what slope to use. These values were guided by Pipe Rules, which can be customized on the Settings Tab of the Toolspace under Pipe Rule Set. There are also Structure Rules, which control elements such as default sump depth and pipe drop across structure. The structure rules can be customized on the Settings Tab of the Toolspace under Structure Rule Set.

Drawing a Sanitary Sewer Network in Profile View

Once the horizontal layout has been completed for a pipe network, the engineer is usually required to produce a representation of the vertical layout in profile.

Sometimes this information is placed on a road profile, especially when the system parallels the road alignment and is contained within the right-of-way. The first leg of the sanitary sewer created in the last exercise meets this criteria — it typically holds a 5′ offset from the Parker Place centerline, and it would be appropriate to show this information on the Parker Place profile view.

The following exercise will lead you through adding the main trunk of the sanitary sewer network to the Parker Place profile view:

1. Open `Pipes2.dwg` (which you can download from `www.sybex.com/go/introducingcivil3d2009`), or continue working in the drawing from the previous exercise.

2. Choose Pipes → Draw Parts in Profile View.

3. At the `Select network(s) to add to profile view or [Selected parts only]:` prompt, enter **S** to choose selected parts only.

4. At the `Select pipe network parts to add to profile view:` prompt, select all of the pipes and structures from MH 1 through MH 5. Press ↵.

5. At the `Select profile view:` prompt, select the Parker Place profile view that is to the right of the site plan. The selected pipes and structures will appear in profile view, similar to what's shown in Figure 13.11 (your profile view might look slightly different).

6. Note that the pipes connecting from runs in the cul-de-sacs show the appropriate manholes as ellipses (see Figure 13.12).

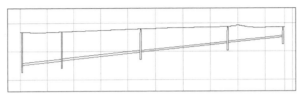

Figure 13.11

The selected pipes will appear in profile view.

Figure 13.12

Pipes that connect to structures from a different angle will be shown as ellipses.

Creating an Alignment from Storm Drainage Network Parts

Although the main leg of the sanitary sewer network was appropriate to show on the Parker Place profile view, the storm drainage network shown on the southern portion of the site would likely require its own profile. Because profiles are always created from an alignment, this network will require an alignment that traces key structures and pipes. Civil 3D provides a tool for creating an alignment from a pipe network.

The following exercise leads you through creating an alignment from network parts and then placing those parts on the resulting profile view:

1. Open `Pipes3.dwg` (which you can download from `www.sybex.com/go/introducingcivil3d2009`), or continue working in the drawing from the previous exercise.

2. Choose Pipes → Utilities → Create Alignment from Network Parts.

3. At the `Select first connected Network Part (Pipe or Structure):` prompt, select CB 1.

4. At the `Select next Network Part or [Undo]:` prompt, select Pipe A, CB 2, Pipe B, CB 4, Pipe D, and SDMH. Press ↵. The Create Alignment - From Pipe Network dialog will appear as shown in Figure 13.13.

Figure 13.13

The Create Alignment - From Pipe Network dialog

5. In the Create Alignment - From Pipe Network dialog, leave all of the default settings and click OK.

6. The Create Profile from Surface dialog will appear. Confirm that the Existing Ground surface is selected, and then click the Add button. The sampled surface entry will appear in the lower part of the dialog. Click the Draw in Profile View button. The Create Profile View dialog will appear.

7. In the Create Profile View dialog, click Next four times to land on the Pipe Network Display screen (see Figure 13.14). Confirm that all of the network elements listed in step 4 are checked in this list. Click the Create Profile View button.

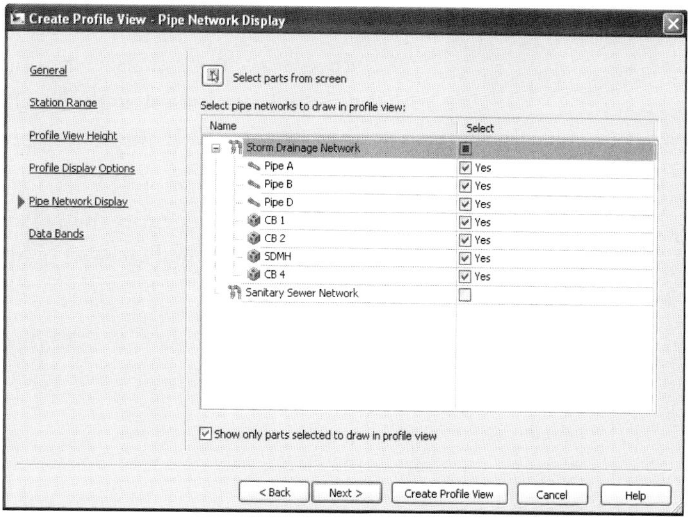

Figure 13.14

Confirm that all of the elements specified in step 4 are checked.

8. At the Select profile view origin: prompt, select a location in the drawing underneath the Parker Place profile view. A new profile view will appear showing the storm pipes and structures (see Figure 13.15). Some of the profile labels specify grade breaks and slopes — you can erase those if you'd like.

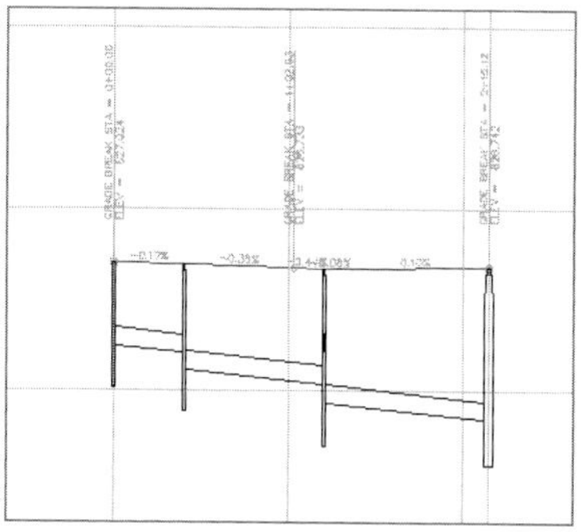

Figure 13.15

A profile view is created for the new alignment.

Labeling a Pipe Network in Profile View

Once pipes and structures have been drawn on a meaningful profile view, it makes sense to add labels. These labels, like their counterparts in plan view, are dynamic to the pipe network model and will react whenever the network changes.

The following exercise shows you how to add labels to the sanitary and storm drainage networks in profile view:

1. Open Pipes4.dwg (which you can download from www.sybex.com/go/introducingcivil3d2009), or continue working in the drawing from the previous exercise.

2. Choose Add Pipe Network Labels → Add Pipe Network Labels → Add Pipe Network Labels. The Add Labels dialog will appear.

3. Use the Label Type pull-down list to choose Entire Network Profile.

4. Use the Pipe Label Style pull-down list to choose Length Material and Slope.

5. Use the Structure Label Style: pull-down list to choose Data with Connected Pipes (Profile). The dialog will look like Figure 13.16. Click the Add button.

6. At the Select part (in profile view) contained in the network to be labeled: prompt, select any pipe or structure in the Parker Place profile view. Labels will appear, as shown in Figure 13.17.

Figure 13.16

The Add Labels dialog

7. In the Add Labels dialog, use the Pipe Label Style: pull-down list to select Name Only. Click the Add button.

8. At the Select part (in profile view) contained in the network to be labeled: prompt, select any pipe or structure in the Alignment - (Storm Drainage Network) profile view. Labels will appear.

Note that the structure labels in this profile view contain question marks (???) for the station and offset information.

9. Zoom in on CB 1 in the Profile View. Select CB 1, right-click, and choose Structure Properties. The Structure Properties dialog will appear.

10. In the Structure Properties dialog, switch to the Part Properties tab.

Figure 13.17

The pipe and structure labels in profile view

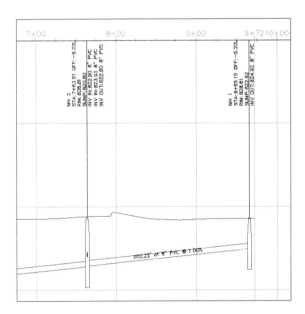

11. On the Properties tab, click inside the field next to Reference Alignment, and then press the ellipsis. The Reference Alignment dialog will appear.

12. Use the pull-down list to select the storm drainage alignment. Click OK.

13. Click OK to dismiss the Structure Properties dialog. The question marks are now replaced with Station and Offset information.

14. Repeat steps 9 through 13 for the other structures in this profile view.

Showing Pipe Crossings in Profile View

One of the most tedious tasks facing pipe network designers is adding pipe crossings to the profile view. It is critical to note where different types of pipes may potentially violate separation guidelines. With traditional methods, the slightest change to one pipe network would trigger a series of manual calculations. It was often easy to forget to check one pipe, or forget to move the crossing in the drawings. Civil 3D provides a means to show how a pipe crosses a profile, and its location will change with any edits to the pipe network.

The following exercise shows you two ways to add pipe crossings to a profile view:

1. Open `Pipes5.dwg` (which you can download from `www.sybex.com/go/introducing civil3d2009`), or continue working in the drawing from the previous exercise.

2. Select the Parker Place profile view. Right-click and choose Profile View Properties. The Profile View Properties dialog appears.

3. Switch to the Pipe Networks tab of the Profile View Properties dialog.

4. On the Pipe Networks tab, locate the entry for Pipe A.

5. In the row for Pipe A, check the Draw box. The Draw column now says Yes, as shown in Figure 13.18.

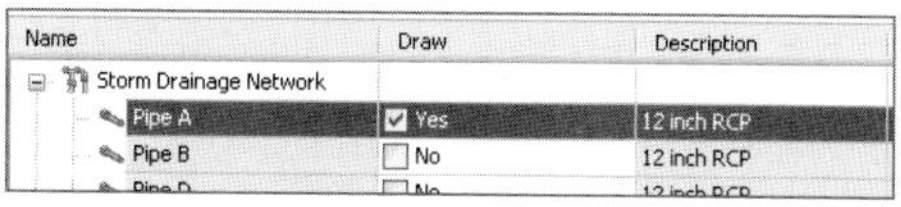

Figure 13.18

Check the box to draw Pipe A in this profile view.

6. In the row for Pipe A, check the Style Override box. The Pick Pipe Style box will appear.

7. Use the pull-down list to choose the Pipe Crossing Pipe (Storm) style. Click OK.

8. Repeat steps 4 through 7 for Pipe C. The dialog should now look like Figure 13.19.

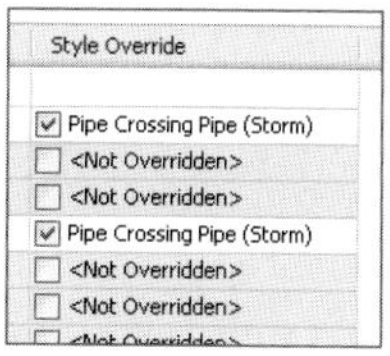

Figure 13.19

Check the style override box for Pipes A and C.

9. Click OK to exit the dialog.

10. Zoom in on the Parker Place profile view to see the two crossing pipes as shown in Figure 13.20.

11. Choose Pipes → Draw Parts in Profile View.

Figure 13.20

Pipes A and C now appear as crossings in the Parker Place profile view.

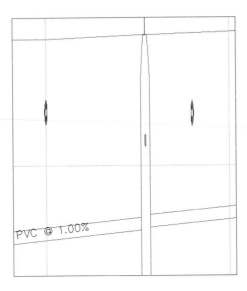

12. At the Select network(s) to add to profile view or [Selected parts only]: prompt, enter **S** to choose selected parts only.

13. At the Select pipe network parts to add to profile view: prompt, select the sanitary pipe that crosses Pipe A (see Figure 13.21). Press ↵.

14. At the Select profile view: prompt, select the Alignment - (Storm Drainage Network) profile view. The selected pipe will appear in profile, as shown in Figure 13.22. It will look strange until you override the style to show the pipe as a crossing.

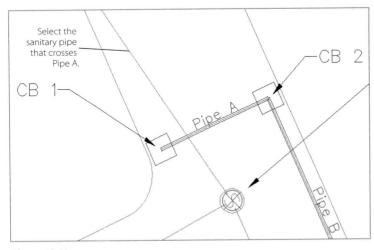

Figure 13.21

Select the sanitary pipe that crosses Pipe A.

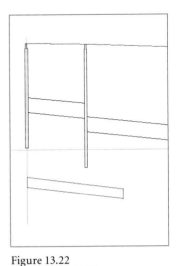

Figure 13.22

At first, the pipe will not appear as a crossing.

15. Select the Alignment - (Storm Drainage Network) profile view. Right-click and choose Profile View Properties. The Profile View Properties dialog appears.

16. Switch to the Pipe Networks tab of the Profile View Properties dialog.

17. On the Pipe Networks tab, locate the Sanitary Sewer Network category. There should be only one pipe checked for this network, as shown in Figure 13.23. (The pipe name will vary from what's shown in this figure, depending on how you drew your network.)

18. In the row for the sanitary pipe, check the Style Override box. The Pick Pipe Style box will appear.

19. Use the pull-down list to choose the Pipe Crossing Pipe (Sanitary) style.

20. Zoom in on the Alignment - (Storm Drainage Network) profile view to see the crossing pipe, as shown in Figure 13.24.

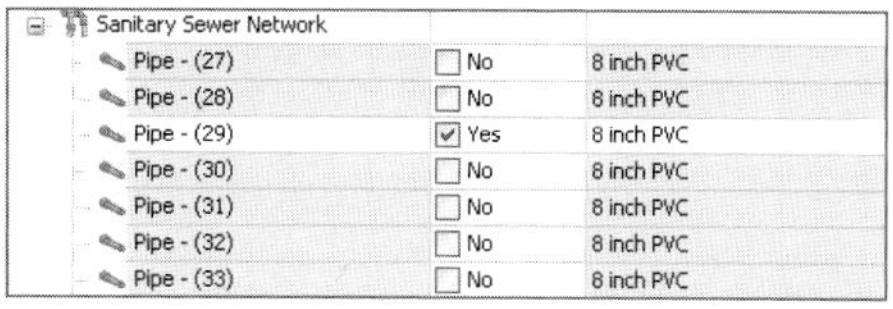

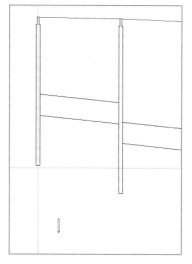

Figure 13.23

Only the one selected sanitary pipe should appear on the list.

Figure 13.24

Once the style is overridden, the pipe will appear as a crossing.

Creating a Dynamic Pipe Table

Sometimes, drawings are crowded with many different types of annotations. Between road labels, several types of pipe networks, grading elevations, and more, it can be tricky to get all of the required information shown in a meaningful way. Tables are a method for showing pipe data in a concise list form without cluttering the plan.

The following exercise leads you through adding a pipe table for both the sanitary and storm networks:

1. Open Pipes6.dwg (which you can download from www.sybex.com/go/introducingcivil3d2009), or continue working in the drawing from the previous exercise.

2. Choose Pipes → Add Tables → Add Pipe. The Pipe Table Creation dialog will appear.

3. In the Pipe Table Creation dialog, make sure that the By Network radio button is selected, and Sanitary Sewer Network is chosen. Leave the remaining default settings (see Figure 13.25). Click OK.

Figure 13.25

The Pipe Table Creation dialog

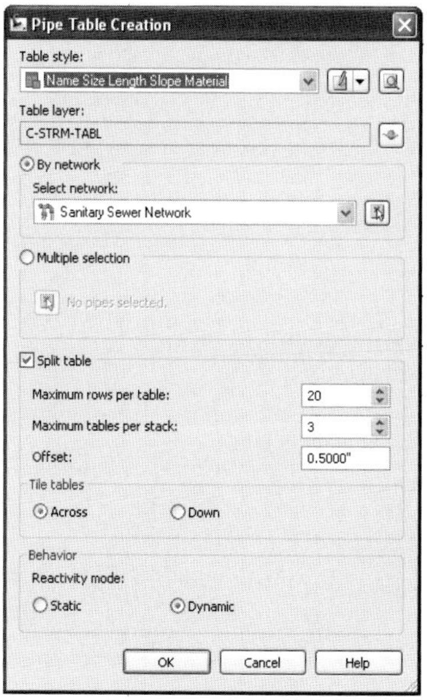

4. At the Select upper left corner: prompt, select a location in the drawing some-where to the right of the profile views. A table will appear that looks similar to Figure 13.26. (The pipe names for your network will vary from the figure, depending on how you drew your network.)

5. Repeat steps 2 through 4 for the Storm Drainage Network.

Figure 13.26

The Sanitary Sewer Network Pipe Table

Sanitary Sewer Network Pipe Table				
NAME	SIZE	LENGTH	SLOPE	MATERIAL
Pipe — (27)	8"	202.22'	1.00%	PVC
Pipe — (28)	8"	309.24'	1.00%	PVC
Pipe — (29)	8"	288.23'	1.00%	PVC
Pipe — (30)	8"	147.01'	1.00%	PVC
Pipe — (31)	8"	171.57'	1.00%	PVC
Pipe — (32)	8"	242.28'	1.00%	PVC
Pipe — (33)	8"	269.61'	1.00%	PVC

Editing a Pipe Network

Whenever pipe networks are designed, it is rare that there won't be any changes. Gravity systems often require modeling to confirm that pipes meet capacity requirements, and pipes may need to be resized based on these results. Structures may need to be changed at the request of regulating agencies. Slopes may need tweaking to ensure appropriate veloc-ity. There are many types of edits, revisions, and adjustments that will occur over the life of the design project. Civil 3D provides several ways to edit your pipe network.

You can make visual edits by stretching, moving, deleting, and spinning both pipes and structures. There are also provisions for tabular editing in Panorama, and more. No matter how you edit your pipe network, the labels, tables, and all views of your pipes and structures will change to match.

The following exercises will lead you through making several different kinds of pipe network edits and give you an opportunity to see the dynamic labeling and profiling mechanism in action.

Editing a Pipe Network Using Grips

The following exercise uses a structure grip to stretch a pipe length, change a pipe invert, and change the structure location:

1. Open Pipes7.dwg (which you can download from www.sybex.com/go/introducing civil3d2009), or continue working in the drawing from the previous exercise.

2. Choose View → Viewports → 2 Viewports.

3. At the Enter a configuration option [Horizontal/Vertical] <Vertical>: prompt, type **H** for horizontal. The view will split into two viewports.

4. Click in the top viewport to activate it. Zoom in on Pipe A from the Storm Drainage network.

5. Click in the bottom viewport to activate it. Zoom in on the Storm Drainage Network Pipe Table. Your screen should look similar to Figure 13.27.

6. Click in the top viewport to activate it. Select CB 1. A grip will appear. Grab the grip and move the structure approximately 10′ to the left. Note that the length and slope of Pipe A has changed in the pipe table, as shown in Figure 13.28.

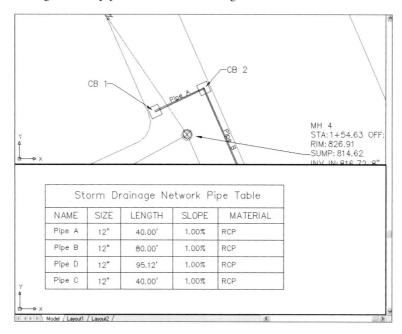

Figure 13.27

The Pipe Table Creation dialog

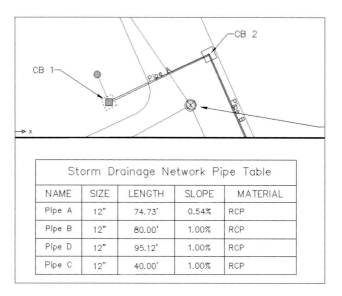

Figure 13.28

Editing the location of the structure in plan changes the pipe length. The pipe table updates dynamically.

7. While still active in the top viewport, pan over to MH 1 so that you can clearly see the structure label.

8. Click in the bottom viewport to activate it. Pan over to MH 1 in profile view. Select the pipe attached to MH 1. Use the diamond-shaped grip at the pipe invert to move the pipe invert approximately 1′ higher, as shown in Figure 13.29. Note that the information in the MH 1 label in the plan changes immediately.

9. Click in the top viewport to active it. Select MH 1. A grip will appear. Use the grip to stretch MH 1 to approximately station 9+00. Note that the structure moves in the profile view, the pipe shortens, and all labels change.

10. Save the drawing — you will need it for the next exercise.

Figure 13.29

Use the diamond-shaped invert grip to raise the start invert approximately 1′.

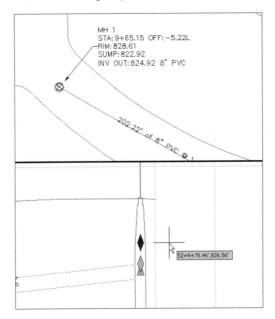

Swapping Parts

The following exercise uses the swap part function to exchange one type of pipe and structure for another:

1. Continue working in Pipes1.dwg.

2. Click in the bottom viewport to activate it. Pan over Pipe D in profile view.

3. Click in the top viewport to activate it. Pan over to Pipe D in plan view.

4. Select Pipe D. Make sure you select the pipe and not the alignment. You may find it easier to select the pipe if you freeze the alignment layer. Right-click and choose Swap Part. The Swap Part Size dialog will appear as shown in Figure 13.30.

5. In the Swap Part Size dialog, choose 18 Inch RCP. Click OK.

6. Note that the pipe style in both plan and profile views changes to reflect the larger diameter.

7. Pan over to CB 4. Select CB 4, right-click, and choose Swap Part. The Swap Part Size dialog will appear. Select the Concentric Manhole. Click OK.

8. Note that the structure style changes in both plan and profile views to reflect the new part. Figure 13.31 shows Pipe D in profile.

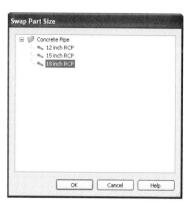

Figure 13.30

The Swap Part Size dialog

Adjusting Sump Depth

Sump depth, structure insertion point, and more can be edited using the Structure Properties dialog. The following exercise has you exploring this interface and using it to adjust a sump depth:

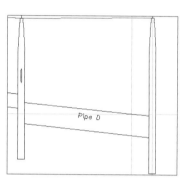

Figure 13.31

The pipe and structure appearance both change to reflect the new parts.

1. Continue working in Pipes1.dwg.

2. Choose View → Viewports → 1 Viewports. The view will return to one viewport.

3. Pan over to MH 6. Select MH 6, right-click, and choose Structure Properties. The Structure Properties dialog will appear.

4. Switch to the Part Properties tab of the Structure Properties dialog. Scroll down to the Sump Behavior section of the dialog. Change the sump depth from 2.000 to **0**. Click OK.

5. Note that the sump depth has been changed to match the invert-out elevation.

Adjusting Sump Depth

Sometimes it's easier to see what's happening with your pipe network in a tabular list. The Pipe Network Vistas Panorama window allows you to see a list of pipes and/or structures for easy editing. The graphics will immediately adjust to match the model changes.

The following exercise will teach you how to adjust the sump depth of a structure using the structure properties dialog:

1. Continue working in Pipes1.dwg.

2. Pan over to the Storm Drainage Network in plan view. Select Pipe D, right-click, and choose Edit Network. The Network Layout Tools dialog will appear.

3. In the Network Layout Tools dialog, click the Pipe Network Vistas button. A Panorama window will appear.

4. Switch to the Pipes tab of the Panorama window. Scroll over to the Slope (Hold Start) column. Change the value for Pipe D from its current value to **-3.00%** (see Figure 13.32). Note that the pipe slope changes in profile view, and any affected labels also change to match the new slope.

Figure 13.32

Change the slope for Pipe D to -3.00%.

t	Reference Surface	Slope (Hold Start)	
	Existing Ground	-0.54%	0
	Existing Ground	-1.00%	1
	Existing Ground	-1.00%	1
	Existing Ground	-3.00%	3

Summary

In this chapter, you learned some basic pipe network creation, annotation, and labeling skills. These skills will assist you in creating gravity systems, such as sanitary sewers and storm drainage. With Civil 3D pipe networks, the plan, profile, crossing, labels, and tables are linked together dynamically. This dynamic interaction reduces the possibility for errors in and omissions from pipe design and drafting.

CHAPTER 14

Projects

Working in an engineering firm generally means working on a team. This team can be as simple as a technician and an engineer, or it can include dozens of people spread across several disciplines such as architecture, civil engineering, landscape architecture, irrigation, and project management. No matter the team size or makeup, it's important that team members communicate and that they're always working with the latest information.

To solve this problem, and to make it more efficient for multiple team members to work on the same project together, Civil 3D contains the data shortcuts (DS) feature. This feature lets you share data between drawings quickly and easily. Although the types of objects are somewhat limited, most users find they suffice, and that their ease of use makes DS a great tool.

This chapter covers the following topics:

- **The difference between data shortcuts and Xrefs**
- **Creating new project template folders**
- **Creating new projects in Civil 3D**
- **Creating new data shortcuts and references**
- **Updating references**
- **Repairing broken or lost references**

What Are Data Shortcuts?

Data shortcuts allow the cross-referencing of design data between drawings. To this end, the data is what is made available, and it's important to note that the appearance can be entirely different between the host and any number of data shortcuts. We'll use the term *data shortcut* or, more simply, *shortcut* when we discuss selecting, modifying, or updating these links between files.

WHAT ABOUT VAULT?

Many users have heard discussions of Vault when they learn about Civil 3D. Vault is part of a system that also includes Autodesk Data Management Server and Microsoft SQL services. As an introductory text, this book will focus on the DS system because most users can use it happily, never needing some of the functions that Vault offers. For more information on Vault, check out *Mastering AutoCAD Civil 3D 2009* by your authors (Sybex, 2008).

There are two primary situations in which you need data or information across drawings, and they are addressed with external references (Xrefs) or shortcuts. These two options are similar but not the same. Let's compare:

- **Xref functionality:** Used when the goal is to get a picture of the information in question. Xrefs can be changed by using the layer control, Xref clips, and other drawing-element controls. Although they can be used for labeling across files in Civil 3D 2009, the fact that you have to bring over the entire file to label one component is a disadvantage.

- **Shortcut functionality:** Brings over the design information, but generally ignores the display. Shortcuts work only with Civil 3D objects, so they will have their own styles applied. This may seem like duplicitous work because you have already assigned styles and labels in one drawing and have to do it again, but it offers the advantage that you can have completely different views of the same data in different drawings.

Only Civil 3D objects can be used with shortcuts, and even then some objects are not available through shortcuts. The following objects are available for use through data shortcuts:

- Alignments
- Surfaces
- Profile data
- Pipe networks
- View frame groups

You might expect that corridor, parcel, assembly, point, or point group information would be available through the shortcut mechanism, but they are not. Parcels and corridors can be accessed only via Xref, but once they've been Xreferenced, you can use the normal labeling techniques and styles. Now that you've looked at what objects you can tackle with shortcuts, you learn how to create them in the next section.

A NOTE ABOUT THE EXERCISES IN THIS CHAPTER

Many of the exercises in this chapter assume you've stepped through the full chapter. It's difficult to simulate the large number of variables that come into play in a live environment. To that end, many of these exercises build on the previous one. For the easiest workflow, don't close any files until the end of the chapter or until you're told to do so in an exercise.

Additionally, you'll have to perform some saves to data files throughout this chapter. Remember that you can always get the original file from the media that you downloaded from www.sybex.com/go/introducingcivil3d2009.

Publishing Data Shortcut Files

Shortcut files are simply XML files that have pointers back to the drawing containing the object in question. These shortcuts are managed through Prospector and are stored in a working folder. Creating shortcuts is a matter of setting a working folder, creating a shortcut folder within that, and then creating the shortcut files. You look at all three steps in this section.

As a precursor to making your first project, you should establish what a typical folder structure looks like. Civil 3D includes a mechanism for copying a typical project folder structure into each new project. By creating a blank copy of the folder structure you'd like to have in place for your projects, you can use that as the starting point when a new project is created in Civil 3D. In this exercise, you'll set up a prototype folder structure for use later in creating new projects.

Figure 14.1

Creating a project template

1. Open Windows Explorer and navigate to
   `C:\Civil 3D Project Templates`.

2. Create a new folder titled `Introducing`.

3. Inside `Introducing`, create folders called `Survey`,
   `Engineering`, `Architecture`, `Word`, and `Con Docs`, as
   shown in Figure 14.1.

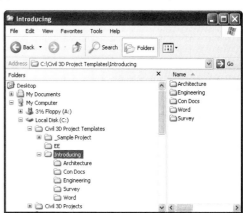

This structure will be displayed inside Civil 3D and in the working folder when a project is created. We've included a `Word` folder as an example of other, non–Civil 3D–related folders you might have in your project setup for users outside the CAD team, such as accountants or the project manager. These files and folders would be added to each new project created via Civil 3D. This is a great way to include project checklists, standard details sheets, or a template cover sheet that contains your logo and company information. You can set up template folders to handle a variety of situations and make life easier on other users.

The Working and Data Shortcuts Folders

For the most part, you can mentally substitute "project folder" for "working folder" when you are working with DS. Then you can substitute "project folder" for "data shortcuts folder," and the whole thing will make a lot more sense. The working folder will contain a number of projects, each in turn having a shortcuts folder where the shortcut files actually reside. Each time you create a new shortcut folder within the Prospector framework, you'll have the opportunity to create a full project structure. In the following exercise, you set the working folder and create a new project:

1. Create a new blank drawing using any template.

2. Within Prospector, make sure the View drop-down list is set to Master View.

3. Right-click the Data Shortcuts branch and select Set Working Folder to display the Browse for Folder dialog shown in Figure 14.2.

4. Click Local Disk (C:) to highlight it, and then click the Make New Folder button.

5. Type **Introducing Shortcuts** as the folder name and click OK to dismiss the dialog.

Figure 14.2

Creating a new working folder

6. Right-click the Data Shortcuts branch in Prospector, and select New Data Shortcuts Folder to display the New Data Shortcut Folder dialog shown in Figure 14.3.

Figure 14.3

Creating a new shortcut folder (aka a project)

7. Type **Timberwilde** for the folder name, and toggle on the Use Project Template option as shown in Figure 14.3.

8. Select the Introducing folder from the list as shown, and click OK to dismiss the dialog. Congratulations! You've made a new Civil 3D project. Notice that the Data Shortcuts branch in Prospector now reflects the path of the Timberwilde project.

If you open Windows Explorer and navigate to C:\Introducing Shortcuts\ Timberwilde, you'll see the folder from the Mastering project template plus a special folder named _Shortcuts, as shown in Figure 14.4. One common issue that arises is that you already have a project folder inside the working folder. This is typically done during some bidding or marketing work, or during contract preparation. If you already have a project folder established, it will not show up in Civil 3D unless there is a _Shortcuts folder inside it. To this end, you can manually make this folder. There's nothing special about it, except that it has to exist.

Figure 14.4

Your new project shown in Windows Explorer

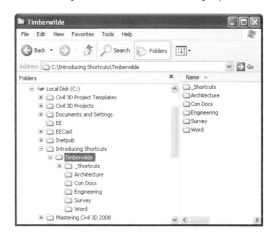

Remember, the *working folder* and *data shortcuts folder* are simply Civil 3D terms for a projects folder and individual projects. If you're familiar with Land Desktop, the working folder is similar to the project path, with various projects. Finally, don't forget that drawing files and working folders aren't tied together. When you change drawings, the data shortcuts folder will not change automatically. You must right-click the Data Shortcuts branch and select a different data shortcuts folder.

ANOTHER WAY TO LOOK AT IT

The other, somewhat common, approach when setting up projects in Civil 3D with shortcuts is to set the working folder path to your particular project folder. The project then has a CAD folder, and within that would be the _Shortcuts folder, which would be the same for every project. This results in a folder structure like H:\Projects*Project Name*\CAD_Shortcuts, which some users may find this more useful and easier to manage, particularly if your company standards dictate that the top level of a project folder shouldn't include something like a _Shortcuts folder. Both methods are workable solutions, but you should decide on one and stick to it! We'll use the more conventional approach shown in the previous exercise throughout this text.

Creating Data Shortcuts

You've created a data shortcuts folder, so it's time to put it to use. One caution when working with data shortcuts: a drawing creating a shortcut for a given project can actually be stored anywhere. This could lead to confusion for users trying to determine what file is tied to what Civil 3D object, so it is really best practice to keep the drawing files in the same rough location as your shortcut files. For the purposes of these exercises though, you'll just leave the data in the default location instead of moving it first. In the following exercise, you'll start working with shortcuts by publishing data shortcuts for the alignments, profiles, and surface in your project:

1. Open the Creating Shortcuts.dwg file. (Remember, all data files can be downloaded from www.sybex.com/go/introducingcivil3d2009.) This drawing contains surface, alignment and profile data, ready to be shared with the rest of the team. (See Figure 14.5.)

Figure 14.5

The Creating Short-cuts drawing file

2. In Prospector, right-click the Data Shortcuts branch, and select Create Data Shortcuts to display the Create Data Shortcuts dialog shown in Figure 14.6.

3. Check the Surfaces and Alignments options, and the subitems will all be selected. Note that the Profiles associated with the Parker Place alignment are also being selected for publishing.

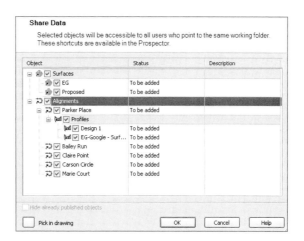

Figure 14.6

The Create Data Shortcuts dialog

4. Click OK to dismiss the dialog and create the data shortcuts.

5. In Prospector, expand the branches under the Data Shortcuts heading as shown in Figure 14.7, and you should see all of the relevant data listed. The listing here indicates that the object is ready to be referenced in another drawing file.

The data shortcut mechanism changed greatly between the 2008 and 2009 releases. In 2008, you had to manually manage the XML data reference files. In 2009, Civil 3D manages these files for you. They are stored in the magic _Shortcuts folder as individual XML files. You can review these XML files using XML Notepad. You can still open and view these files, but notice that the first comment in the XML file is PLEASE DO NOT EDIT THIS FILE! In the past, some users found they needed to edit XML files to fix broken or lost references. This is no longer necessary with the addition of the Data Shortcuts Editor, which you look at later in this chapter.

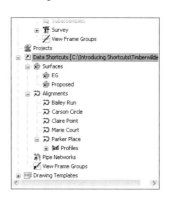

Figure 14.7

Data shortcuts listed in Prospector

Using Data Shortcuts

Now that you've created the shortcut XML files to act as pointers back to the original drawing, you'll use them in other ways and locations. Once a reference is in place, it's a simple matter to update the reference and see any changes in the original file reflected in the reference object. In this section, you look at creating and exploring these references, and then learn about updating or editing them.

Creating Shortcut References

Shortcut references are made using the Data Shortcuts branch within Prospector. In the following exercise, you create references to the objects you previously published to the Timberwilde project:

1. Open the Creating References.dwg file. This is an empty file built on the Extended template.

2. In Prospector, expand Data Shortcuts → Alignments.

3. Right-click the Bailey Run alignment and select Create Reference to display the Create Alignment Reference dialog shown in Figure 14.8.

4. Set the Alignment Style to Proposed and the Alignment Label Set to Major Minor and Geometry Points as shown in Figure 14.8.

5. Click OK to close the dialog.

6. Perform a zoom extents to find this new alignment.

7. Repeat steps 3 through 5 for the Carson Circle, Claire Point, Marie Court, and Parker Place alignments in the shortcuts list. When complete, your screen should look similar to Figure 14.9.

Figure 14.8

The Create Alignment Reference dialog

Figure 14.9

Completed creation of alignments references

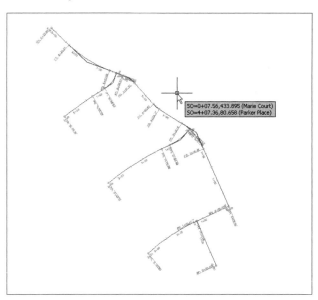

Note the tooltip in Figure 14.9 indicates station and offset data, reflecting the fact that data references bring data, not just pictures of data. Each of these alignments is simply a pointer back to the original file. They can be stylized, stationed, or labeled, but the definition of the alignment cannot be changed. This is more clearly illustrated in a surface, so you'll add a surface reference in the following exercise:

1. Expand Data Shortcuts → Surfaces.

2. Right-click the EG surface and select Create Reference to display the Create Surface Reference dialog.

3. Change the Surface Style to Contours 1′ & 5′ (Background), and then click OK. Your screen should look like Figure 14.10.

4. Expand the Surfaces branch of Prospector and the EG surface as shown in Figure 14.11.

5. Right-click the EG surface and select Surface Properties.

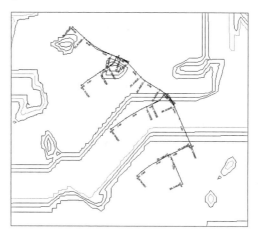

Figure 14.10

The EG surface reference

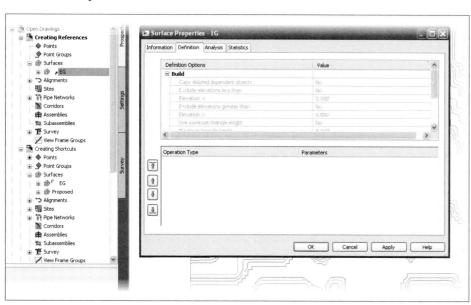

Figure 14.11

The EG surface in Prospector and the EG Surface Properties dialog

Here are a couple of important things to note:

- The small arrow next to the EG surface name indicates that the surface is a shortcut.
- There's no Definition branch under the EG surface. Additionally, in the Surface Properties dialog, the entire Definition tab is grayed out, making it impossible to change by using a shortcut.

6. Click OK to close the dialog.

To make a reference into a live object in the current drawing, simply right-click its name and select Promote. This breaks the link to the source information and creates an editable object in the current drawing. This technique can be very handy for playing with alternative designs, copying profile or alignment data into a temporary drawing, and editing without concern that you are destroying the currently valid design data.

Now that you've created a file with a group of references, you'll look at how changes in the source drawing are reflected in this file.

Updating and Managing References

As it is, if the reference were just a copy of the original data, you'd have done nothing more than cut and paste the object from one drawing to another. The benefit of using shortcuts is just like Xrefs: when a change is made in the source, it's reflected in the reference drawing. In this section, you make a few changes and look at the updating process, and then you see how to add to the data shortcut listings in Prospector.

Updating the Source and Reference

When it's necessary to make a change, it can sometimes be confusing to remember which file you were in when you originally created a now-referenced object. Thankfully, you can use the tools in the Data Shortcut palette to very simply jump back to that file, make the changes, and refresh the reference, which is what you'll be doing in the following exercise:

1. In Prospector, expand Data Shortcuts → Alignments.

2. Right-click Bailey Run, and select Open Source Drawing. You can also do this by selecting the object in the drawing window and right-clicking to access the shortcut menu. The Open Source Drawing command is on the shortcut menu when a reference object is selected.

3. Select the Parker Place alignment and make a grip-edit to Parker Place's northern end, dragging it up and further north, as shown in Figure 14.12.

4. Save the drawing.

Once a change is made in the source drawing, Civil 3D will synchronize references the next time they are opened. In the current exercise, the reference drawing is already open. The following steps show you how the alert mechanism works in this situation.

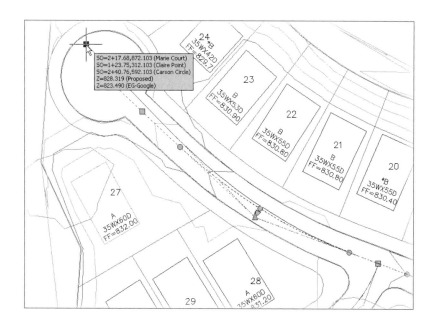

Figure 14.12

Grip-editing Parker Place

5. Using the Window menu, select the Creating References.dwg file to make it active. An alert bubble like the one shown in Figure 14.13 should appear. This may take a few minutes, but if you expand Creating References → Alignments in Prospector, you will also see a series of warning chevrons. You might look for this change manually if one of your team members e-mails or calls to tell you they've made a design change and you don't want to wait for the alert bubble.

> ⓘ **Data shortcut definitions may have changed**   ✖
> References to data shortcut definitions may have changed and may require synchronization
> Synchronize

Figure 14.13

Data reference change alert bubble

6. Click Synchronize in the alert bubble to bring your drawing current with the design file and dismiss the Panorama window if you'd like. If you don't see the alert bubble, right-click each alignment branch in Prospector and select Synchronize. Your drawing will update, and the Parker Place alignment will reflect the change in the source. If you do not get the bubble, you can select individual references within Prospector and right-click them to access the Synchronize command.

Shockingly enough, the Open Source Drawing command is the only way to track down the source of a shortcut. There is no way to simply list the object and recognize the file name, or see the file name in a table.

Updating references as in the preceding exercise is simple enough and works well once file relationships are established. But suppose there is a change in the file structure of the source information and you need to make a change? You look at that in the next section.

Managing Changes in the Source Data

Designs change often—there's no question about that. And using shortcuts to keep all the members of the design team on the same page is a great idea. But in the scenario you're working with in this chapter, what happens if new, additional alignment data is added to the source file? You explore that in this exercise:

1. Return to the Creating Shortcuts.dwg file.

2. Create a new alignment, named **Loop Road**, extending from the Claire Point cul-de-sac to the Carson Circle cul-de-sac, ignoring the fact that it crosses a number of parcels. (Part of the fun with Civil 3D is the ability to quickly experiment!) Your screen should look like Figure 14.14, with the new alignment circled.

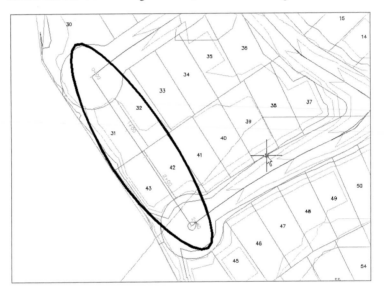

Figure 14.14

Loop Road alignment drawn and completed

3. Save the file.

4. In Prospector, right-click Data Shortcuts and select Create Data Shortcuts to display the Create Data Shortcuts dialog.

5. Check the Hide Already Published Objects option in the lower-left corner of the dialog to make finding the new object easier.

6. Check the Loop Road alignment, and then click OK to dismiss the dialog. Save the Creating Shortcuts drawing!

7. Switch back to Creating References file, and add the Loop Road alignment to your data shortcuts as in earlier examples.

By using shortcuts to handle and distribute design information, it's quite simple to keep adding information to the design as it progresses. This means that designs really don't have to be complete before other team members can begin working with the data. It's important to remember that simply saving a file does not create new shortcut files for all of the Civil 3D objects contained in that file—they have to be created from the Data Shortcuts branch.

Fixing Broken Shortcuts

One of the dangers of linking things together is that eventually you'll have to deal with broken links. As files are renamed, or moved from the Preliminary folder to the Production folder, the data shortcut files that point back simply get lost. Thankfully, Civil 3D includes a tool for handling broken or edited links: the Data Shortcuts Editor. You explore that tool in the following exercise:

1. Open the file `Repairing References.dwg`. This file contains a number of references pointing to a file that no longer exists, and Panorama should appear to tell you that four problems were found. Close the Panorama window.

2. In Prospector, expand Repairing References → Surfaces and you will see that Proposed has a warning chevron next to it.

3. Right-click Proposed and select Repair Broken References from the shortcut menu to display the Choose the File Containing the Referenced Object dialog.

4. Navigate to the `Creating Shortcuts.dwg` file in the data set. Click OK to dismiss the Choose the File Containing the Referenced Object dialog. An Additional Broken References dialog will appear as shown in Figure 14.15, offering you the option to repair all the references or cancel.

5. Click the Repair All Broken References button to close the Additional Broken References dialog. Civil 3D will crawl through the file linked in step 4, and attempt to match the Civil 3D objects with broken references to objects in the selected drawing.

Additional Broken References

More broken references were detected in this file.

You can attempt to repair all broken references.

Note: This process may take some time.

→ Repair all broken references

Cancel

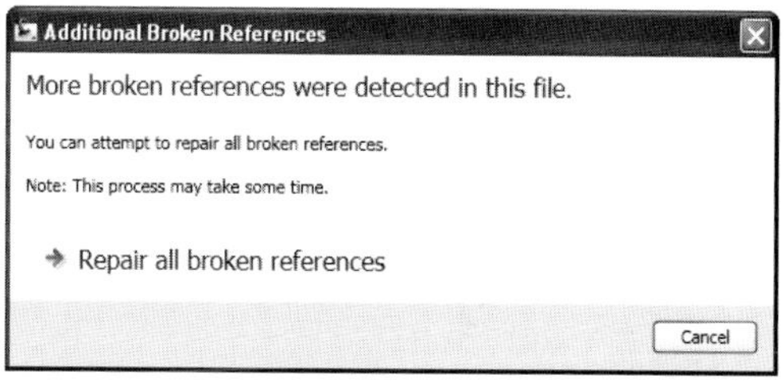

Figure 14.15

The Additional Broken References dialog

6. Perform a zoom extents, and your drawing should look like Figure 14.16, with a surface, alignment, and profile view.

The ability to repair broken links helps make file management a bit easier, but there will be times when you need to completely change the path of a shortcut to point to a new file. To do this, you need to use the Data Shortcuts Editor.

Figure 14.16

Repaired references within an older file

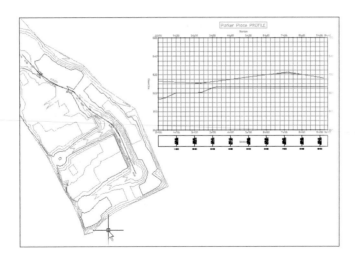

The Data Shortcuts Editor

The Data Shortcuts Editor (DSE) is used to update or change the file to which a shortcut points. This can happen when an alternative design file is approved, or when you move from preliminary to final design. In the following exercise, you change the EG surface shortcut to point at a surveyed site surface instead of the Google Earth surface the shortcut file was previously using:

1. Make sure `Creating References.dwg` is still open.

2. In Windows, go to Start → All Programs → Autodesk → Autodesk Civil 3D 2009 → Data Shortcuts Editor to load DSE.

3. Select File → Open Data Shortcuts Folder to display the Browse for Folder dialog.

4. Navigate to `C:\Introducing Shortcuts\Timberwilde`, and then click OK to dismiss the Browse for Folder dialog. Your DSE should look like Figure 14.17. (Your paths will be different from ours.)

Figure 14.17

Editing the Timber-wilde data shortcuts

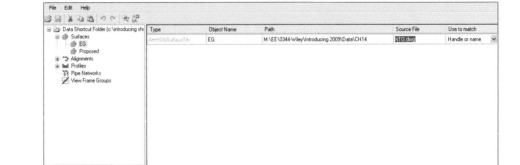

5. On the left, select the Surfaces branch to isolate the surfaces.

6. Click the Source File column on the EG row, and type **XTO.dwg** as the Source File Name.

PICKING A NEW FILE IN A NEW PATH

Unfortunately, you can't browse to a new file in this dialog, setting the path and file name at the same time. If you want to change both parts of the source data, the path and the file containing the new data, it takes two steps. You will need to place a copy of your old data file in the new path and change the path. The Data Shortcuts Editor will then find that file in the new path and validate the path. Then you can change to a different file in that path. It's a bit cumbersome, but it's better than not being able to change it at all!

7. Click the Handle Only drop-down menu and change it to Handle or Name.

8. Click the Save button in the DSE and switch back to Civil 3D. You should still be in the Creating References drawing file.

9. In Prospector, select the Data Shortcuts → Surfaces → EG branch and note that the Source File Name is shown as Creating Shortcuts (see Figure 14.18).

Figure 14.18

The Source File Name is shown in Prospector's preview area.

10. Right-click the Data Shortcuts branch and select Validate Data Shortcuts. Prospector will alert you of a broken reference.

11. Expand Data Shortcuts → Surfaces. Right-click EG and select Repair Broken Shortcut.

12. Scroll up within Prospector, and expand the Surfaces branch.

13. Right-click EG and select Synchronize. Your screen should look like Figure 14.19, showing a completely different surface as the EG surface.

The ability to modify and repoint the shortcut files to new and improved information during a project without losing style or label settings is invaluable. However, when you use this function, be sure to validate and then synchronize.

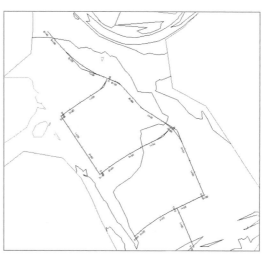

Figure 14.19

Completed repathing of the EG surface shortcut

Summary

Working with data across projects and data files is part of working with Civil 3D in a team environment. You should set up this process slowly: get a project template in place, add the design files, and then create references to bring your design into the construction documents. The ability to begin this third process while the design is still in flux is the real power of the application, making it possible to begin the task of documentation shortly after a conceptual design is begun. The ability to add and refine data throughout the process without having to start over on the documents process is where Civil 3D shines and lets your team work in new, more efficient ways.

More Exercises for Exploring AutoCAD Civil 3D 2009

Although the main text has numerous exercises and examples, hundreds of tools and options are not covered. In this appendix, you'll find a collection of exercises to take you a little further into Civil 3D. Remember, you can download all data files from www.sybex.com/go/introducingcivil3d2009, except for the exercises in the "Surveying" section of this appendix. For those, you'll need to use the files you created in Chapter 4, "Survey."

Lines and Curves

These exercises give you hands-on practice using the Best Fit tools as well as performing a map check analysis.

Making a Curve by Best Fit

In this exercise, you'll use the Best Fit tools to fit an arc to Civil 3D points.

1. Open the More Lines and Curves1.dwg file.

2. Zoom in on the Civil 3D points marked PL.

3. Choose Lines/Curves → Create Best Fit Entities → Create Arc. The Arc by Best Fit dialog will appear.

4. In the Arc by Best Fit dialog, choose the radio button next to From Civil 3D Points. Click OK.

5. At the Select point objects or [Numbers/Groups]: prompt, select the first PL point.

6. At the Select point objects or [Numbers/Groups/Undo]: prompt, continue selecting the remaining PL points from left to right. As you select the points, a dashed, red preview arc will appear as shown in Figure A.1. After all of the points are selected, press ↵. The Regression Data Panorama will appear.

7. Click the green checkmark in the upper-right corner of the Regression Data Panorama. An arc appears that is a best fit for the point data, as shown in Figure A.2.

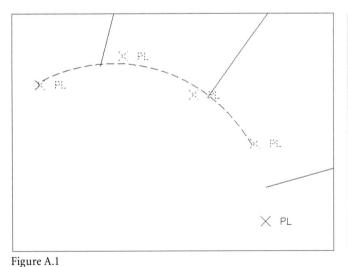

Figure A.1

As you select each point, a dashed curve will appear showing a preview of the best fit arc.

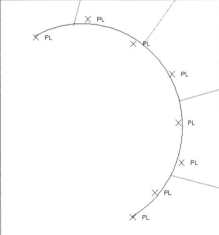

Figure A.2

The best fit arc

Making a Parabola by Best Fit

In this exercise, you'll fit a parabolic vertical curve based on segments.

1. Open the `More Lines and Curves2.dwg` file.

2. Zoom in on lines drawn in profile, as shown in Figure A.3.

3. Choose Lines/Curves ➔ Create Best Fit Entities ➔ Create Parabola. The Parabola by Best Fit dialog will appear.

4. In the Parabola by Best Fit dialog, confirm that the From Entities radio button is selected. Click OK.

5. At the `Select lines, arcs, polylines or profile objects:` prompt, select the first magenta line.

6. At the `Select lines, arcs, polylines or profile objects or [Undo]:` prompt, continue selecting the remaining magenta lines from left to right. As you select the lines, a red, dashed preview parabola will appear, as shown in Figure A.3.

7. In the Parabola by Best Fit dialog, confirm that the From Entities radio button is selected. Click OK. After all of the lines are selected, press ↵. The Regression Data Panorama will appear.

8. Click the green checkmark in the upper-right corner of the Regression Data Panorama. A parabola appears that is a best fit for the line data, as shown in Figure A.4.

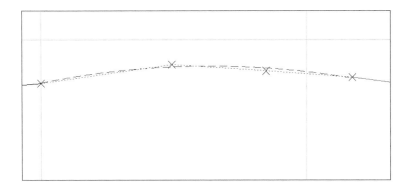

Figure A.3

As you select each line, a dashed curve will appear showing a preview of the best fit parabola.

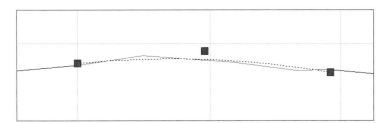

Figure A.4

The best fit parabola

Performing a Map Check

A common surveying task is performing a map check on already-drawn lines. You'll do that in this exercise.

1. Open the More Lines and Curves3.dwg file. The drawing contains labeled linework that represents a property.

2. Choose General → Mapcheck Analysis. The Mapcheck Analysis palette will appear.

3. Click the New Mapcheck Analysis button, as shown in Figure A.5.

4. At the Enter name of mapcheck: prompt, type **Deed**. Press ↵.

5. At the Specify point of beginning (POB): prompt, use your endpoint osnap to choose the northwest corner of the property.

6. At the Select a label or [Clear/New]: prompt, select the label on the next line to the east, as shown in Figure A.6.

7. At the Select a label or [Clear/New/Reverse]: prompt, continue picking the labels around the property going clockwise. A preview arrow will appear with each selection. If at any time the preview arrow does not trace the correct line, type **R** to reverse the arrow.

8. After all of the labels have been selected, press ↵. Entries for six sides will appear in the Mapcheck Analysis palette, as in Figure A.7.

Figure A.5

Starting a new map check analysis

Figure A.6

Select the label on the next line to the east.

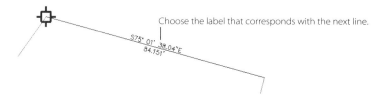

Choose the label that corresponds with the next line.

Figure A.7

The Mapcheck Analysis palette populated with data

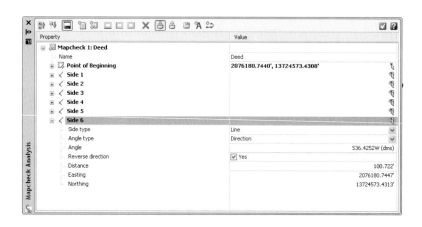

9. Click the Output View button on the Mapcheck Analysis palette, as shown in Figure A.8.

10. In the Mapcheck Analysis palette, expand the Closure Summary entry, as shown in Figure A.9, to see the results of the mapcheck analysis.

Figure A.8

Selecting the Output View button

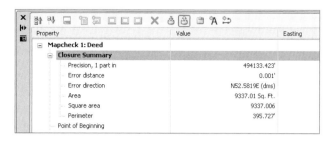

Figure A.9

The closure summary provides information about errors in direction and distance.

Surveying

For these exercises, you will be working with the survey database created in Chapter 4. (If you have not completed the exercises in that chapter, please do so now.)

Remove Elements from a Survey Network Style

In this exercise, you'll modify a Network style and apply the change.

1. Continue working in the Survey.dwg file that was created as part of the Chapter 4 exercises.

2. Switch to the Settings tab of the Toolspace.

3. On the Settings tab, locate the Network Styles branch of the Survey tree.

4. Right-click the Basic entry under the Network Styles branch, and select Copy. The Network Style dialog will appear.

5. Type **Clean** in the Name field, as shown in Figure A.10.

6. Switch to the Display tab of the Network Style dialog.

7. Turn off the lightbulbs next to Network Lines, Direction Lines, and Sideshot Lines as shown in Figure A.11. Click OK to dismiss the dialog. A new style has been created.

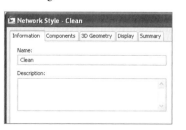

Figure A.10

Name the new style "Clean."

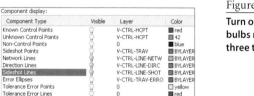

Figure A.11

Turn off the light-bulbs next to the three types of lines.

8. Select the survey network object. Right-click and choose Survey Network Properties from the shortcut menu, as shown in Figure A.12. The Network Properties dialog will appear.

9. Use the Object Style drop-down list to change the object style from Basic to Clean. Click OK to dismiss the dialog. The survey figure lines will turn off and the screen will appear as shown in Figure A.13.

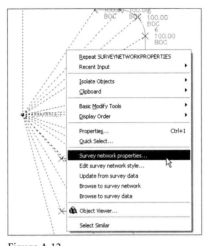

Figure A.12

Select the survey network properties.

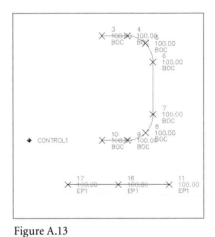

Figure A.13

The Clean figure style removes the network, direction, and sideshot lines.

Editing a Figure

The following short exercise will lead you through editing a survey figure that was incorrectly drawn. In this case, the field crew connected points 6 and 7 when there should have been a curb cut.

1. Continue working in the Survey.dwg file.

2. Zoom in on the BOC figure.

3. Choose Survey → Edit Figure Geometry → Break.

4. At the Select an object to break: prompt, select anywhere on the BOC figure.

5. At the Select second break point or [First point]: prompt, type **F**.

6. At the Specify first break point: prompt, use your node osnap to select point number 6, as shown in Figure A.14.

7. At the Specify second break point: prompt, use your node osnap to select point number 7, as shown in Figure A.14. The figure will break into two pieces, leaving an opening, as shown in Figure A.15.

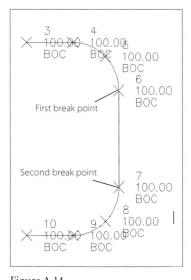

Figure A.14

Select point 6 as the first break point, and select point 7 as the second break point.

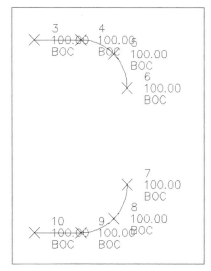

Figure A.15

The survey figure after executing the Break command

8. Select the northern half of the BC figure. Right-click and choose Update Survey Data from Drawing. The edited figure will be written back to the survey database; however, now there is another BOC figure that must be added.

9. Right-click the Figures entry on the Survey tab of the Toolspace. Choose Create Figure from Object, as shown in Figure A.16.

10. At the `Select object from which to create figure:` prompt, choose the southern half of the BOC line. The Create Figure from Object dialog appears.

11. Type **BOC2** in the Name field. Confirm that the checkbox next to Associate Survey Points to Vertices is selected. The Create Figure from Object dialog should now look like Figure A.17.

12. Click OK. A new figure entry appears on the Survey tab of the Toolspace, as shown in Figure A.18.

Figure A.16

Choose the Create Figure from Object option.

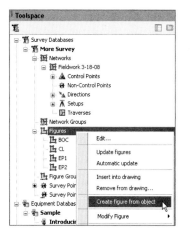

Figure A.17

The Create Figure from Object dialog.

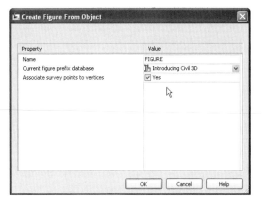

Figure A.18

The new figure is shown on the Survey tab of the Toolspace.

Exporting a Fieldbook

In this exercise, you'll export a fieldbook file for use in another drawing or database.

1. Continue working in the Survey.dwg file.

2. Right-click the Fieldwork 3-18-08 entry on the Survey Toolspace and choose Export Fieldbook, as shown in Figure A.19. The Save As dialog will appear.

3. Navigate to any folder on your computer. Type **MoreFieldbook** in the File Name field, and then click Save. A fieldbook is exported and can be used to create a network in a new survey database or drawing.

Figure A.19

Right-click the desired network entry and choose Export Fieldbook.

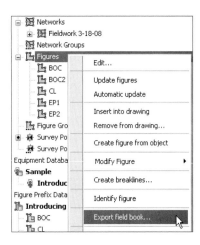

Points

In this collection of exercises, you'll look at four more common methods for creating points and how to renumber existing points.

Creating Points from AutoCAD Objects

In this short exercise, you'll create points along AutoCAD polylines using the point creation tools.

1. Open the More Points.dwg file.

2. Choose Points → Create Points. The Create Points dialog will appear.

3. Click the chevrons button on the far-right side of the Create Points dialog to expand the parameter options.

4. Click the plus sign (+) next to Points Creation to expose additional options.

5. Confirm that Prompt for Elevations is set as None.

6. Confirm that Prompt for Descriptions is set as Automatic. If necessary, use the pull-down list to change the setting from Manual to Automatic.

7. Click inside the field next to Default Description. Change the default description by typing **SPOT**.

8. Click the chevrons button on the far-right side of the Create Points dialog to roll up the parameter options.

9. Click the arrow on the first button from the left (the Miscellaneous Point Creation tools) in the Create Points dialog and choose On Line/Curve.

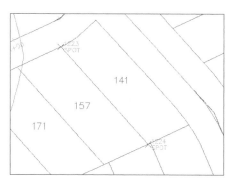

Figure A.20

Points will appear on the polyline.

10. At the Select an arc, line, polyline, lot line or feature line prompt, select the polyline between lots 141 and 157. Points will appear at the start point and endpoint of the lot line, as shown in Figure A.20.

11. At the Select an arc, line, polyline, lot line or feature line prompt, select additional internal lot lines as desired. Press ↵ to exit the command.

Creating Points from a Surface

In this short exercise, you'll create points along a polyline. These points will acquire an elevation from the existing ground surface.

1. Open the More Points2.dwg file, or continue working in the drawing from the previous exercise.

2. Choose Points → Create Points. The Create Points dialog will appear.

3. Click the chevrons button on the far-right side of the Create Points dialog to expand the parameter options.

4. Click the plus sign (+) next to Points Creation to expose additional options.

5. Click inside the Prompt for Elevations field to reveal a pull-down list, and change the setting from None to Manual.

6. Confirm that Prompt for Descriptions is set as Automatic. If necessary, use the pull-down list to change the setting from Manual to Automatic.

7. Confirm that the Default Description is set as SPOT.

8. Click the chevrons button on the far-right side of the Create Points dialog to roll up the parameter options.

9. Click the arrow on the fourth button from the left (the Surface Point Creation tools) in the Create Points dialog and choose Polyline/Contour Vertices.

10. At the Select a surface object: prompt, select any contour from the Existing Ground surface.

11. At the Select a polyline or contour: prompt, select the polyline that represents the road right-of-way. Points will appear at each vertex of the polyline with corresponding surface elevations, as shown in Figure A.21.

Figure A.21

Points appear at each vertex of the polyline.

Creating Points by Incremental Distance and Incremental Elevation

In this exercise, you'll use two of the incremental point creation tools. The first tool creates points between two known elevations at a horizontal interval, and the second tool creates points between two known elevations at a vertical interval.

1. Open the More Points3.dwg file, or continue working in the drawing from the previous exercise.

2. Zoom in on the east lot line for lot 155.

3. Choose Points → Create Points. The Create Points dialog will appear.

4. Click the arrow on the fifth button from the left (the Interpolation Point Creation tools) in the Create Points dialog and choose Incremental Distance.

5. At the `Specify first point or [Entity]:` prompt, click the Point Object button on the Transparent Commands toolbar, and then select the point object at the northern end of the east lot line for lot 155.

6. At the `Specify an elevation for the first control point <826.707'>:` prompt, press ↵ to accept the elevation.

7. At the `Specify second point >> Select point object:` prompt, select the point object at the southern end of the east lot line for lot 155.

8. At the `Specify an elevation for the second control point or [Difference/Slope/Grade] <826.082'>:` prompt, press ↵ to accept the elevation.

9. At the `Distance between points <10.00>:` prompt, type **15** and then press ↵.

10. At the `Specify an offset <0.000>:` prompt, press ↵ to accept the offset. Points will appear every 10′ along the lot line with elevations calculated from the start point and endpoint elevations, as shown in Figure A.22. Press ↵ to exit the command.

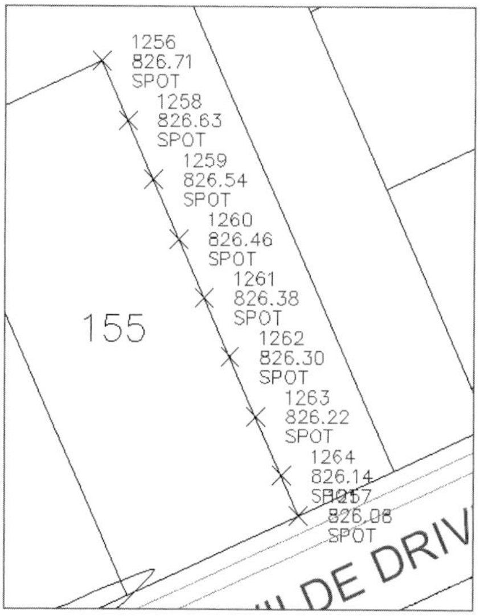

11. Zoom in on the line that runs along the front of lots 158 through 139.

12. Click the arrow on the fifth button from the left (the Interpolation Point Creation tools) in the Create Points dialog and choose Incremental Elevation.

13. At the `Specify first point or [Entity]:` prompt, click the Point Object button on the Transparent Commands toolbar, and then select the point object at the southwest corner of lot 158.

14. At the `Specify an elevation for the first control point <826.104'>:` prompt, press ↵ to accept the elevation.

15. At the `Specify second point >> Select point object:` prompt, select the point object on the frontage of lot 139.

16. At the `Specify an elevation for the second control point or [Difference/Slope/Grade] <827.147'>:` prompt, press ↵ to accept the elevation.

Figure A.22

Points appear between the start point and endpoint at the specified interval.

17. At the Elevation Difference <0.000'>: prompt, type **0.25** and press ↵.

18. At the Specify an offset <0.000>: prompt, press ↵ to accept the offset. Points will appear at 0.25´ vertical intervals along the lot line with elevations calculated from the start point and endpoint elevations, as shown in Figure A.23. Press ↵ to exit the command.

Figure A.23

Points appear between the start point and endpoint at the specified vertical interval.

Creating Points by High/Low Point

In this exercise, you'll create a high point between two points using design grades.

1. Open the More Points4.dwg file, or continue working in the drawing from the previous exercise.

2. Zoom in on the shared lot line between lots 169 and 161.

3. Choose Points ➔ Create Points. The Create Points dialog will appear.

4. Click the arrow on the fourth button from the left (the Surface Point Creation tools) in the Create Points dialog and choose Polyline/Contour Vertices.

5. At the Select a surface object: prompt, select any contour from the Existing Ground surface.

6. At the Select a polyline or contour: prompt, select the polyline between lots 169 and 161. Points will appear at each vertex of the polyline with corresponding surface elevations.

7. Click the arrow on the sixth button from the left (the Slope Point Creation tools) in the Create Points dialog and choose High/Low Point.

8. At the `Specify start point:` prompt, click the Point Object button on the Transparent Commands toolbar, and then select the point object at the southern end of the lot line between lots 169 and 161.

9. At the `Specify end point:` prompt, click the Point Object button on the Transparent Commands toolbar, and then select the point object at the northern end of the lot line between lots 169 and 161.

10. At the `First Slope (run:rise) or [Grade] <Horizontal>:` prompt, type **G** to indicate Grade. Press ⏎.

11. At the `Grade (percent) or [Slope] <0.00>:` prompt, type **20** to indicate a grade of 10 percent, and then press ⏎.

12. At the `Second Grade (percent) or [Slope] <20.00>:` prompt, type **10** to indicate a grade of 10 percent. Press ⏎. A green X will appear giving you a preview of where the high point between the two locations will fall.

13. At the `Add point [Yes/No] <Yes>:` prompt, press ⏎ to accept Yes. A point will appear that represents the horizontal location of a high spot between the two original points using 20 percent and 10 percent grades, as shown in Figure A.24.

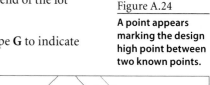

Figure A.24

A point appears marking the design high point between two known points.

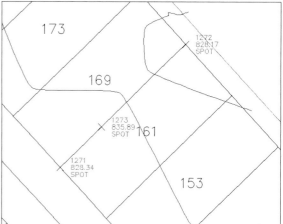

Renumbering Points

In this short exercise, you'll renumber all of the points from the previous exercises.

1. Open the `More Points5.dwg` file, or continue working in the drawing from the previous exercise.

2. Choose Points ➔ Edit Points ➔ Renumber.

3. At the `Points [All/Numbers/Group/Selection] <All>:` prompt, press ⏎ to accept all points.

4. At the `Enter an additive factor for point numbers:` prompt, type **-1000**. All of the point numbers in the drawing will change by negative one thousand—for example, point number 1245 will become point number 245.

Parcels

In these exercises, you'll edit parcel segments, and then explore a number of options you might need for labeling your parcel maps.

Editing Rear Lot Lines

In this exercise, you will edit parcel segments to eliminate arcs.

1. Open the More Parcels.dwg file.

2. Zoom in on lots 28 through 30. Note that lots 27, 28, and 29 have arcs in their rear segments, as shown in Figure A.25.

3. Use your endpoint osnap to draw a polyline like the one shown in Figure A.26.

4. Choose Parcels → Create Parcel from Objects. The Create Parcel from Objects dialog will appear.

Figure A.25

Lots 27, 28, and 29 have curved rear segments.

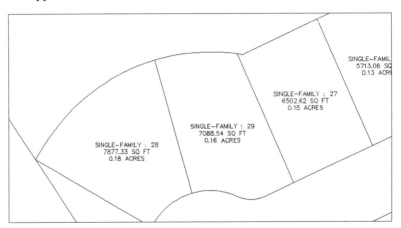

Figure A.26

Draw a polyline that will become rear parcel segments.

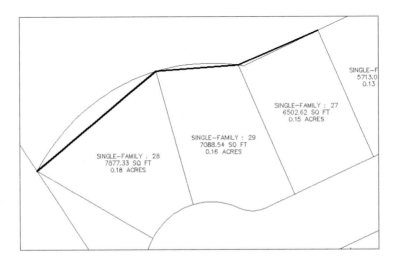

5. Use the Parcel Style drop-drown list to choose Single Family.

6. Use the Area Label Style drop-down list to choose Number Only.

7. Click OK. Three small parcels are formed at the rear of lots 27, 28, and 29.

8. Choose Parcels → Edit Parcel → Edit Parcel Segments.

9. At the Select lot line: prompt, select any parcel segment in the drawing. The Parcel Layout Tools dialog will appear.

10. Click the Delete Sub-entity button from the Parcel Layout Tools as shown in Figure A.27.

11. At the Select subentity to remove: prompt, select each arc segment from the original rear lot line one by one until they are all deleted. The original lots will now have straight rear lot lines as shown in Figure A.28.

Replacing Multiple Segment Labels

In this short exercise, you'll change parcel line segment labels from a detailed label style to a simple length-only style.

1. Open the More Parcels2.dwg file, or continue working in your drawing from the previous exercise.

2. Choose Parcels → Add Parcel Labels → Add Parcel Labels. The Add Labels dialog will appear.

3. Use the Label Type pull-down list to choose Replace Multiple Segment.

4. Use the Line Label Style pull-down list to choose Distance, as shown in Figure A.29.

5. Click Add.

6. At the Select parcel to be labeled by click on area label: prompt, select the Single-Family: 1 parcel in the drawing. The line segment labels will change from a length and bearing label to a length-only label.

7. Continue selecting all of the parcels from Single-Family: 2 through Single Family: 21. Labels will appear as shown in Figure A.30.

Figure A.27

Click the Delete Sub-entity button.

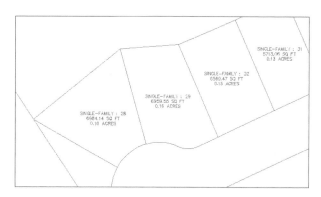

Figure A.28

The curved segments are deleted, leaving the line segments to serve as the rear lot lines.

Figure A.29

Change the line label style to Distance.

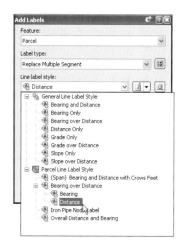

Figure A.30

New distance labels applied to a series of parcels

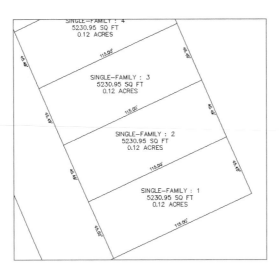

Figure A.30

New distance labels applied to a series of parcels

Replacing Multiple Area Labels

In this short exercise, you'll swap a simple Number Only parcel area label for the more detailed Name and Area label.

1. Open the More Parcels3.dwg file, or continue working in your drawing from the previous exercise.

2. Choose Parcels → Add Parcel Labels → Add Parcel Labels. The Add Labels dialog will appear.

3. Use the Label Type pull-down list to choose Replace Area.

4. Use the Area Label Style pull-down list to choose Parcel Number.

5. Click Add.

6. At the Select parcel area selection label or [sTartpoint/Polylines/aLL/Site]: prompt, type **t** for sTart-point and then press ↵.

7. At the Start point: prompt, click inside Single-Family: 1.

8. At the End point: prompt, click inside Single-Family: 10, and then click inside Single-Family: 21. Press ↵ to end the command. The parcel labels will change to Number Only, as shown in Figure A.31.

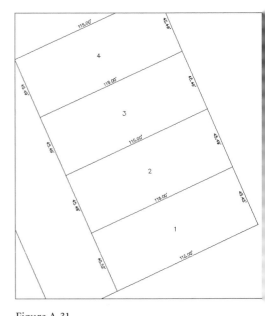

Figure A.31

The Parcel Area labels displayed as Number Only

Labeling Overall Distance

In this short exercise, you'll add an overall distance label to a continuous rear lot line.

1. Open the `More Parcels4.dwg` file, or continue working in your drawing from the previous exercise.

2. Choose Parcels ➔ Add Parcel Labels ➔ Add Parcel Labels. The Add Labels dialog will appear.

3. Use the Label Type pull-down list to choose Single Segment.

4. Use the Line Label Style pull-down list to choose Overall Distance and Bearing.

5. Click Add.

6. At the `Select point on entity:` prompt, click the east lot line for lot 5. A label will appear that labels the full length of the segment that spans from lot 1 through lot 10, as shown in Figure A.32. Continue labeling by clicking the east lot line for lot 14.

7. Press ↵ to end the command.

Figure A.32

The overall distance is labeled.

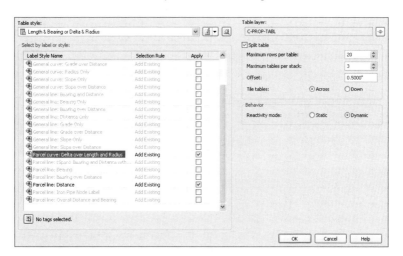

Creating a Segment Table

In this short exercise, you'll create a segment table for all labeled parcel line and curve segments.

1. Open the `More Parcels5.dwg` file, or continue working in your drawing from the previous exercise.

2. Choose Parcels ➔ Add Tables ➔ Add Segments. The Table Creation dialog will appear.

3. Check the Apply boxes next to the Parcel Curve: Delta over Length and Radius label style and the Parcel Line: Distance label style, as shown in Figure A.33. Click OK.

Figure A.33

Check the Apply box next to the label styles that are currently labeling segments in the drawing.

4. At the Select upper left corner: prompt, click in the drawing somewhere to the right of the site plan. A Parcel Line and Curve Table will appear, similar to Figure A.34.

5. Zoom in on lot 21 and note that all of the segment labels have converted to tags, as shown in Figure A.35.

Parcel Line and Curve Table			
Line #/Curve #	Length	Bearing/Delta	Radius
C1	25.28	4.98	290.75
C2	12.85	2.53	290.75
C3	53.22	7.51	405.75
C4	53.22	7.51	405.75
C5	17.60	3.47	290.75
C6	20.54	4.05	290.75
C7	53.22	7.51	405.75
C8	7.86	1.55	290.75
C9	30.27	5.97	290.75
C10	41.72	5.89	405.75
C11	7.12	2.72	150.00
C12	42.50	8.37	290.75
C13	45.49	17.37	150.00
C14	50.73	10.00	290.75
C15	1.45	0.29	290.75
C16	30.96	11.83	150.00
C17	44.56	12.76	200.00
C18	21.95	6.29	200.00
L1	115.00	N43° 08' 45.26"E	
L2	115.00	N35° 37' 51.96"E	

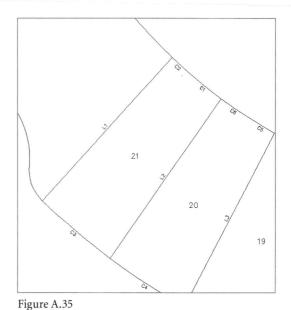

Figure A.34

The segment table

Figure A.35

The segment labels convert to tags.

Surfaces

In this collection of exercises, you'll look at another method of creating surfaces, using the simplify tools, and adding labels in a grid arrangement.

Creating Surfaces from DEM Data

In Chapter 7, "Surfaces," you looked at creating a surface from Google Earth and point data. In this exercise, you'll create a new surface from a DEM file. DEM files are commonly available from government agencies and represent large area topographic information in a grid format.

1. Start a new blank drawing from the NCS Imperial Extended template that ships with Civil 3D.

2. Switch to the Settings tab of Toolspace, right-click on the drawing name, and select Drawing Settings. Set the coordinate system as shown in Figure A.36 via the Drawing Settings dialog, and click OK. The coordinate system of the DEM file that you will import will be set to match the coordinate system of our drawing.

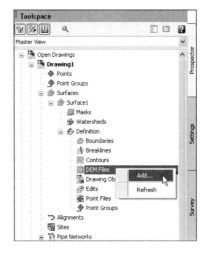

Civil 3D coordinate settings for DEM import

3. In Prospector, right-click the Surfaces collection and select the Create Surface option. The Create Surface dialog appears.

4. Accept the options in the dialog, and click OK to create the surface. This surface is added as Surface 1 to the Surfaces collection.

5. Expand the Surfaces → Surface 1 → Definition branch, as shown in Figure A.37.

6. Right-click DEM Files and select the Add option (see Figure A.37). The Add DEM File dialog appears.

7. Navigate to the `McKinneyWest.DEM` file and click Open.

8. Set the values in the DEM File Properties dialog as shown in Figure A.38, and then click OK. This translates the DEM's coordinate system to the drawing's coordinate system.

9. Right-click Surface 1 in Prospector and select Surface Properties. (You could also right-click Surface 1 in Prospector and select Zoom To, and then right-click on

Figure A.37

Adding DEM data to a surface

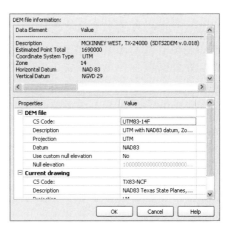

Figure A.38

Setting the `McKinney West.DEM` file properties

the surface in your drawing and select Surface Properties.) The Surface Properties dialog appears.

10. On the Information tab, change the Name field to **McKinney W**. Close the dialog.

Simplifying Surfaces

In this exercise, you'll use a new feature in Civil 3D 2009—the Surface Simplify tools—to reduce the file size and point data of a surface created from aerial information.

1. Open the More Surfaces1.dwg file. The surface statistics for the Aerial Points surface are shown in Figure A.39.

2. Within Prospector, expand Surfaces → Aerial Points → Definition.

3. Right-click Edits and select Simplify Surface to display the Simplify Surface Wizard.

4. Select the Point Removal radio button as shown in Figure A.40, and then click Next to move to the Region Options.

Figure A.39

Aerial Points surface statistics before simplification

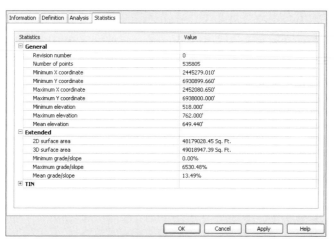

Figure A.40

The Simplify Surfaces dialog

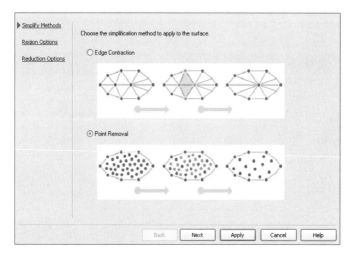

5. Leave the Region Option set to Use Existing Surface Border. There are also options for selecting areas with a window or polygon, as well as selecting based on an existing CAD element. Click Next to move to the Reduction Options.

6. Set the Percentage of Points to Remove to 10 percent, and then uncheck the Maximum Change in Elevation option. This value is the maximum allowed change between the surface elevation at any point before and after the Simplify process has run.

7. Click Apply. The program will process this calculation and display a Total Points Removed number as shown in Figure A.41. You can adjust the slider or toggle on the Maximum Change in Elevation button to experiment with different values.

8. Click Finish to dismiss the wizard and fully commit to the Simplify edit.

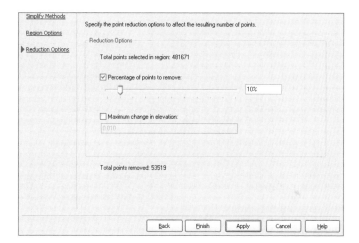

Figure A.41

Reduction Options in the Simplify Surface Wizard

Surface Volume Grid Labels

In this exercise, you'll add grid labels to a volume surface.

1. Open the More Surfaces2.dwg file.

2. Select Surfaces → Add Surface Labels → Spot Elevations on Grid.

3. Click one of the red or green cut-fill contours to pick the Volume surface.

4. Pick a point in the southwest of the surface to set a base point for the grid.

5. Press ↵ to set the grid rotation to 0.

6. Enter **25** at the command line to set the X spacing.

7. Enter **25** at the command line to set the Y spacing.

8. Click to the northeast of the surface to set the area for the labels.

9. Verify that the preview box contains the Volume surface, and then press ⏎ at the command line to continue.

10. Wait a few moments as Civil 3D generates all the labels you just specified. When it's finished, your drawing should look similar to Figure A.42.

Figure A.42

Volume surface with grid labels

Alignments

In this collection of exercises, you'll look at another method of creating alignments, and then explore a number of options for editing the stationing and geometry of the alignment.

Converting a Line to an Alignment

In this short exercise, you'll create an alignment from existing linework. However, this linework won't be a polyline; instead, it will be a simple line. You just have to use some built-in right-click functionality to convert the street to a polyline first.

1. Open the More Alignments.dwg file.

2. Zoom in on the line at the subdivision entrance representing another road, as shown in Figure A.43.

3. Select the line and right-click to display the shortcut menu.

4. Select Convert to Polyline.

5. Select Alignments → Convert Alignment from Polyline, and then select the newly converted polyline to display the Create Alignment – From Polyline dialog.

6. Change the Name: to **Entrance**, and then click OK to dismiss the dialog. Your drawing should look like Figure A.44.

Figure A.43

The entrance road centerline

Figure A.44

Converted Entrance road alignment

Changing the Starting Station

In this exercise, you'll use a quick editing tool to change the starting station of an alignment.

1. Continue using the More Alignments1.dwg file.

2. Select the Entrance road alignment you created in the previous exercise, right-click, and select Alignment Properties from the shortcut menu.

3. Change to the Station Control tab.

4. Change the Station to **5+35** (as shown in the circled area in Figure A.45). This matches up the stationing with an existing road on adjacent development. An alert will appear warning you that a change in stationing could and will affect other items. Click OK to close this warning.

5. Click OK to close the dialog. Your screen should look like Figure A.46.

Figure A.45

The Station Control tab in the Alignment Properties dialog

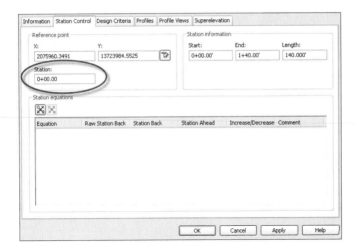

Figure A.45

The Station Control tab in the Alignment Properties dialog

Figure A.46

Entrance road with a new start station

Reversing the Alignment Direction

In this exercise, you'll use the built-in tool to reverse the Parker Place alignment so you can see how quick and easy it is to change alignment direction.

1. Continue using the More Alignments1.dwg file.

2. Select Alignments → Reverse Alignment Direction.

3. Select the Parker Place alignment (it's the longest one, running north-south), and a warning will appear alerting you to the fact that reversing will remove station equations.

4. Click OK to dismiss the warning.

5. Pan to the southern end. The stationing should be reversed, reflecting a new starting point on the north end of the alignment, as shown in Figure A.47.

Figure A.47

Parker Place stationing after station reversal

Editing Individual Alignment Segment Properties

In this exercise, you'll examine the concept of component-level editing, using the Alignment Layout Parameters dialog to make changes to an individual component piece within an alignment.

1. Open the More Alignments2.dwg file.

2. Zoom to Maalouf Mile (the only alignment in the drawing), and select it to activate the grips.

3. Right-click and select Edit Alignment Geometry from the context menu. The Alignment Layout Tools toolbar appears.

4. Select the Sub-entity Editor tool, shown in Figure A.48, to open the Alignment Layout Parameters dialog.

5. Select the Pick Sub-entity tool (just to the left of the Sub-entity Editor tool) on the Alignment Layout Tools toolbar.

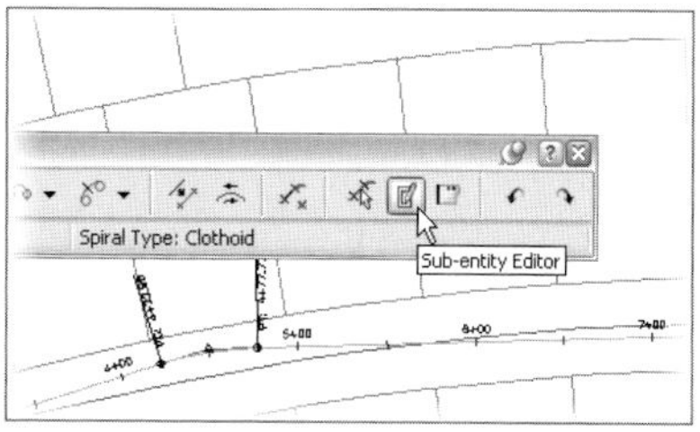

Figure A.48

The Sub-entity Editor tool

6. Pick the first curve on the southwest corner of the site to display its properties in the Alignment Layout Parameters dialog. The properties are mostly grayed out, which indicates that the values for this curve are being derived from other parameters. This curve was drawn so that it would be tangent from the end of a line and would pass through a point in space. These parameters control every other aspect of the curve.

7. Zoom in and pick the second curve in the reverse curve. Notice that the Radius field is now black (see Figure A.49) and is available for editing.

Figure A.49

The Alignment
Layout Parameters
toolbar for the first
curve (on the left)
and the second
curve (on the right)
on Maalouf Mile

8. Change the value in the Radius field to **2000** and watch the screen update. This value is too far from the original design intent to be a valid alternative.

9. Change the value in the Radius field to **1400** and again watch the update. This value is closer to the design and is acceptable.

10. Close the Alignment Layout Parameters dialog and the Alignments Layout Tools toolbar.

Removing and Adding Alignment Components

In this exercise, you'll take out the reverse curve using tools to remove one component and add another pair of components back in to the alignment.

1. Continue using or open the More Alignments 2.dwg file.

2. Zoom to and select Rose Drive to activate the grips.

3. Right-click and select Edit Alignment Geometry. The Alignment Layout Tools toolbar appears.

4. Select the Delete Sub-entity tool as shown in Figure A.50.

Figure A.50

The Delete Sub-
entity Tool on the
Alignment Layout
toolbar

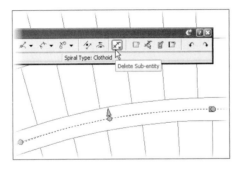

5. Pick the two curves in Maalouf Mile to remove them. Note that the last tangent is still part of the alignment—it just isn't connected.

6. Select the Draw Fixed Line - Two Points tool, and snap to the center of the two circles shown in Figure A.51. Be sure to pick from left to right to get the direction correct.

7. Click the down arrow next to Add Fixed Curve - Three Points, and select the Free Curve Fillet (Between Two Entities, Radius) option.

8. Pick the line on the western edge, and then pick the left end of the short line you just created.

9. Press ↵ at the command line to accept the option of Lessthan180 for the curve solution angle.

10. Enter **200**↵ at the command line to set the radius. The arc should be placed as shown in Figure A.52.

11. Repeat steps 7 through 10 to complete the other curve (use a radius of 1380), and then connect the full alignment.

12. When you're finished, close the Alignment Layout Tools toolbar. Your alignment should look like Figure A.53.

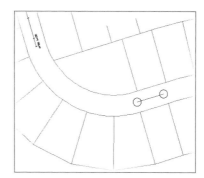

Figure A.51

After adding a new tangent to the Maalouf Mile alignment

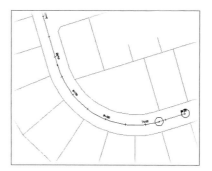

Figure A.52

Adding an arc to the alignment

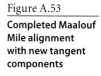

Figure A.53

Completed Maalouf Mile alignment with new tangent components

Creating an Alignment Table

In this exercise, you will create an alignment segment table in lieu of direct labeling. This can be helpful in making dense drawings a little easier to read.

1. Open the More Alignments 3.dwg file.

2. Select Alignments → Add Alignment Labels → Add Alignment Labels to open the Add Labels dialog.

3. In the Label Type field, select Multiple Segment from the drop-down list. With this, you'll click the alignment one time, and every subcomponent will be labeled with the style selected here.

4. Verify that the Line Label Style field is set to Bearing Over Distance and that the Curve Label Style is set to Delta over Length and Radius. (You won't be stuck with these labels—you just need them for selecting elements later.)

5. Click Add, and select the alignment.

6. Click Close to close the Add Labels dialog.

7. Select Alignments → Add Tables → Add Segments to display the Alignment Table Creation dialog shown in Figure A.54.

8. Click OK to close the dialog.

9. Pick a point somewhere in the drawing space to place the table.

Figure A.54

The Alignment Table Creation dialog

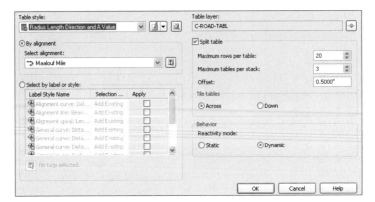

Profiles

In this series of exercises, you'll look at some alternative creation methods and then some more labeling and profile view options.

Creating a Profile Layout by Entity

Similar to using fixed, floating, and free alignment components, profiles can be made with these relationships. In this exercise, you'll explore this additional method of creating a profile.

1. Open the More Profiles 1.dwg file.

2. From the main menu, choose Profiles → Create Profile by Layout.

3. Pick a grid line on the Alignment - (1) profile view to display the Create Profile dialog.

4. Click OK to accept the default settings and open the Profile Layout Tools toolbar.

5. Click the down arrow next to the Draw Fixed Tangent by Two Points tool, and select the Fixed Tangent (Two Points) option, as shown in Figure A.55.

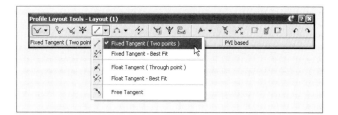

Figure A.55

Selecting the Fixed Tangent (Two Points) tool on the Profile Layout Tools toolbar

6. Using a center osnap, pick the circle on the left edge of the profile view. A rubber-banding line will appear.

7. Using a center osnap, pick the circle located at approximately station 2+30. A tangent will be drawn between these two circles.

8. Using a center osnap, pick the circle located at approximately 8+00. Another rubber-banding line appears.

9. Using a center osnap, pick the circle located on the right edge of the profile view. A second tangent will be drawn. Right-click to exit the Fixed Line (Two Points) command, and your drawing should look like Figure A.56. Note that there are no station labels on the second tangent, because it is not yet tied to the first segment. The labeling begins at station 0 +00 and continues until there is a break, as there was at the end of the first tangent.

Figure A.56

Layout profile with two tangents drawn

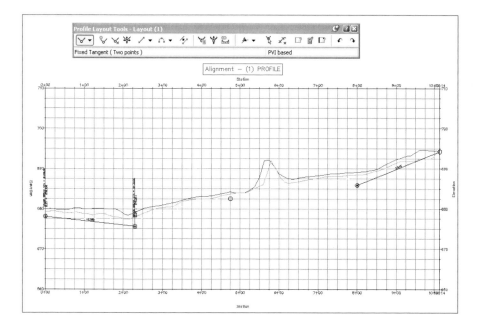

10. Select the down arrow next to the Draw Fixed Parabola by Three Points tool on the Profile Layout Tools toolbar. Choose the More Fixed Vertical Curves → Fixed Vertical Curve (Entity End, Through Point) option, as shown in Figure A.57.

11. Pick the left tangent to attach the fixed vertical curve. (Remember to pick the tangent line and not the end circle.) A rubberbanding line appears.

12. Using a center osnap, select the circle located at approximately station 4+50.

13. Right-click to exit the Fixed Vertical Curve (Entity End, Through Point) command. Your drawing should look like Figure A.58.

14. Click the down arrow next to the Draw Fixed Tangent by Two Points tool, and select the Float Tangent (Through Point) option as shown in Figure A.59.

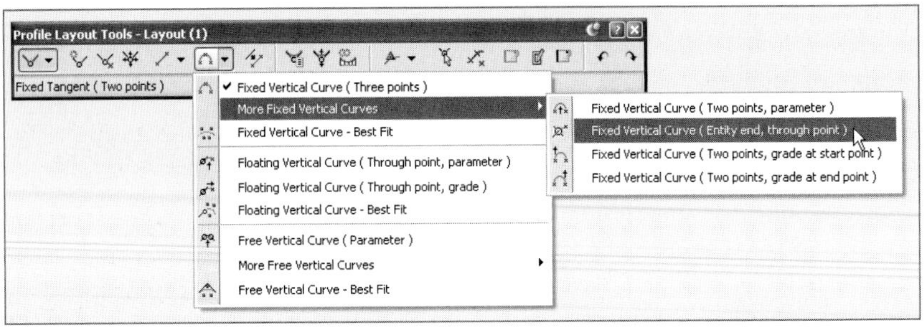

Figure A.57

The Fixed Vertical Curve (Entity End, Through Point) tool on the Profile Layout Tools toolbar

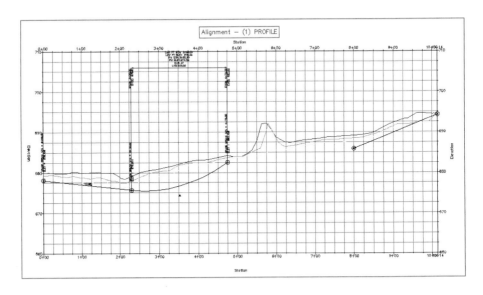

Figure A.58

Completed curve from the entity end

Figure A.59

Selecting the Float Tangent (Through Point) tool on the Profile Layout Tools toolbar

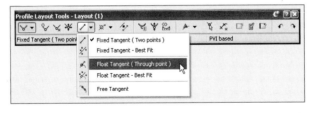

15. Pick the curve you just created, and then pick the beginning of the tangent you created on the far right.

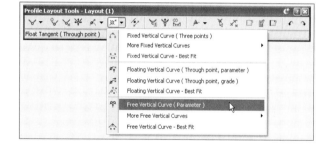

Figure A.60

Selecting the Free Vertical Curve (Parameter) tool on the Profile Layout Tools toolbar

16. Click the down arrow next to the tool labeled Draw Fixed Parabola Tangential to End of an Entity and Passing through a Point, and then select the Free Vertical Curve (Parameter) option as shown in Figure A.60.

17. Pick the tangent just created, and then pick the tangent that ends your layout profile.

18. Enter 150 ↵ at the command line for a curve length.

19. Right-click to complete the profile, and close the Profile Layout Tools toolbar by clicking on the red X button. Your drawing should look like Figure A.61.

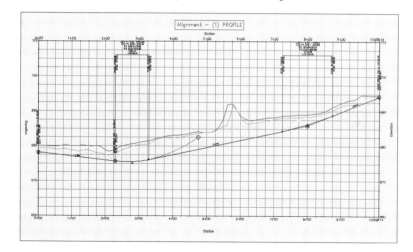

Figure A.61

Completed layout profile created with entity tools

Creating a Layout Profile from a File

Profiles can also be made from text files. This can be helpful for re-creating profile information from older plans or importing from other data sources. You'll import a file to create a layout profile in this exercise.

Figure A.62

Profile defined in a text file

1. Open the file Profile1.txt in Notepad. Civil 3D has a very specific format. Each line is a PVI definition (station and elevation). Curve information is an optional third bit of data on any line. This file is shown in Figure A.62.

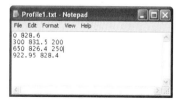

2. Open the More Profiles2.dwg file.

3. From the main menu, choose Profiles → Create Profile from File.

4. Select the TextProfile.txt file and click Open. The Create Profile dialog appears.

5. In the dialog, set the alignment drop-down list to Parker Place.

6. Set the Profile Style to Layout.

7. Set the Profile Label Set list box to Complete Label Set.

8. Click OK. Your drawing should look like Figure A.63.

Figure A.63

**A completed profile
created from a file**

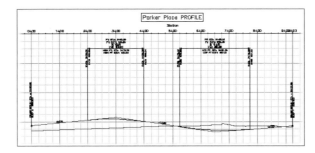

Labeling Stations Along a Profile

Labeling along the profile at major, minor, and alignment geometry points allows the user to insert labels similar to a horizontal alignment. In this exercise, you modify a style to reflect a plan-readable approach and remove the stationing from the first and last points along the profile.

1. Open the More Profiles 3.dwg file.

2. Pick the layout profile, right-click, and select the Edit Labels option to display the Profile Labels dialog.

3. Uncheck the Start and End station checkboxes for the Major Stations label.

4. Change the value for the Start Station to **50** and the value of the End Station to **950**, as shown in Figure A.64.

Figure A.64

**Modifying the val-
ues of the starting
and ending stations
for the major labels**

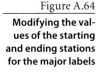

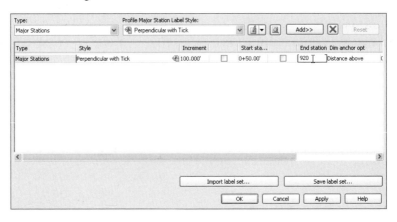

5. Click the icon in the Style field to display the Pick Label Style dialog.

6. On the button to the right of the Style list box, click the down arrow and select the Edit Current Selection option. The Label Style Composer dialog appears.

7. On the General tab, change the value of the Orientation Reference to View, as shown in Figure A.65.

8. Click OK to close the Label Style Composer dialog. Click OK again to close the Pick Label Style dialog.

9. Click OK to close the Profile Labels dialog. Instead of each station label being oriented so that it is perpendicular to the profile at the station, all station labels are now oriented vertically along the top of the profile at the station.

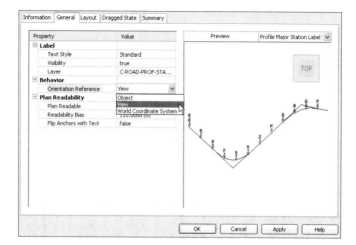

Figure A.65

Changing the orientation reference of a label

Creating Gapped Profile Views

Profile views must often be limited in length and height to fit a given sheet size. Gapped views are a way to show the entire length and height of the profile, by breaking the profile into different sections with gaps (spaces) between each view. In this exercise, you use a variation of the Create Profile View Wizard to create gapped views automatically.

1. Open the Profile View 4.dwg file.

2. From the main menu, select Profiles → Create Multiple Profile Views to display the Create Multiple Profile Views Wizard.

3. In the Select Alignment drop-down list, select Parker Place, and in the Profile View Style drop-down list, select the Full Grid option, as shown in Figure A.66. Click Next.

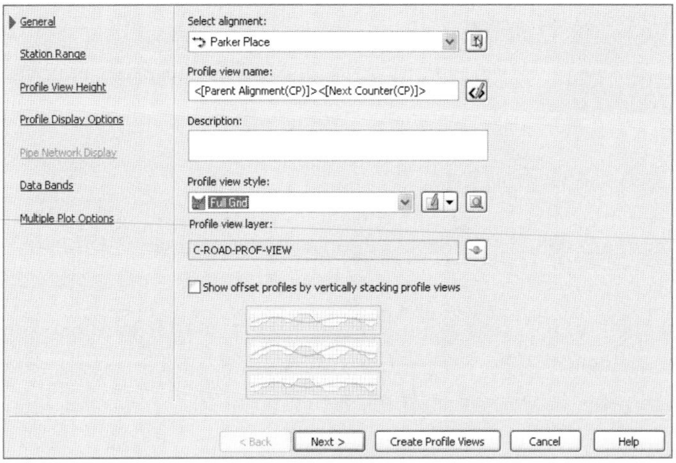

Figure A.66

**The Create Multiple
Profile Views Wizard**

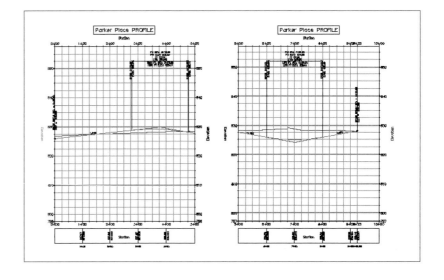

4. In the Station Range area, make sure the Automatic option is selected. This area
   is also where the Length of Each View is set. Change the Length value to **500**.
   Click Next.

5. Turn on the User Specified radio button for Profile View Height and set the value
   to **60**. Click Next.

6. Scroll to the right in the Specify Profile Display Options until you see the Labels
   column. Click the Labels cell for the top row (the Existing Ground profile) to
   display the Pick Profile Label Set dialog. Set the drop-down list to _No Labels
   and click OK.

7. Click the Create Profile Views button, and then pick a point on screen to create a
   view similar to Figure A.67.

Figure A.67

**The gapped profile
views of the Parker
Place alignment**

Assemblies and Corridors

In these exercises, you'll create a new assembly, and then model a cul-de-sac, build a surface boundary, and hatch the design.

Building a Main Road Assembly

The following exercise will give you hands-on experience building assemblies.

1. Open the More Corridors1.dwg file.

2. Choose Corridors → Create Assembly. The Create Assembly dialog opens.

3. Enter **Main Road** in the Name text box. Make sure the Assembly Style text box is set to Basic and the Code Set Style text box is set to All Codes. Click OK.

4. Pick a location in your drawing for the assembly near the other assemblies that are in the drawing.

5. Choose Corridors → Subassembly Tool Palettes, and locate the Imperial-Roadway tool palette. Position the palette on your screen so that you can clearly see the assembly baseline.

6. Click the LaneOutsideSuper button on the tool palette. The AutoCAD Properties palette will appear. Position the palette on your screen so that you can clearly see both the assembly baseline and the Imperial-Roadway tool palette.

7. Locate the Advanced section on the Design tab of the AutoCAD Properties palette. This section will list the LaneOutsideSuper parameters. Make sure the Side parameter says Right, and change the Width parameter to **15′**. This will prepare you to place a 15′-wide lane on the right side of the assembly.

8. Note that the command line states Select marker point within assembly or [RETURN for Detached]. Click the assembly on the right side of the center point marker to place a 15′-wide lane on the right side of the assembly, as shown in Figure A.68.

Figure A.68

Add a LaneOutsideSuper on the right side of the assembly.

9. Return to the AutoCAD Properties palette and change the Side parameter to Left. Click the assembly on the left side of the center point marker to place a 15′ lane on the left side of the assembly. (Be sure to click the assembly baseline marker itself and not any part of the right LaneOutsideSuper.) If you lost the AutoCAD Properties palette, you can resume the LaneOutsideSuper subassembly placement by clicking the LaneOutsideSuper button on your tool palette and then changing the Width parameter again.

10. Switch to the Imperial-Structures tool palette. Click the UrbanCurbGutterValley1 button on the tool palette. The Advanced section of the AutoCAD Properties Palette Design tab will list the UrbanCurbGutterValley1 parameters. Change the Side

parameter to Right. Note that the Insertion Point parameter has been established at the Gutter Edge, meaning the curb will attach to your lane at the desired gutter edge location. This would typically be at the edge of the pavement.

11. Note that the command line states Select marker point within assembly or [RETURN for Detached]. Click the circular point marker on the right LaneOutsideSuper subassembly that represents the edge of the pavement to place an UrbanCurbGutterValley1 subassembly at the edge of the pavement (see Figure A.69). If you misplace your UrbanCurbGutterValley1, simply use the AutoCAD Erase command to erase the misplaced subassembly and return to step 10.

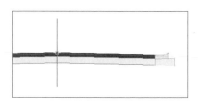

Figure A.69

The UrbanCurbGutterValley1 subassembly placed on the LaneOutsideSuper subassembly

12. Change the Side parameter on the AutoCAD Properties palette to Left. Click the circular point marker on the left of the LaneOutsideSuper subassembly that represents the edge of the pavement.

13. Switch to the Imperial-Generic tool palette. Click the LinkWidthAndSlope button on the tool palette. In the Advanced section of the Design tab on the AutoCAD Properties palette, change the Side parameter to Right, the Width parameter to **4.5′**, and slope parameters to **2.00** percent.

14. Note that the command line states Select marker point within assembly or [RETURN for Detached]. Click the circular point marker on the right UrbanCurbGutterValley1 subassembly that represents the top rear of the curb to attach the LinkWidthAndSlope subassembly (see Figure A.70). If you misplace the subassembly, use the AutoCAD Erase command to erase the misplaced subassembly and return to step 13.

15. Change the Side parameter on the AutoCAD Properties palette to Left. Click the circular point marker on the right of the UrbanCurbGutterValley1 subassembly that represents the top rear of the curb. The finished assembly will look like Figure A.71.

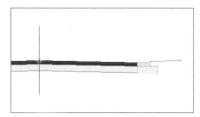

Figure A.70

The LinkWidthAndSlope subassembly placed on the LaneOutsideSuper subassembly

Figure A.71

The completed Main Road assembly

Building a Cul-De-Sac Assembly

In this exercise, you'll build the assembly required for modeling a cul-de-sac.

1. Open the More Corridors2.dwg file, or continue working in your drawing from the previous exercise.

2. Zoom in on the assemblies, and locate the Intersection or Cul-de-Sac assembly. Note that the assembly does not yet include a lane, as shown in Figure A.72.

3. Choose Corridors → Subassembly Tool Palettes, and locate the Imperial-Roadway tool palette. Position the palette on your screen so that you can clearly see the assembly baseline.

4. Click the LaneOutsideSuper button on the tool palette, as shown in Figure A.73. The AutoCAD Properties palette will appear. Position the palette on your screen so that you can clearly see both the assembly baseline and the Imperial-Roadway tool palette.

5. Add the LaneOutsideSuper subassembly to the left side of the assembly. The completed assembly will look like Figure A.74.

Modeling a Cul-de-Sac Corridor

In this exercise, you'll model a cul-de-sac using different regions and baselines as part of the process.

1. Open the More Corridors2.dwg file. Note that there is an alignment that follows the EOP for a cul-de-sac, as well as a corresponding profile. There is also a corridor, a corridor surface, a few assemblies, and some Intersection EOP labels, as shown in Figure A.75.

Figure A.72

The partially completed Cul-de-Sac assembly

Figure A.73

The LaneOutsideSuper button on the Imperial-Roadway tool palette.

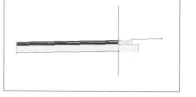

Figure A.74

The completed Cul-de-Sac assembly

Figure A.75

The drawing contains a corridor, corridor surface, alignments, profiles, and some labels.

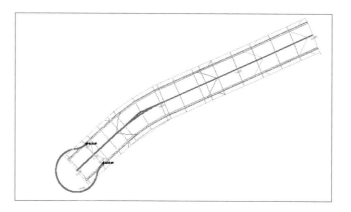

2. Select the corridor. Grab the diamond-shaped grip that corresponds with station 3+27.75. Using your endpoint osnap, stretch the grip to the station corresponding to the cul-de-sac point of curvature as shown in Figure A.76.

3. Select the corridor, right-click, and choose Rebuild Corridor. The resulting corridor will look like Figure A.77.

Figure A.76

Use your endpoint osnap to line up the diamond-shaped grip with the cul-de-sac point of curvature.

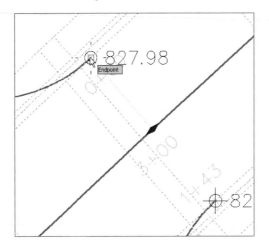

Figure A.77

When the corridor is rebuilt, it will stop at the cul-de-sac point of curvature.

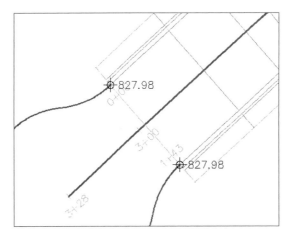

4. Zoom over to the cul-de-sac in plan view. Select the corridor, right-click, and choose Corridor Properties. In the Corridor Properties dialog, switch to the Parameters tab.

5. Click Add Baseline. Select Cul-de-Sac EOP as the baseline alignment in the Pick Horizontal Alignment dialog. Click OK.

6. Click in the Profile field. Select Cul-de-Sac EOP FG as the baseline profile in the Select a Profile dialog. Click OK.

7. Right-click the baseline you just created, and select Add Region. Select the Intersection or Cul de Sac Assembly in the Pick an Assembly dialog. Click OK.

8. Expand your baseline to see the new region you just created, as shown in Figure A.78.

Figure A.78

A new baseline and new region are created.

9. Click the Frequency button for your region. In the Frequency to Apply to Assemblies dialog, set all the frequency intervals to **5′**, and change the At Profile High/Low Points to Yes. Click OK.

10. Click the Target button for your region. In the Target Mapping dialog, click inside the Width Alignment field. The Set Width or Offset Target dialog will appear.

11. Select the Marie Court alignment, and then press the Add>> button. The Marie Court alignment will appear in the Selected Entities to Target area of the dialog, as shown in Figure A.79. Click OK.

12. Click in the Outside Elevation Profile field. The Set Slope or Elevation Target dialog will appear.

13. Select the Marie Court alignment from the drop-down list, select the Marie Court FG profile, and press the Add>> button. The Marie Court FG profile entry will appear in the Selected Entities to Target area of the dialog, as shown in Figure A.80. Click OK.

14. Click OK to dismiss the Target Mapping dialog.

15. Click OK to dismiss the Corridor Properties dialog. The corridor will rebuild and reflect the addition of the cul-de-sac, as shown in Figure A.81.

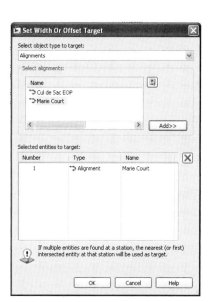

Figure A.79

The Set Width or Offset Target dialog

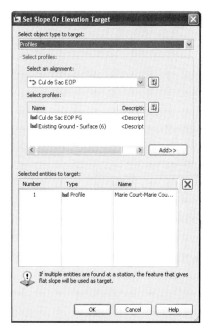

Figure A.80

The Set Slope or Elevation Target dialog

Figure A.81

The corridor is
rebuilt to reflect
the new baselines,
regions, targets,
and frequencies.

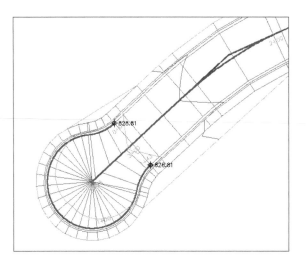

Adding an Interactive Corridor Surface Boundary

In this exercise, you'll trace the boundary of a corridor surface using an interactive jig to guide your selections.

1. Open the More Corridors3.dwg file, or continue working in your drawing from the previous exercise.

2. Pick your corridor surface in the drawing. Right-click and choose Surface Properties. The Surface Properties dialog opens. Change the Surface Style to No Display so that you don't accidentally pick it when choosing a corridor boundary. Click OK to dismiss the Surface Properties dialog.

3. Select the corridor, right-click, and choose Corridor Properties. The Corridor Properties dialog appears.

4. Switch to the Boundaries tab of the Corridor Properties dialog.

5. Pick the corridor surface entry, right-click, and choose Add Interactively as in Figure A.82.

Figure A.82

Select the surface
entry, right-click,
and choose Add
Interactively.

6. Zoom down to the Start Station of Marie Court. The command line will prompt you `To define boundary, select the first point on a corridor feature line.` Use your endpoint osnap to pick the leftmost feature line on the corridor. The command line will then prompt you to `Select next point on this feature line or click on another feature line or [Undo/Close].`

7. Move your mouse and notice that a red jig follows your cursor along the chosen feature line, as shown in Figure A.83. It will continue to follow you until the end of a region.

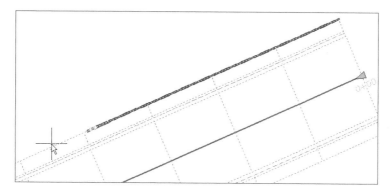

Figure A.83

A red jig will trace the proposed boundary path.

8. When you reach the next region, simply pick the leftmost feature line in that region. Continue the process around the entire corridor. As you progress, the jig will continue to follow your cursor and picks.

9. When you come back to the Start Station of Marie Court, type **C** to close the boundary. The Boundaries tab of the Corridor Properties dialog will return.

10. Click OK to dismiss the dialog, and your corridor will automatically rebuild, along with your corridor surface.

11. Select your corridor surface under the Surfaces branch in Prospector. Right-click and choose Surface Properties. The Surface Properties dialog opens. Change the Surface Style to Contours 1′ And 5′ (Design), and click OK. Click OK to dismiss the Surface Properties dialog.

12. Note that your surface is now limited to the area inside the interactive boundary. Temporarily freeze the C-ROAD-CORR layer to see the results, as shown in Figure A.84.

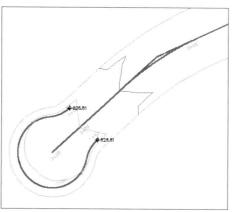

Figure A.84

The finished corridor surface contours

Using a Hatch Code Set Style

In this exercise, you will hatch a corridor based on the pieces in the assemblies.

1. Open the More Corridors4.dwg file or continue working in your drawing from the previous exercise.

2. Select the corridor, right-click, and select Corridor Properties.

3. In the Corridor Properties dialog, switch to the Codes tab. Select All Codes with Hatching from the drop-down list in the Code Set Style selection box, as shown in Figure A.85.

4. Click OK to dismiss the Corridor Properties dialog. Your corridor should now have hatching applied per the code set style, similar to Figure A.86.

5. Expand the General → Multipurpose Styles → Code Set Styles branches on the Settings tab of Toolspace, as shown in Figure A.87.

Figure A.85

Use the drop-down list to choose All Codes with Hatching.

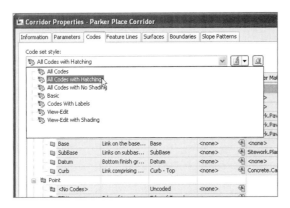

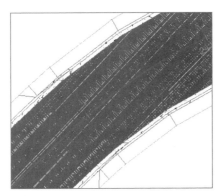

Figure A.86

The corridor with the default hatching applied from the All Codes with Hatching code set style

Figure A.87

Make changes to the Code Set Style on the Settings tab of the Toolspace.

6. Double-click the All Codes with Hatching code set style to open the Code Set Style dialog. Switch to the Codes tab.

7. Scroll to the right until you see the Material Area Fill Style column. The Material Area Fill Style specifies the hatch pattern for each link code. You can customize these hatch patterns by clicking any entry in this column and modifying the style.

Sections

In this collection of exercises, you'll adjust the sample line swath width, along with adding a new sample line and sample view.

Editing Swath Width of a Sample Line Group

The following short exercise will lead you through changing the swath width of a sample line group.

1. Open the More Sections1.dwg file.

2. Zoom in on the sample lines.

3. Select any sample line, right-click, and choose Sample Line Group Properties, as shown in Figure A.88. The Sample Line Group Properties dialog will appear.

4. Switch to the Sample Line tab of the Sample Line Group Properties dialog.

5. Use the Shift key to select all of the sample line entries.

6. Type **50** in the Left Offset column.

7. Type **50** in the Right Offset column, as shown in Figure A.89.

8. Click OK. The sample lines will become shorter. Zoom over to the Section Views in the drawing and note that each section view is now 50′ offset on either side of the road centerline, as shown in Figure A.90.

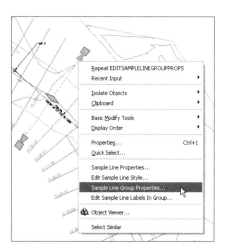

Figure A.88

Select any sample line and right-click to bring up the shortcut menu.

Figure A.89

After all of the rows are selected, change the Left and Right Offset values to 50.

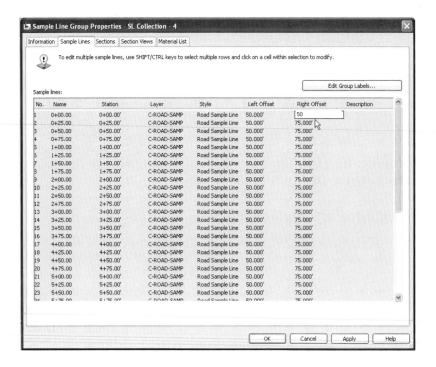

Figure A.90

When the sample line swath width is adjusted, the Section Views will change to match.

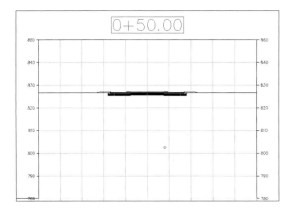

Adding a New Sample Line to a Sample Line Group

This short exercise will show you how to add a new sample line to a sample line group from a polyline.

1. Open the More Sections2.dwg file, or continue working in your drawing from the previous exercise.

2. Choose Sections → Edit Sample Lines. The Sample Line Tools dialog will appear.

3. Use the pull-down menu to choose Select Existing Polylines, as shown in Figure A.91.

4. At the `Select polylines:` prompt, choose the magenta polyline that is drawn at station 7+17.22 (see Figure A.92). Press ↵. A sample line is created.

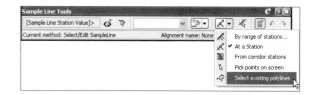

Figure A.91

Use the pull-down menu to choose Select Existing Polylines.

Creating a New Section View

The following short exercise will teach you how to make a section view for the newly created sample line.

1. Open the `More Sections3.dwg` file, or continue working in your drawing from the previous exercise.

2. Choose Sections → Create Section View. The Create Section View dialog will appear.

3. Use the Sample Line pull-down list to choose station 7+17.22. Note that this sample line may be at the top of the list instead of in station order. The dialog will look like Figure A.93. Click Next three times.

4. On the Create Section View - Section Display Options dialog, change the labels for the Existing Ground surface to _No Labels, as shown in Figure A.94. Click the Create Section View button.

5. At the `Identify section view origin:` prompt, pick a location in the drawing under the other section views. A section view will appear, as shown in Figure A.95.

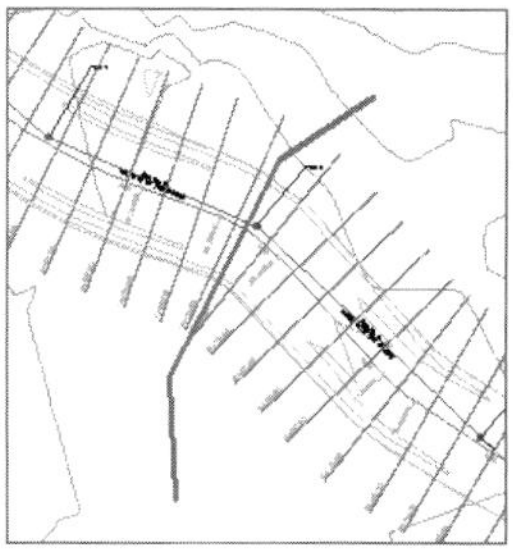

Figure A.92

Choose the magenta polyline that is drawn at station 7+17.22.

Figure A.93

Select the 7+17.22 sample line.

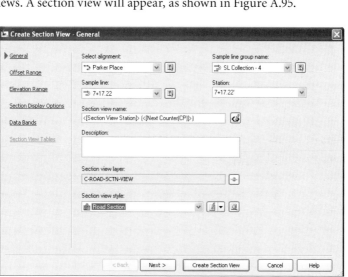

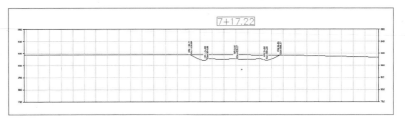

Adding a Grade Label to a Section View

The following short exercise will teach you how to add a grade label to a section view.

1. Open the `More Sections4.dwg` file, or continue working in your drawing from the previous exercise.

2. Choose Sections → Add Section View Labels → Add Section View Labels. The Add Labels dialog will appear.

3. Use the Label Type pull-down list to choose Grade, and then use the Grade Label Style pull-down list to choose Grade, as shown in Figure A.96.

4. At the `Select a section view:` prompt, select the newly created station 7+17.22 section view.

5. At the `Pick first point:` prompt, use your endpoint snap to select the bottom of the backslope of the right ditch.

6. At the `Pick second point:` prompt, use your endpoint snap to select the top of the backslope of the right ditch. Press ↵ to end the command.

7. A label will appear, as shown in Figure A.97.

Figure A.96

Set the Add Labels dialog to add section view grade labels.

Grading

In this collection of exercises, you'll work more with feature lines to edit the design and elevation, and explore another use of grading groups.

Working with Feature Lines and Slopes

Pulling all the pieces of a pond together can take some work. In this exercise, you'll step through the grading of a feature line.

1. Make sure your Feature Line toolbar is open.

2. Pick the pond outline feature line.

3. Right-click and select Elevation Editor to open the Grading Elevation Editor in Panorama.

4. Click in the Station cells in the Grading Elevation Editor to highlight and ascertain the elevation at the outfall, as shown in Figure A.98. In this case, the elevation is 654.095′. Some minor variation might occur, depending on your pick points and the length of your pilot channel. Notice also that the icon for this point in the Panorama display is a white triangle, indicating that this point is derived from a feature line intersection.

5. Click the Insert Elevation Point tool and select the pond outline.

6. Using an intersection snap, set a new elevation point at the intersection of the pilot channel and the flowline, and enter the elevation of **654.095′** (or the elevation you ascertained earlier). (This has to be added after the pilot channel has been created because otherwise, the fillet process would tweak the location.)

7. Close Panorama.

Figure A.98

Finding elevations using the Grading Elevation Editor

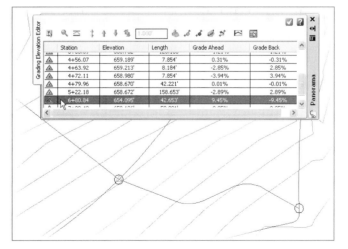

8. Click the Set Grade/Slope between Points tool, and then pick the pond bottom again.

9. Pick the PI near the southwest corner of the pond bottom. Enter **657.**⏎ for the elevation.

10. Pick the PI at the southern inflow. This should register an elevation of 655.50.

11. Press ⏎ to accept the grade. This sets all the elevations between the two selected PIs to fall at the same grade.

12. Pick the pond bottom again.

13. Pick the same initial PI. Press ⏎ to accept the elevation of 657.

14. Moving your mouse clockwise to set the direction of the grading change you're about to make, use a center snap and pick the PI near the outflow shown in Figure A.99.

Figure A.99

Setting slopes between points

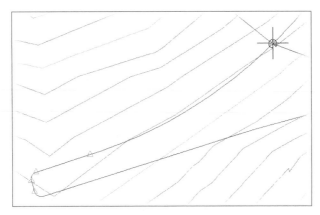

15. Press Enter to accept the elevation (it should be the 694.095 entered earlier) and to tie to the pilot channel elevation.

16. Pick the pond bottom again. Pick the PI at the northern inflow, and press ⏎ to accept the elevation (it should be 655.5).

17. Pick the outfall PI.

18. Enter **E** to accept the elevation value. The entire outline of the pond bottom is graded except the area between the two inflows. Because you want to avoid a low spot, you'll now force a high point.

19. Click the Insert High/Low Elevation Point tool.

20. Pick the pond outline.

21. Pick the PI near the north inflow as the start point, and pick the PI near the southern inflow as the endpoint. Enter **0.5.**⏎ as the grade ahead.

22. Enter **0.5.**⏎ as the grade behind. A new elevation point will be created as shown in Figure A.100.

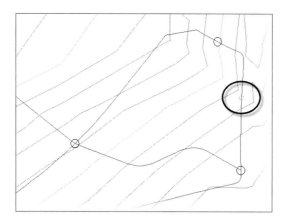

Figure A.100

Creating a high point on the eastern edge

Creating a Detention Pond

Another common use for grading objects is the creation of detention ponds. In this exercise, you'll create a pond from a given outline and calculate the volume of the pond.

1. Open the More Grading 2.dwg file.

2. Select Grading → Create Grading to display the Grading Creation Tools toolbar.

3. Select the Grade to Elevation criteria from the drop-down list as shown in Figure A.101.

4. Click the Create Grading button.

5. Select the pond outline drawn on lot 19. An alert will pop up asking if you want to weed the feature line. Select the Continue Grading without Feature Line Weeding option.

6. Click to the inside of the pond to set the grading side.

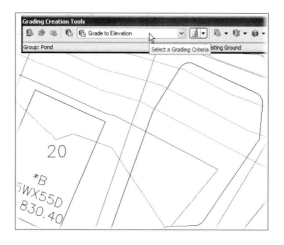

Figure A.101

Selecting the Grade to Elevation criteria on the Create Grading Tools toolbar

7. Press ↵ at the command line to accept grading over the entire length of the feature line.

8. Enter **825** at the command line as the target elevation.

9. Press ↵ to accept the Slope format of entry for cuts.

10. Enter **3** as the Cut Slope.

11. Press ↵ to accept the Slope format of entry for fills.

12. Enter **3** as the Fill Slope. Civil 3D will calculate the grading, and your pond should now look like Figure A.102.

Figure A.102

Completed 3:1 slope grading of the pond

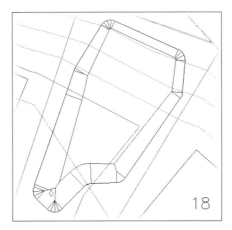

13. Select the arrow next to Create Grading to display the drop-down list of commands, and select Create Infill.

14. Click in the middle of the pond you just created. This essentially puts a bottom on the pond, connecting all the slopes into a solid surface.

15. Press ↵ to exit the command.

16. Select the diamond that now appears in the middle of the pond to select the grading group, right-click, and select Grading Group Properties.

17. On the Information tab, check the Automatic Surface Creation checkbox. The Create Surface dialog will appear.

18. Click OK to dismiss the Create Surface dialog, accepting the default values.

19. Click the Volume Base Surface checkbox within the Grading Group properties dialog to tell Civil 3D to calculate a volume between the newly created Pond surface and the Existing Ground surface.

20. Click OK to dismiss the dialog, and your pond should look like Figure A.103.

21. Open the Grading Group properties dialog again, and switch to the Properties tab as shown in Figure A.104. The volume of your pond should be 215.5 cubic yards of cut.

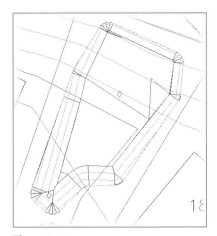

Figure A.103

Completed pond surface creation

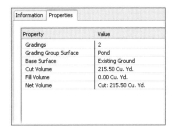

Figure A.104

Calculated pond volumes in the grading group

Pipes

In this series of exercises, you'll make a parts list and use a feature line to create a pipe network, and then look at a new labeling option.

Making a Parts List

The following exercise will lead you through making a parts list that will be used to create a water network.

1. Open the More Pipes.dwg file, or continue working in your drawing from the previous exercise.

2. Switch to the Settings tab of the Toolspace. If the Toolspace is not visible, choose General → Toolspace.

3. Locate the Parts List entry under the Pipe Network tree on the Settings tab, as shown in Figure A.105.

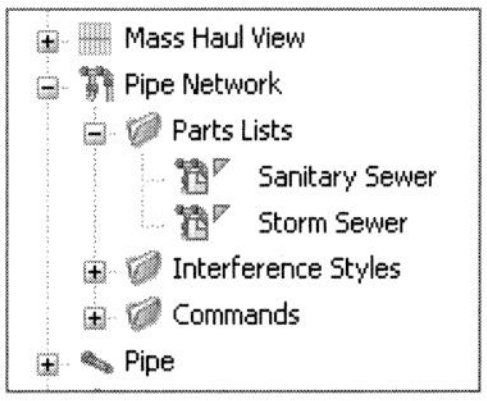

4. Right-click the Parts Lists entry and choose Create Parts List. The Network Parts List dialog will appear.

Figure A.105

The Parts List entry under the Pipe Network tree

5. Switch to the Information tab of the Network Parts List dialog. Type **Water** in the Name field.

6. Switch to the Pipes tab. Select the New Parts List entry, right-click, and choose Add Part Family. The Part Catalog dialog will appear.

7. In the Part Catalog dialog, check the box next to PVC Pipe. Click OK to dismiss the dialog.

8. In the Network Parts List dialog, use the + next to the Water entry to expose the PVC Pipe entry.

9. Select the PVC Pipe entry, right-click, and choose Add Part Size. The Part Size Creator dialog will appear.

10. Click inside the Inner Pipe Diameter field to reveal the pull-down list, and select 8.000000 from the list. The result will look like Figure A.106. Click OK.

Figure A.106

Select an inner diameter of 8 inches, and set the material to PVC.

Property	Value	Units	Source
Wall Thickness	0.240000	inch	Calculation
Inner Pipe Diameter	8.000000	inch	Table
Cross Sectional Shape	SweptShape_Circular		Constant
Minimum Curve Radius	0.000000	in	Optional Property
Manning Coefficient	0.000000		Optional Property
Hazen Williams Coefficient	0.000000		Optional Property
Darcy Weisbach Factor	0.000000		Optional Property
Material	PVC		Optional Property

11. In the Network Parts List dialog, use the + next to the PVC Pipe entry to expose the 8 Inch PVC Pipe entry.

12. Click inside the Style column next to the 8 Inch PVC Pipe entry. The Pipe Style dialog appears.

13. Use the pull-down list to choose the Double Line (Water) style. Click OK.

14. Click inside the Rules column next to the 8 Inch PVC Pipe entry. The Pipe Rule Set dialog will appear.

15. Use the pull-down list to choose the Water Pipe rule set. Click OK. The dialog will now look like Figure A.107.

Figure A.107

Set the 8-inch pipe to use the Double Line (Water) style and the Water Pipe rule set.

Name	Style	Rules	Render Material
⊟ Water			
⊟ PVC Pipe			
8 Inch PVC Pipe	Double Line (Water)	Water Pipe	ByLayer

16. Switch to the Structures tab.

17. If necessary, use the + next to the Null Structure entry to expose a second Null Structure entry.

18. Click inside the Style column next to the Null Structure entry. The Structure Style dialog appears.

19. Use the pull-down list to choose the Null style. Click OK.

20. Click inside the Rules column next to the Null Structure entry. The Structure Rule Set dialog will appear.

21. Use the pull-down list to choose the Water Null Structure rule set. Click OK. The dialog will now look like Figure A.108.

22. Click OK to dismiss the Network Parts List dialog. A parts list has now been created for water networks and is available for future pipe network creation.

Figure A.108

Set the Null struc-
ture to use the Null
style and the Water
Null Structure style.

Creating a Pipe Network from a Feature Line

The following exercise leads you through converting a feature line into a water network.

Figure A.109

Choose the blue fea-
ture line to become
the water network.

1. Open the More Pipes2.dwg file, or continue working in your drawing from the previous exercise.

2. Choose Pipes → Create Pipe Network from Objects.

3. At the Select object or [Xref]: prompt, select the blue feature line located just east of the road right-of-way, as shown in Figure A.109. Arrow glyphs will appear showing a flow direction.

4. At the Flow Direction [Ok/Reverse] <Ok>: prompt, press ↵ to accept the flow direction. The Create Pipe Network from Object dialog will appear.

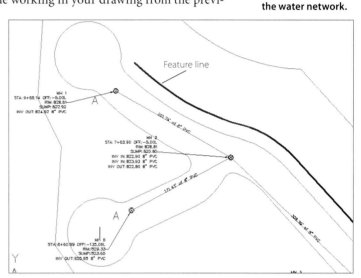

Feature line

5. In the Network name: field, type **Water**.

6. In the Network Parts List field, use the pull-down list to choose Water.

7. In the Surface Name field, use the pull-down list to choose Existing Ground.

8. Check the box next to Erase Existing Entity.

9. Check the box next to Use Vertex Elevations. The dialog box should now look like Figure A.110.

10. Click OK. The feature line is converted to a series of pipes and null structures, as show in Figure A.111. The null structures are invisible because the Null style has been composed as a "no show."

Figure A.110

Establish settings
for the Water
network

Figure A.111

**The feature line is
converted to a pipe
network.**

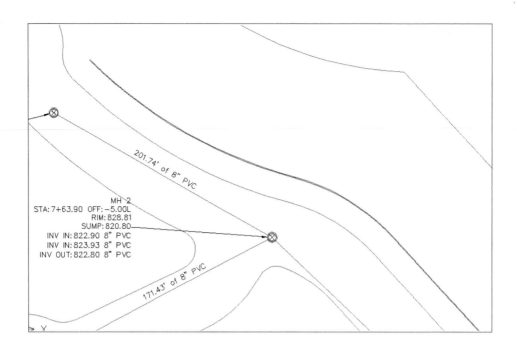

Adding a Pipe Spanning Label

In this short exercise, you'll add a label to the water pipes that lists their combined length.

1. Open the More Pipes3.dwg file, or continue working in your drawing from the previous exercise.

2. Choose Pipes → Add Pipe Network Labels. The Add Labels dialog will appear.

3. In the Add Labels dialog, change the Label Type to Spanning Pipes Plan using the pull-down list, as shown in Figure A.112.

4. Change the Pipe label Style to Length and Material using the pull-down list.

Figure A.112

**Choose the Spanning Pipes Plan
label type in the
Add Labels dialog.**

5. Click Add.

6. At the `Select first Network Part (Pipe or Structure):` prompt, select the northernmost water pipe.

7. At the `Select next Network Part or [Undo]:` prompt, select the next water pipe to the south, and continue selecting pipes until all five are selected. Press ↵.

8. At the `Specify label location on pipe:` prompt, click anywhere on one of the middle pipes. A label will appear that lists the combined length of all five pipes, as shown in Figure A.113.

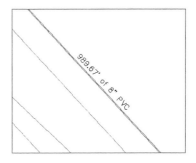

Figure A.113

After applying a spanning label to the pipe network

Index

Note to reader: **Bolded** page locators refer to main discussions of a topic. *Italicized* page locators refer to illustrations.